HITLER'S PRIESTESS

NICHOLAS GOODRICK-CLARKE

HITLER'S PRIESTESS

Savitri Devi, the Hindu-Aryan Myth,
and Neo-Nazism

NEW YORK UNIVERSITY PRESS

NEW YORK AND LONDON

NEW YORK UNIVERSITY PRESS
New York and London

Library of Congress Cataloging-in-Publication Data
Goodrick-Clarke, Nicholas.
Hitler's priestess : Savitri Devi, the Hindu-Aryan myth, and neo-
Nazism / Nicholas Goodrick-Clarke.
p.   cm.
Includes bibliographical references (p.   ) and index.
ISBN 0-8147-3110-4 (acid-free paper)
1. Neo-Nazism.   2. Savitri Devi.   I. Title.
JC481.G57 1998
320.53'3'092—dc21   97-45407
                                        CIP

New York University Press books are printed on acid-free paper,
and their binding materials are chosen for strength and durability.

Manufactured in the United States of America

10 9 8 7 6 5 4 3 2 1

CONTENTS

ACKNOWLEDGMENTS

When writing the biography of an underground figure, one can only benefit from the help of persons in the milieu. Here I would like to thank Ernst Zündel for initially drawing my attention to Savitri Devi in 1982 and sending me a copy of *The Lightning and the Sun.* I also wish to acknowledge Samisdat Publishers of Toronto for allowing me to quote at length from Savitri Devi's books.

Former comrades of Savitri Devi were generous with their memories, as well as with the loan of books and photographs. I am grateful to Beryl Cheetham, Lotte Asmus, Matt Koehl, and Colin Jordan. My researches were greatly aided by Muriel Gantry, at whose Essex cottage Savitri Devi died en route for America in 1982. A friend since 1946, her nonpartisan memoirs over several decades revealed much of Savitri Devi's personality, as well as providing amusing anecdotes. I am much indebted to Miguel Serrano, who kindly sent me books and translations, and his correspondence with Savitri Devi, and otherwise clarified the nature of his "Esoteric Hitlerism."

This study has also benefited from scholarly encouragement and debate. Warm thanks are due to my friends Professor Joscelyn Godwin and Dr. Hans Thomas Hakl for their generous help with sources and leads. An earlier review of Savitri Devi and her Hitler cult was the subject of my plenary lecture at the ninth international conference of CESNUR (Centre for Studies of New Religions, Turin) held at the University of Rome in May 1995.

I owe thanks to the librarians and staffs of the British Library; the India Office Library and Records, London; the Bodleian Library, Oxford; the Taylor Institution Library, Oxford; and Indian Institute Library, Oxford.

INTRODUCTION

"Discovered Alive in India: Hitler's Guru!"

The young German sat on the threadbare sofa listening to the words of the old woman before him. Through windows opening onto a balcony, shafts of dust-flecked sunlight shone into the darkened space of her humble, spartanly furnished room. Outside the strange, heady tumult of India resounded in the full glare of the midday heat. All around he could hear the street sounds and raucous, bustling squalor of this back alley in Delhi. Occasionally, her narrative was interrupted by the songs of the exotic birds she kept in her room and the young man was distracted by the sudden darting movement of the many cats, her inseparable companions, that lay at her feet or dozed out on the balcony in the warm air.

His attention fixed on the worn and crinkled face of the old woman as she carefully chose her words to tell the story of her life. She was dressed in the fashion of Indian women, wearing a loose white sari and a thin cotton shift over her shoulders. Soft gray hair framed her high forehead and was gathered behind her ears. While her brow was barely lined, her cheeks, chin, and neck blurred in a mass of furrows and wrinkles. Her lips were thin, and her mouth looked twisted, pointing downward at the right side. But it was her eyes that held him. Her eyes burned with a strange luminous quality, the light of inner vision and missionary zeal. But he also noticed that the left eye stared with a pained expression, while the right appeared tired and liquid, and he remembered with a start that she was now almost blind with cataracts.

The old woman's name was Savitri Devi and the young man had traveled all the way from Frankfurt to find her in this small bare room in old India and to hear in her own words the story of her sacred

1

mission for Hitler and Nazism. This elderly and infirm prophetess of Aryan revival, a philosopher of Hitler's cosmic purpose and Nazi pilgrim in the ruins of the German Reich at the end of the Second World War, had lived for years in poverty and obscurity in Calcutta and Delhi. Now in November 1978, at the end of a long life devoted to the Aryan cause, she had found a new publisher.

In late 1982 Ernst Zündel, the founder-proprietor of the neo-Nazi Samisdat Publishers in Toronto, publicized the availability of a set of five two-hour cassettes of live interviews with Savitri Devi and a brand-new edition of her out-of-print classic *The Lightning and the Sun* (1958). The notice was mailed worldwide on card flyers and it is worth quoting in its breathless entirety:

> THE HITLER CULT REVEALED. Discovered alive in India: Hitler's guru! For serious students of the occult: You can now purchase the complete set of tape cassette recorded, live interviews with Hitler guru Savitri Devi at her home in India. Hear in her own words the narration of a prophetic pilgrimage along the edge of the cosmic abyss. Watch the clouds of evil scatter under the lightning of Cosmic Justice and the sun of Cosmic Truth.
>
> Read her shocking and most recently published manuscript, "The Lightning and the Sun," which exposes the tangled roots of Nazism for all to see. Discover through her the secret Nazi pyramid connection with Pharaoh Akhnaton and the ancient cult of the sun. Learn the real significance of Genghis Khan's evil role in history, his incredible significance in the present. Discover the hidden springs of Hitler's manic will to power, his mystical bond with the dark forces of time and destiny. Pursue the outlines of evil in its awesome cosmic context.
>
> Decipher now the encoded workings of the Nazi mind. Perceive how Hitler saw the workings of the universe through: Human sacrifice. Vegetarianism. Aryanism. The cyclic view of history. The children of violence. The will to survive and to conquer. The seat of truth. Gods on earth. Kalki, the avenger.
>
> Were ancient sanskrit laws of the universe compiled in the Bhagavad Gita the secret source of Nazi strength? The amazing answers to these riddles are now at hand. Read them in "The Lightning and the Sun," Hitler guru Savitri Devi's huge, illustrated 448 page illumination of occult Nazi wisdom and prophecy.[1]

The Samisdat publicity was a resounding finale to a long and eventful life, begun early in the century in the beautiful, old walled city of Lyons.

* * *

When I first read these lines on the card flyer, I knew very little of Savitri Devi. But Samisdat Publishers was known to me as a far-right press owned by Ernst Zündel, notorious for the publication in 1974 of the first English-language translation of *The Auschwitz Lie*, a short book that denied the very fact of the Holocaust. However, the Samisdat catalogue mingled efforts to glorify the Third Reich, minimize war crimes, and deny the extermination of the Jews with odd books about UFOs, incredible German secret weapons, and postwar Nazi bases in Antarctica. Ernst Zündel clearly offered these topics as a potent myth of apocalyptic Nazi revival backed by astonishing resources. This myth might appeal to an older generation of unrepentant Nazis seeking imaginative relief from the division of Germany since 1945. At the same time it introduced a young generation of Germans to the idea of the Third Reich's achievement and technological superiority against a backdrop of neo-Nazi science fiction.

Samisdat's presentation of Savitri Devi was evidently part of this strategy designed to entice new audiences with the neo-Nazi message. Ancient mythology and pyramid secrets, Eastern religion, vegetarianism, and Green ideas—the very currency of the burgeoning New Age with its interest in exotic religion, spiritual truths, and a worship of nature—could be exploited as bait for the young, unwary, or simply curious. By the late 1970s the historical experience of the Third Reich was quickly receding into the past. As popular literature and films ably demonstrated, Nazism was becoming something mythical, even fantastic and also plastic, that could be molded and combined with novel associations and thereby given new meanings. By republishing the work of Savitri Devi, Zündel aimed to create a new cultic interest in Hitler, linking him to ancient mysteries, the world of nature, and powerful religious symbols drawn from the Orient.

Her ideas have since built unlikely bridges between neo-Nazism and the New Age. Savitri Devi viewed nature in the Hindu fashion, as a violent pageant of creation and destruction in which man held no special rights. A cloyingly sentimental love of animals stood in marked contrast to her misanthropic contempt for non-Aryan humans, the weak, and infirm. Himmler and Rosenberg, among other leading Nazis, also combined a concern for animals with their monstrous blueprints to eliminate all "unworthy" human life. *The Impeachment of Man*

(1959), her book devoted to a thoroughgoing rejection of the "man-centered creeds" of Judaism and Christianity, was republished by the far-right Noontide Press in America in 1991. Here the brutality of Social Darwinism meets both the Green cult of nature and the antisocial excesses of "animal rights" activists. Again, the amoral worship of beauty and force implicit in Nazi thinking finds new alliances with Hinduism, the cult of Shiva, and Deep Ecology, that radical current of ecological thought that condemns modern man as the scourge of nature.

Savitri Devi was a Frenchwoman of Greek-English birth who had become an admirer of German National Socialism in the late 1920s and was obsessed by the Aryan myth. Deeply impressed by its racial heritage and caste system, she had emigrated to India in the early 1930s to acquaint herself at firsthand with what she regarded as the cradle of the Aryan race. There she spent the years of the Third Reich and the Second World War in expectation of a global Axis victory, after which she and her Brahmin husband expected to help in the establishment of a racial New Order in the subcontinent.

During these years Savitri Devi elaborated an extraordinary synthesis of Hindu religion and Nordic racial ideology involving the polar origin of the Aryans, the cycle of the ages, and the incarnation of the last avatar of Vishnu in Adolf Hitler. She regarded the Third Reich as "the holy Land of the West, the Stronghold of regenerate Aryandom." Her ideas were actually representative of a certain section of high-caste Brahmin Indian society that hated the Raj and was impressed by Hitler's dramatic challenge of British imperial power. Such Indians were fascinated by the Nazi swastika—a holy Indian symbol—and fondly recalled the German tradition of Sanskrit scholarship since the early nineteenth century. However, it seemed unlikely that these ideas, so foreign to the actuality of National Socialism, could ever find supporters in the West.

The situation changed with the total defeat and collapse of the Third Reich in 1945. In its wake Savitri Devi pursued a long and busy career as a neo-Nazi apologist and ideologue in Europe. She was arrested by the British occupational forces in Germany for Nazi propaganda activities and imprisoned. Her extravagant Hitler cult, her Hindu-Nordicist doctrine of the Aryan race, and unswerving loyalty to the Nazi cause found numerous devotees among her fellow prisoners and demoralized Germans. After her release she befriended leading personalities of the Nazi regime such as the air ace Hans-Ulrich Rudel and the commando leader Otto Skorzeny, who both played an active role in maintaining a global Nazi support network. She met with Nazi émigrés and fugitives in Spain, Egypt, and the Middle East. She wrote books hymning the Third Reich and National Socialism, accounts of her propaganda campaign and detention, and a highly charged emotional memoir of her "pilgrimage" to Hitler shrines and other places of Nazi association in Austria and Germany during the 1950s.

Savitri Devi, a foreigner who had not even directly experienced life under National Socialism, supplied a new religious cult for the vanished Führer and an international rationale for Nazi-Aryan ideology that effectively transcended the narrow realities of German nationalism and anti-Semitism in the Third Reich. Defeated and humiliated Germans who could neither grasp the disgrace of their country nor accept the vilification of an idolized leader found comfort in Savitri Devi's rapturous approval. Hardened practitioners of Nazi terror and persecution were flattered by her doctrine of universal Aryan mission. The prosaic and gruesome aspects of Nazi practice during the years of tyranny yielded before a mythological tableau in which Hitler was deified and his regime invested with new religious significance.

Nor was her appeal confined to die-hard German Nazis and survivors of the Third Reich. The existence of small but persistent neofascist and neo-Nazi movements after 1945 in Europe, the United States, and South America is a well-documented fact. While these tiny groups and parties continue to peddle racism, anti-Semitism, and appeals for an authoritarian state, the universal postwar condemnation of Hitler and National Socialism is a major obstacle to their ever gaining popular acceptance. The extermination of European Jewry has become the horrific hallmark of the Third Reich, forever tainting any attempts to rehabilitate National Socialist ideology. By her outright inversion of this accepted moral scheme, Savitri Devi became a heroine of the neo-Nazi scene. In emotionally laden prose she transformed the negative attributes of Nazism into a religious cult of cosmic significance. The Third Reich was presented as a rehearsal for the Aryan paradise, and Adolf Hitler was celebrated as an avatar, a supernatural figure whose intervention in the cycle of the ages was essential to the restoration of the Golden Age.

Powerful ideas of anti-Semitism as a form of world-rejecting gnosis, Aryan paganism as a global religion of white supremacism, and Hitler as a divine being within a cosmic order together compose an unholy theology of the Aryan myth. Seen in this light, neo-Nazism has all the characteristics of an international sect with a religious cult. There are devotional practices, initiates and martyrs, prophecies and millennial expectations, and even relics. By entering the strange world of Savitri Devi, we catch a glimpse of the fatal attraction of neo-Nazism and Hitler cults for their followers. Above all, we may understand their perennial capacity to transmute religious energies and hopes for cultural revival into anger and violence.

Through her divinization of Hitler and National Socialism, Savitri Devi became a leading light of the international neo-Nazi underground from the early 1960s onward. She was a confidante of Colin Jordan, the flamboyant leader of the National Socialist Movement in Britain, and his henchman John Tyndall, who heads the British National Party today. She knew Lincoln Rockwell, the founder of the American Nazi Party, and in August 1962 she attended the notorious Cotswold Camp in Gloucestershire that acted as the founding meeting of the World Union of National Socialists (WUNS). In the late 1960s her books were reprinted in *National Socialist World*, the organ of the WUNS published by Lincoln Rockwell and William Pierce. In the pages of the magazine she was credited with a "mysterious and unfailing wisdom according to which Nature lives and creates: the impersonal wisdom of the primeval forest and of the ocean depths and of the spheres in the dark fields of space . . . [which Adolf Hitler made] the basis of a practical regeneration policy of worldwide scope."[2]

By the 1980s Savitri Devi had assumed the status of a cult figure herself on the neo-Nazi scene. Her eclectic ideas deriving from Hinduism, the myth of the Aryan race, Germanophilia, and adoration (the word is not too strong) for Adolf Hitler supplied a new mystique for that sinister minority of Nazi apologists in various countries around the world. Following her death in 1982, her ashes were placed in a Nazi shrine at Lincoln Rockwell's headquarters in Arlington, Virginia. Ernst Zündel, the German-Canadian publisher of Holocaust revisionism, sold her books and taped interviews in mass editions to young German neo-Nazis. Miguel Serrano, the former Chilean ambassador and pioneer of "Esoteric Hitlerism," paid fulsome tribute to her inspiration in his own books about the Hitler avatar. Nazi satanist groups and skinheads in Europe, America, and New Zealand cultivate her memory and ideas today. In Savitri Devi and her entourage one finds an articulate statement of the Hitler cult that defines the unholy theology of neo-Nazism.

1

HELLAS AND JUDAH

Savitri Devi was born Maximiani Portas on 30 September 1905 in Lyons. Her mother, Julia née Nash, came from Cornwall, one of two surviving daughters of one William Nash, an Englishman, who had married his first cousin. Her father was of mixed Mediterranean stock with an Italian mother from London and a Greek father who had acquired French citizenship on account of his residence in France.[1] Although Maximiani was a French national by birth, her early sympathies lay with Greece. Her father was a respected member of the sizeable Greek community in Lyons, and she enjoyed their company. Her given name Maximiani, the female form of Maximian, a name borne by several Roman emperors including Marcus Aurelius, also reinforced her own sense of Greek identity.

Her mixed ancestry and residence in an adoptive country was quite possibly a strong factor in her long quest for a true fatherland. In her youth Maximiani sought her roots in Greece, but later she embraced the idea of a supranational Aryan race, first in India and then in Germany, the country of her idol and exemplar, Adolf Hitler. Although her physical appearance was Mediterranean, she later comforted herself that she was of predominantly Nordic stock. Her maternal grandfather was the descendant of tenth-century Vikings from Jutland, while her father's Italian forebears came from Lombardy, a part of north Italy settled by the Germanic Langobard tribe during the migrations of the Dark Ages.[2]

Maximiani Portas was a willful and often insolent child with strong opinions. Her mother's English friends bored her with their endless conversation of relatives and illnesses, and this helped her form a neg-

7

ative image of England. France fared no better in her estimation. She was contemptuous of the French Revolution and the republican pride of the French. She regarded the ideals of equality, liberty, and fraternity as specious and was once punished at school for making an obscene gesture at the plaque displaying the Declaration of the Rights of Man. Above all, she had a great love of animals. From the age of five she voiced concern about man's cruelty to animals, animal experiments, circuses, and the fur trade. While still a schoolgirl, she abjured meat-eating and insisted that her mother prepare vegetarian food for her. The peasant torture of cats in France, a folk practice based on medieval superstition, disgusted her and turned her further against mankind.[3] This special affection for animals and her feelings of misanthropy led her to mistrust and eventually reject the man-centered nature of Western beliefs and values. This attitude became the hallmark of her Weltanschauung.

During her adolescence she discovered the French poet Charles Leconte de Lisle (1818–1894), who had been elected to the Academy in 1886 in succession to Victor Hugo. Leconte de Lisle's own tragic view of the universe, his romantic colors always tinged with somber pessimism, strongly appealed to Maximiani. He regarded all religious symbols as fragments of a divine truth, but the profusion of faiths over time convinced him of the relative value and ultimate vanity of every doctrine. Beset by a sense of cosmic futility, Leconte de Lisle rejected Christianity and evoked the stoical heroism of barbarian and exotic peoples in his famous cycle *Poèmes barbares* (1862). He was also powerfully attracted to Hinduism, following the translation of its sacred texts in the 1840s.[4] Maximiani felt a profound sympathy with Leconte de Lisle's view of life's fragility, the vanity of existence, and the illusion of the world. His romantic poems about the ancient Egyptians, the Scandinavians, Celts, and Hindus, their proud paganism, and heroic action yet final resignation in the face of death and oblivion confirmed her own aversion to Christianity and helped form her own fatalistic worldview. She continued to quote the verse of Leconte de Lisle throughout her life.

After the outbreak of World War I, Maximiani Portas soon found political reasons for rejecting England and France, while passionately defending their rivals and enemies. She detested the Allies for their treatment of Greece during the war. In August 1914 England and France had made valuable propaganda about the barbarian conduct of imperial Germany, which had invaded Belgium and thereby violated its neutrality. Young Maximiani regarded their protests as pure hypocrisy in light of their subsequent disregard for Greek sovereignty when the Entente (Britain, France, and Russia) landed troops in Greece and attempted to force its alliance. The constitutional crisis surrounding Greece's entry into the war and its ill-fated postwar occupation of Anatolia had a major bearing on Maximiani's profound sympathy for Greece and her burgeoning hatred of Britain and France during the 1920s.

During the war years a so-called National Schism prevailed in Greece between the pro-German King Constantine, who favored a policy of neutrality between the Entente and the Central Powers (Germany, Austria-Hungary, and Ottoman Turkey), and Prime Minister Eleftherios Venizelos, who was an enthusiastic champion of Greece's traditional British connection. The king forced Venizelos's resignation on two occasions in 1915 over this dispute in policy, and in August 1916 a group of pro-Venizelos officers staged a coup against the royalist government. Meanwhile, French troops had first landed at Salonika in October 1915, and the Entente then intervened with a landing of British and French troops in Athens in November and December 1916 to back up its demands for weapons and for Entente access to the Macedonian front to aid Serbia against Austria-Hungary. After formally recognizing the Venizelos government, Britain and France mounted a ten-month blockade of those provinces of the kingdom that remained loyal to the king until Constantine gave up his throne and the Venizelos government was firmly installed in Athens in June 1917.[5]

The events in Greece were watched with mounting concern by the émigré community in Lyons, and opinion was often bitterly divided between loyalty to the king and support for the Entente. The Allied intervention in the domestic affairs of Greece, involving the deposition of the king, was understandably condemned by many Greeks as an intolerable interference with the sovereignty and neutrality of their country. As a young girl Maximiani harbored strong anti-Entente feelings and demonstrated them by chalking the slogan "A bas des Alliés. Vive l'Allemagne" on the wall of Lyons railway station in late 1916. She also vividly remembered reports of demonstrations in Constitution Square in Athens, when the royalist crowds protested against the Allied blockade and support of Venizelos against the king. Young Maximiani reviled the Allies for their treatment of Greece during the war, but her contempt increased after their betrayal of their former ally Venizelos and his imperial adventure in Anatolia in the period from 1919 to 1923.[6]

This Anatolian campaign had its roots in the *Megali Idea*, or Great Idea, the irredentist aspiration to absorb all the Greek communities of the declining Ottoman Empire into a single Greek state. These ambitions owed their inspiration to the former glories of the medieval Byzantine Empire, which had been the great power of Eastern Europe until its final conquest by the Ottoman Turks after the fall of Constantinople in 1453. After the Greek War of Independence in the 1820s, the idea of a neo-Byzantine Greater Greece held a magical appeal for many Greek nationalists. In 1844 the Greek statesman John Kolletis outlined this vision of a Greater Greece: "The Kingdom of Greece is not Greece. Greece constitutes only one part, the smallest and poorest. A Greek is not only a man who lives within this kingdom but also one who lives in Jannina, in Salonica, in Serres, in Adrianople, in Constantinople, in Smyrna, in Trebizond, in Crete, in Samos and in any land associated with Greek history or the Greek race. . . . There are two main centres of Hellenism: Athens, the capital of the Greek kingdom, and 'The City' [Constantinople], the dream and hope of all Greeks."[7] These sentiments were often strongest among émigré Greeks due to their more acute sense of nationality. The *Megali Idea* was widely current among the Greeks of Lyons at the end of the Great War, and Maximiani rejoiced in its chauvinism and extravagant claims, not least the traditional last toast at dinners: "Let us go to Constantinople!"

Following the armistice of November 1918 and the proclamation of Allied victory, Venizelos was eager to reap rewards for his long-standing support of the Entente. He acted as Greece's chief negotiator at the Versailles peace conference, where his prime concern was the status of the Greek population of Asia Minor, hitherto part of Ottoman Turkey, which amounted to more than a million and a half persons. Venizelos's goal at Versailles was the incorporation of Smyrna (İzmir) and its hinterland within an independent Greek national state. By giving political expression to the *Megali Idea*, he hoped to increase his domestic popularity. Before the war there had been a Turkish majority in the Aydin province of Ottoman Turkey, which included the Smyrna region (950,000 Turks and 620,000 Greeks), but Venizelos speculated that a Greek province of Smyrna would attract a large influx of Greeks resident elsewhere in Asia Minor, which combined with the high birth rate of the Anatolian Greeks would soon give a substantial Greek majority in the region.[8]

The Greek annexation of Smyrna and its hinterland was accepted at Versailles, and the Greek occupation forces began to disembark at Smyrna under the protection of Allied warships in May 1919. However, the occupation was no easy matter; rival bands of Greek and Turkish guerrillas were soon fighting, and by the end of the summer there was already a strong revival of Turkish national feeling in Anatolia, which ultimately made the acclaimed Greek-Turkish Treaty of Sèvres in August 1920 a hollow truce. The Western powers also reacted with displeasure to the restoration of King Constantine in December 1920 and began to undermine the Greek advantage. In February 1921 the French and Italian governments weakened the Greek position in Asia Minor by their agreements with Mustafa Kemal, the leader of the Turkish nationalists. But Greece still expected British support for a further Greek offensive in Asia Minor, which was launched in March 1921. However, in April came the proclamation of an Allied policy of strict neutrality; Britain accordingly forbade any arms sales to the Greeks, while the French turned a blind eye to private sales to the Turkish nationalists. Because Greece had embarked on the occupation of Smyrna with Allied approval at Versailles, these developments appeared to the Greeks as the height of hypocrisy and double-dealing on the part of Britain and France.

Throughout 1921 and 1922 there was a growing realization in Greece that the Greek occupation in Asia Minor was no longer politically or militarily tenable. When Mustafa Kemal launched his major offensive in August 1922, the Turkish attack swiftly developed into a Greek rout, with the Greek forces retreating in chaos to Smyrna and the coast. On 8 September the Greek army evacuated the city and the Turkish army entered it the next day. Killing and looting soon began, followed by a full-scale massacre of the Christian population. As many as 30,000 Christians lost their lives and the Armenian, Greek, and Frankish quarters were destroyed by a great fire that raged unchecked through the city. A quarter of a million people fled to the waterfront, but the Allied ships in the harbor maintained a studied position of neutrality and neither help nor quarter was given to the hapless Greeks and Armenians. The scale of the debacle was inconceivable: within a few days the Greek army had withdrawn to the Greek islands and mainland and the 2,500–year Greek presence on the coast of Asia Minor had suddenly ended.

More than a million Greek refugees, many of them destitute, often with no possessions other than their holy icons, and a great number speaking no other language than Turkish, flooded into Athens, Thessalonica, and other cities on the Greek mainland. This enormous influx, of both rural peasants and middle-class merchants and traders, placed great strain on the social fabric and economy of a war-weary Greece that had already experienced six years of international hostilities. The population of Athens itself almost doubled between 1920 and 1928, with refugees living in wretched shantytowns all around the city that survived for many decades. The painful period of political and economic adjustment was difficult for all Greeks and lasted well into the late 1920s. This debacle signaled the absolute defeat of Greek territorial ambitions in Asia Minor and the final betrayal of the *Megali Idea* that had shone for a century on the Greek nationalist horizon.

By her own account, Maximiani had lived for the *Megali Idea* as a child and young girl. With its ignominious defeat, Greece seemed to her a martyr of all that was highest and most ideal in humanity. Greece had once been the fount of classical civilization with its emphasis on idealistic philosophy, aesthetic perfection, the attainment of physical and intellectual prowess. Now Greece was exhausted, its cities and meager farmland overwhelmed by the wave of Anatolian refugees, and its fond imperial hopes dashed by resurgent Turkish nationalism. In Maximiani's view, Allied treachery had led to the destruction of a Greek culture that had endured and flourished in Asia Minor throughout classical antiquity and the early Christian era. She was convinced that the French and British were the enemies of Greece. For the rest of her life she regarded the Allies' trumpeting of democracy and liberalism as so much cant and a mere pretext for the extension of their own political and commercial interests.

After the defeat of Germany, Maximiani's resentment of the Allies increasingly involved the demonstration of pro-German sympathies. In 1919 she and her family visited a POW camp near Lyons, where she proudly expressed her solidarity with a young German prisoner. When the Versailles Treaty was signed, she was repelled by the sight of French crowds in Lyons screaming their approval of the tough settlement and immense German reparations. Now that hostilities had ceased, these demands seemed intended only to humiliate a former enemy. She was also appalled by the French government's use of black Senegalese troops to occupy the Ruhr and to help enforce reparations under the terms of the treaty. Occasional reports in the French press of German resistance and its forceful suppression only served to increase her anger with the French. After the catastrophe in Anatolia, she saw no reason that she should support a settlement that favored the Allies after they had undermined the Treaty of Sèvres, which had been welcomed by the Greeks. She rejected the Versailles Treaty as an undue burden on Germany and noted the rise of revanchist movements including the National Socialists with approval. The Allies' conduct toward Greece remained all the while an important factor in her feelings of solidarity with defeated Germany.

After completing her secondary schooling, Maximiani Portas made her first visit to Greece in the second half of 1923. She was not yet eighteen years old and her head was full of wonderful ideas and the gilded memories of old Greek émigrés in Lyons. She sailed on a Greek steamer of the Piræus-Marseilles line and landed at the port in early August. She was soon made painfully aware of the recent disaster in Asia Minor by the severe hardships of the Anatolian refugees who were crowded into the poorer districts of the capital, Plaka, Kerameikos, and the shabby suburbs to the west of the Larissa railway station. She stayed at the "International Home," a hostel at 54 Leophoros Amalias, the thoroughfare that runs from the Arch of Hadrian past the Anglican Church of St. Paul to Syntagma (Constitution Square) along the eastern perimeter of the old-city quarter of Plaka, distinguished by its narrow streets, alleys, little squares, and long flights of steps spread around the footslopes of the great limestone crag of the Acropolis hill. Opposite the hostel across the Leophoros Amalias stood a large expanse of trees, shrubs, and colorful flower beds, extending as far north as the Old Parliament building. This was the National Garden, originally laid out by Queen Amalia, wife of the Bavarian King Otto of Greece (1832–1862), which offered the hostel residents a welcome relief from the hot and dusty confines of nearby Plaka.

Here in Greece after World War I, Maximiani began her lifelong odyssey toward the Aryan racial philosophy, which would lead her ultimately to India and the ruins of the Third Reich. As yet, however, she spoke only of "Hellenism," which she understood to be "a civilisation of iron, rooted in truth; a civilisation with all the virtues of the

Ancient World, none of its weaknesses, and all the technical achievements of the modern age without modern hypocrisy, pettiness and
moral squalor."⁹

During the mild autumn days the young girl would wander among
the dramatic ruins of ancient Athens. She often climbed the Acropolis,
marveling at the massive fluted Doric columns and sculptured friezes
of the Parthenon, its bleached white stone bathed in warm sunshine;
the delicate roofed temple of the Erechteion with the Porch of the Caryatids, its entablature borne by six figures of maidens in place of columns; and the great marble surfaces of the Propylaea gateways,
surmounted by residences, bastions, and defensive walls. The gleaming
fragments of scattered masonry, capitals, friezes, and broken columns
lay all around her, an eloquent testimony to the art, beauty, and vigor
of the "Hellenism" she so admired.

Facing north, she could survey the expanse of the city, its crowded
districts of traditional and modern buildings dotted with green hills,
parkland, and squares. At her left the grassy slopes of the Arios Pagos,
the famous Tribunal, ran down toward the Greek Agora and the disorderly ruins of the Stoa overlooked by the well-preserved Temple of
Hephaistos on a scrubby knoll. Further still lay the tangled undergrowth of the Kerameikos cemetery with its great Dipylon gate, ruined
walls, and scattered tombs in the midst of a rundown quarter. To her
right, at the foot of the Acropolis rock, stood the Arch of Hadrian near
her hostel, beside it the lofty columns of the Temple of Olympian Zeus
on the gentle slopes of the Olympieion hill. Further east she saw the
steep white marble terraces of the Stadion built for the first Olympic
Games of modern times in 1896. Far away in the northeast she
glimpsed the tiny whitewashed chapel of St. George perched high atop
the dominant Lykabettos hill rising to more than 900 feet above the
suburb of Kolonaki.

Maximiani was exalted by her view of Athens. The unparalleled ruins resplendent in the bright autumn sunshine, the ethereal landscape,
and the deep-blue skies inspired her to forget her bitterness at the
misery of postwar Greece and anger with the Western Allies. The
beauty of Athens conjured a vision of its ancient society before her
mind's eye: the physical perfection of the slim and athletic Grecian
youths, the order and simplicity of daily life, and the martial bearing
and courage of the soldiers. She saw the merchants and townspeople
in loose-fitting white garments going about their business on the con-

courses of the Agora, where philosophers sat conversing on its low stone walls. Everywhere she perceived beauty, order, and light, an image of classical man in harmony with nature, creating admirable buildings and great public spaces. In her opinion, this noble culture of "Hellenism," "an out and out beautiful world of warriors and artists," could be the product only of a pure race. In due course, she would claim that Greece was the oldest Aryan nation in Europe, with its origins in the Nordic Mycenaean invasions of circa 1400 B.C.[10]

It is noteworthy that Savitri Devi's enthusiasm for Greece also reflected a vital and long-standing German tradition of philohellenism. Once the Bavarian Prince Otto had ascended the Greek throne, a busy traffic in culture and ideas flourished between Bavaria and Greece. Leopold von Klenze (1784–1864), the Bavarian court architect to King Ludwig I, had designed Munich's Ludwigstraße and Siegestor (triumphal arch) on neoclassical lines. He also planned the layout of the restored Greek capital and many other German and Danish architects supplied public buildings for the new Athens after centuries of Ottoman neglect and ruin.[11] This German-Greek cultural axis continued a German intellectual tradition dating from the late eighteenth century when Johann Joachim Winckelmann (1717–1768) revived an appreciation of Greek art in German letters.[12] Savitri Devi's nascent Germanophilia was awakened in her ancestral country by German idealism made manifest in the very stones of Athens. When she finally visited Munich and saw Klenze's neoclassical Glyptothek and Propylaea (1846–1862) on the Königsplatz, she interpreted the nineteenth century exchange between Greece and Germany as proof of their common Aryan ancestry.

Years later, she would recall that she spent such a sunlit afternoon upon the Acropolis on 9 November 1923, the fateful day of Hitler's putsch, when he and his followers had attempted a coup against the Bavarian government and staged a march to the Feldherrnhalle in the center of Munich. The police successfully broke up the march, and sixteen martyrs of the early Nazi movement fell beneath a hail of bullets. When details of the incident were published in the world press the following day, there was some discussion over lunch at the "International Home" hostel. Maximiani admits that she did not yet connect Hitler with her own dream of a new racial order based on her view of classical Greek antiquity. However, she strongly sympathized with him as an enemy of the Allies on account of his contempt for the Versailles

Treaty and saw a parallel between his nationalist idea of one state for all Germans and the *Megali Idea* among the Greeks. She engaged in a heated argument in defense of Hitler with the French manageress of the hostel.[13]

In early December she returned to France to commence her undergraduate studies in philosophy at Lyons in January 1924. Her academic courses embraced a wide range of humanities, and she was fortunate in being able to study under several renowned scholars. In June 1924 she passed her first university examination in psychology. After studying logic under Professor Edmond Goblot, she took papers in this subject in February 1925. She passed her third examination in ethics and sociology and submitted an extended essay on the subject of progress in June 1925. In 1926 she passed her finals for the M.A. degree (license-ès-lettres). Her outstanding results throughout her undergraduate studies encouraged her and her parents to consider a scholarly career at a French university. In this case it was necessary to take a higher doctoral degree, for which the candidate was required to submit two theses. The continuation of her studies also combined with a desire to deepen her knowledge of Greece, and she decided to work on a Greek subject for her shorter complementary thesis.

The memories of her first visit to Athens had remained undimmed throughout Maximiani Portas's undergraduate years, and her Greek nationalism continued to burgeon in the mid-1920s. She wrote herself that she "chose" Greece on the attainment of her majority in September 1926. Portas finally renounced French citizenship and formally acquired Greek nationality from the Greek consulate in Lyons in early 1928.[14] After some preliminary studies in modern Greek history, she chose as the subject of her first thesis the life and thought of the pious educator, reformer, and philosopher Theophilos Kaïres (1784–1853).[15] This research project happily necessitated her residence in Athens, and she traveled once again to Greece in the early months of 1928. As a postgraduate student, she chiefly frequented the University, the Academy, and the National Library, a fine trio of neoclassical buildings designed by the Hansen brothers of Copenhagen between 1839 and 1891 on Panepistimíou Street between Omonia and Syntagma. Among the rich holdings of the National Library she found an abundance of sources on her subject. She now settled into her new scholarly life at Athens and remained there for almost two years before returning to France in November 1929.

Hailed by his admirers as Greece's new Socrates, Theophilos Kaïres was a gifted scholar and teacher whose dedication and tireless efforts on behalf of his countrymen were widely acclaimed but ultimately repaid with controversy, persecution, and excommunication from the Greek Orthodox Church. Born on 19 October 1788 on the island of Andros, he showed early promise in schools on Patmos and Chios and was ordained a deacon at the age of eighteen. He continued his studies at the University of Pisa and in Paris between 1802 and 1810, returning to teach at the Cydonian Academy in Asia Minor. The reputation of this college was greatly enhanced by his activities there from 1812 until 1820. When the Greek War of Independence broke out in 1821, Kaïres fought under Prince Alexander Ypsilantis, receiving serious wounds in the expedition to Olympus. Following his recovery, he became the political representative of Andros and the Cycladic Islands in the National Assembly of the newly liberated country. However, in 1826 he conceived a project to assist the numerous orphans of the war, which became his life's work. After a successful fund-raising campaign among his circle of international acquaintance in Europe, Russia, and Asia Minor, he established an orphan asylum and educational institute on Andros. Kaïres's new foundation swiftly developed into one of the foremost schools of Hellenic education in the embryonic state beset by chaos and factional strife during its first years of independence.

In 1831 Count John Capodistrias, the first president of Greece, who had helped Kaïres with suggestions and funding, was assassinated, and the country lapsed once again into near anarchy. To stabilize the situation, the Allied Powers (Russia, Great Britain, and France) offered the crown of Greece to Prince Otto von Wittelsbach, the son of King Ludwig of Bavaria. In the late 1830s King Otto conferred honors and a senior appointment at the University of Athens upon Kaïres, but he courteously declined both. Immersed in his own educational project on Andros and enjoying widespread national popularity, Kaïres failed to see that such conduct could easily be interpreted by unsympathetic observers as political hostility to the new regime. His charismatic status as a teacher and the success of his school had aroused envy, and his enemies lost no time in exploiting the king's uncertainty regarding his person.

When it was learned that Kaïres was giving courses on the history of mankind and comparative religion and, moreover, his own variety of theology called Theoseveia, charges of unorthodox teaching were soon brought against him by the renowned theologian Constantinos Economous. These charges were groundless because Kaïres had not set himself up as religious teacher but lectured mainly on philosophy and history. However, the political faction opposed to him was quick to incite the clergy against him, and he was arrested in October 1839 and brought before the Holy Synod in Athens. Neither charged nor convicted, he was exiled for a period of reflection to a monastery on the island of Skiathos, where he endured neglect and ill-treatment at the hands of the ignorant monks. He was later detained on the island of Thera and formally excommunicated from the Greek Orthodox Church in November 1841. Finally released in 1842, Kaïres went into exile by way of Constantinople, Malta, Paris, and London, where he was able to meet many old friends and received great encouragement for his advocacy of educational freedom.

When the new constitution of 1844 granted freedom of conscience, Kaïres decided to return to Greece and resume teaching at his orphan asylum in July 1844. He was not to be granted a lengthy respite from persecution. Once his schoolfriend and patron, Minister John Kolletis, had died in 1847, his old enemy Economous unleashed a new wave of religious accusation against him. In December 1852 Kaïres was charged with having instituted a religion contrary to that recognized by the kingdom and with being a proselytizer of unorthodox teachings. His trial took place on the remote island of Syros, where he faced a hostile audience of prejudiced clerics and political opponents who quickly found him guilty and sentenced him to two years' imprisonment, seven years' probation, and a heavy fine. He was immediately confined in a filthy and damp cell. Weakened by a bout of pneumonia earlier in the year, Kaïres soon suffered a nervous collapse, exhaustion, and other complications. He died in prison on 10 January 1853.

During the two years (1928–1929) spent working on her thesis at Athens, Maximiani Portas had ample opportunity to immerse herself in the history and culture of her fatherland, both in the classical age and in the era of independence and nation building that formed the background of her subject. The theological content of her thesis also deepened Maximiani's contact with the Greek Orthodox Church, which she attended regularly in the capital. Despite her mother's Anglicanism, Maximiani had always preferred to worship in the small Greek church at Lyons with her father and other members of the Greek community. She felt a great attraction for the Greek Orthodox Church and Byzantine culture, as expressed in the chanting and hymns of the Greek rite. Above all, she revered the Orthodox Church for its preservation of Greek national identity during the long centuries of Turkish domination. Indeed, much of her feeling for the church owed more to Greek nationalism and her enthusiasm for the neo-Byzantine aspirations of the *Megali Idea* than to Christian piety. Even as a child she had felt ambiguous about Christianity itself; as a student she increasingly questioned the apparent man-centeredness and relegation of nature implicit in Christian teachings. In this skeptical frame of mind she joined a Greek pilgrimage to the Holy Land during Lent 1929. She wanted to see for herself the people and places most intimately associated with the roots of Christianity.

Thanks to a thorough grounding in Scripture knowledge at her Catholic schools in Lyons, Portas knew her Bible well. She was well familiar with the history of Israel with its unfolding sense of election through the Exodus under Moses, the Sinaitic covenant, and the return under Joshua into Canaan. She knew the story of the early monarchy under Saul, David, and Solomon, followed by the division of the kingdom into Israel and Judah, their turbulent histories marked by rebellion, internecine strife, and recurrent relapses from the worship of Yahweh into pagan idolatry until the destruction of Jerusalem and the first Temple by Nebuchadnezzar in 586 B.C. The exile of Israel in Babylon, the return of the Jews to Judaea, and their subsequent history under the Persian, Greek, and Roman world empires were an integral part of her educational background. Her mother's sister was also an avid Bible reader and had encouraged her niece in its study. However, this knowledge had not taught Maximiani to revere the Jews as "the chosen people." On the contrary, her Bible knowledge had instilled in her a repugnance for the Jews, in whose ethical monotheism she identified the original and ultimate enemy of her own pagan, pantheistic tendencies. She utterly rejected the Jewish emphasis on the one and only God, transcendent and wholly apart from nature. Above all, she resented in Judaism a national presumptiveness coupled with universal aspiration: the fact that Yahweh was the God of Israel yet entrusted them with a universal mission for mankind.

Her anti-Semitic prejudice was further strengthened by the political circumstances of modern Palestine. The Zionist movement to create a Jewish state had been gathering force since the latter decades of the nineteenth century, when East European Jews began settling in the country that had been under Turkish rule since the early sixteenth century. In November 1917 as the British army invaded Palestine, the famous Balfour Declaration was issued, promising that the British would facilitate the establishment there of a national home for the Jewish people. In July 1922 the League of Nations had given Britain a mandate to rule Palestine and charged it with a responsibility to secure that objective. However, the British were anxious to retain the goodwill of the Arab majority, which viewed these developments with misgiving and was greatly concerned at the increased level of Jewish immigration during the 1920s. Armed Arab attacks on Jewish settlements had become frequent by the end of the decade. However, the Jews were determined to redeem the earlier promises made and pursued a policy of continuing immigration and property acquisition, combined with shrill demands for more self-determination. Given the messianic background of Zionism, Maximiani Portas was antagonistic toward these trends, which in turn darkened her perception of the Holy Land as a national Jewish prize.

The pilgrimage party sailed from Piræus to Haifa in mid-March and proceeded, in the course of the next forty days leading up to Easter, to visit many of the places associated with the Bible and the life of Jesus. After passing through Bethlehem and Nazareth, the pilgrims made their way to Jerusalem, where they were able to see at first hand the stones that bore witness to more than two thousand years of Jewish history as well as the dramatic events involved in the birth of Christianity. As her fellow pilgrims reverently viewed the City of David and paced the stations of the Cross on the Via Dolorosa leading to the Church of the Holy Sepulchre on the reputed site of the Crucifixion, Portas felt repelled by what she regarded as their servile conduct before these alien shrines, seeing in such behavior a telling symbol of the Jewish-Christian overlordship of Europe. She dismissed the numerous sites of Christian association as a mere accumulation of legend and wryly recalled the story of the original pilgrimage of Helena, the mother of Emperor Constantine, who in A.D. 326 visited Jerusalem, where she found the True Cross and the Holy Sepulchre. Portas contemptuously rejected the subsequent proliferation of "Holy Places" as an invention of the credulous Christians who had been coming to Jerusalem ever since.

This Lenten pilgrimage to Palestine in 1929 cannot be underestimated for its influence on Portas's religious outlook. Her hostile confrontation with the Judaeo-Christian tradition at its fount and origin marks a crucial point in the development of her anti-Judaism, anti-Christianity, and general predisposition away from man-centered monotheism toward a nature-centered pantheism. At the same time, her encounter with large numbers of Jews in their national community transformed her political anti-Semitism into a lifelong article of faith. As Portas wandered in the Jewish quarter of the Old City, she felt overwhelmed and repelled by the exotic nature of the Jews, their attire, their customs, observances, and festivals. The strange dark men in broad-brimmed hats and long black coats hastening to prayers at the Wailing Wall; the apparent paradox of a national or tribal God claiming universal significance; and the ubiquitous references to the immemorial history of Israel and the fulfilment of Scripture all filled her with utter disbelief that the Jews were indeed "the chosen people," as her English aunt had so often insisted during her childhood. Against the background of her fierce Hellenistic nationalism and budding paganism, Portas heartily resented the central importance of this Jewish history in European thought and belief.

By her later account, she recalled the extraordinary paradox that she should have been reminded of Adolf Hitler's vehement nationalism and anti-Semitism at the heart of Jewry in Palestine. Suddenly, she related, it occurred to her that Hitler's campaign against Jewish influence in Germany was not just a German affair but an issue of international significance. She reflected that all the formerly pagan nations of Europe must throw off their superimposed Judaeo-Christian heritage and make renewed contact with their old ethnic religions. For the first time she realized that she was a National Socialist herself, indeed that she had always been a National Socialist. Henceforth her admiration for Hitler was complete. Although she now entertained thoughts of settling in Germany and joining the Nazi movement, she reflected that her French birth and recent adoption of Greek nationality might arouse suspicion there. She resolved instead to realize her newfound political philosophy closer to home by reviving Greek nationalism and paganism.

Returning to Athens after Easter, she attempted to develop a coherent alternative belief based on the gods of ancient Greece. Her background studies in antiquity and ancient history had furnished her with much material for a pagan-national conception of religion that would focus on a race other than the Jews. At this stage, she still identified this race as the Hellenes, the people of Alexander the Great. On the basis of its racial and military superiority such a people should enjoy a wide sphere of influence and regional hegemony. Many of her ideas were still obviously bound up with the irredentism of the *Megali Idea*. However, she soon discovered that her pagan ideas evoked little response among the Greeks, who remained intensely loyal to their Christianity and its Byzantine associations. She therefore spent the latter half of 1929 completing her thesis, which was appropriately prefaced with a memorial to Iôn Dragoumis, the thinker and Hellenic patriot in Macedonia who had been assassinated in Athens in 1920. During the late summer she traveled all around the Peloponnese alone on foot and on horseback. The ancient sites of Arcadia, the ruins of Sparta, and the rugged beauty of the peninsula deepened her love of the country and its proud past. The thesis on Kaïres was completed as a draft in the autumn and she returned to Lyons in November 1929.[16]

Portas now began work on her main doctoral thesis on a purely philosophical topic. The subject was the nature of simplicity in mathematics and natural science and had been suggested by her teacher in logic, Edmond Goblot. However, in order to write upon the philosophy of science, she realized that she would have to study science and accordingly began courses in the science faculty at Lyons University. This polymathic endeavor is all the more remarkable for its swift and successful conclusion. She took the university examinations in physical chemistry and mineralogy in July 1930, followed by papers in general chemistry in November 1930 and in biological chemistry in July 1931. She received her M.Sc. (license-ès-science) in 1931, whereupon she sat down to write her doctoral thesis. Professor Goblot had died in the meantime, and her new supervisor was Professor Étienne Souriau at the Sorbonne, who advised her to confine her subject to mathematical simplicity after all. She completed her five-hundred-page thesis *La simplicité mathématique*, including a discussion of the contemporary Sorbonne philosopher Léon Brunschvicq, by the end of 1931. These studies in mathematics and philosophy drew upon the work of George Boole, Gottlob Frege, and Bertrand Russell in symbolic logic, Henri Poincaré in topology and geometry, and Alfred North Whitehead in the philosophy of science. While remote from her interests in religion and history, this thesis has some bearing on her philosophical development toward a deistic cosmology of energy in nature. Meanwhile she had visited Athens once again in the early autumn of 1931 to revise her Kaïres thesis.

Her aversion to the Jews and the Judaic origins of Christianity still remained a strong motive in her search for a pagan religion. Following her visit to Palestine in 1929, she had taken increasing note of the rise of the National Socialist movement in neighboring Germany. Occasional reports of Hitler's speeches had appeared in the French press since the mid-1920s, and she could not but be impressed by the central importance of anti-Semitism in his political view of the world. Having earlier regarded Hitler first and foremost as a German nationalist politician committed to revising the restrictive conditions of the Versailles Treaty, her view of him altered after reading a German edition of *Mein Kampf*. Here Hitler summarized his views on the race and the nation in terms of a Manichaean dualism between the Aryans and the Jews. Behind Hitler's commonplace eulogy of the Aryans lay more than a century of racial speculation in Europe. Portas decided to find out all she could about the Aryans and their pagan polytheistic religions. But who were the Aryans and where were they to be found in the modern world?

Given her prolonged periods of study in Athens, it would be surprising if Portas had not been influenced by the memory of the famous German archaeologist Heinrich Schliemann (1822–1890), the discoverer of Troy and Mycenaean culture. In the course of his pioneering excavations at Hissarlik in 1871–1875, he had uncovered the greatest treasure trove of gold, silver, and bronze objects ever found. His discoveries confirming the site of Troy, the Trojan War, and the events of Homeric poetry made a deep and lasting impression on the European mind. After his success Schliemann and his young beautiful Greek wife Sophia settled at Athens in a palatial mansion called the Ilíou Mélathron (Palace of Ilion) built by Ernst Ziller in 1878–1879 at 12 Panepstimíou Street. Here they became the center of Athenian society, hosting lavish banquets at which Sophia presided wearing Mycenaean gold and the diadem that had once belonged to Helen of Troy. In due course much of Schliemann's Mycenaean treasure found a home in the National Archaelological Museum in Athens, and he donated much of the Trojan hoard to the German National Museum in Berlin.

At the Hissarlik site of Troy, Schliemann had also found hundreds of objects ranging from pottery fragments and terra-cotta whorls to ornaments bearing the sign of the swastika. He immediately recognized this symbol from similar signs on pots found near Königswalde on the River Oder in Germany and speculated that the swastika was a "significant religious symbol of our remote ancestors," which linked the ancient Teutons, the Homeric Greeks, and Vedic India.[17] The extraordinary publicity surrounding Schliemann's finds at Troy guaranteed a wide European audience for his speculations about an ancient Aryan symbol bridging the mythological and religious traditions of East and West. His book *Troja* (1884) contained a dissertation identifying the Trojans as Thrakians, who were in turn regarded as Teutons. Thanks to Schliemann's extensive scholarly contacts in Germany, England, and France the swastika was swiftly launched as the Aryan symbol in the European mind. Michael Zmigrodzki, a Polish librarian, addressed major international congresses of anthropologists and archaeologists on the subject of the Aryan swastika in 1889, attended by Schliemann, his anti-Semitic collaborator Emile Burnouf, and Professor Ludvig Müller of Copenhagen, who claimed that the swastika was the emblem of the supreme Aryan god.[18] So great was Schliemann's fascination with this symbol that he adorned the external walls of his great house in Athens with a continuous border of decorative swastikas.

Almost every day during her student years in Athens Portas had walked past these swastikas on Heinrich Schliemann's Palace of Ilion (since 1927 the Supreme Court of the Appeal) in Panepistimíou Street, the thoroughfare that ran across the frontage of the University, the Academy, and the National Library. Given her profound interest in Greek antiquities, she was most likely familiar with Schliemann's reputation and work, as well as his speculations on the links between the Homeric myths and the Vedas of India in a common Aryan tradition. It is indeed tempting to speculate that Schliemann's Aryan swastikas were an important motivating factor, specifically present in Athens, that led her to think about the Aryan tradition in India. What is certain, in any case, is that Portas's pursuit of the Aryan myth in late 1931 led her beyond Greece and Europe to the cradle of the Indo-European race in Vedic India.

Following the recent death of her father in February 1932, Portas inherited a legacy that enabled her to visit India. She was now convinced that she could rediscover a living Aryan world only in contemporary India. In 1926 the renowned European Indologist Sir Charles Eliot had written: "Hinduism has not been made, but has grown. It is a jungle, not a building. It is a living example of a great national paganism such as might have existed in Europe if Christianity had not become the state religion of the Roman Empire, if there had remained an incongruous jumble of old local superstitions, Greek philosophy, and oriental cults such as the worship of Sarapis or Mithras."[19] Her journey to the East was inspired by an interest in the Hindu caste system and a desire to learn more about eugenics. Above all, she hoped to find in the religious rites, customs, and beliefs of India something of a living equivalent to the old Aryan cults of Europe—both of ancient Greece and of the Teutonic North—which she believed Christianity had abolished and obscured as a result of the state edict of Emperor Constantine.[20] Her subsequent experience of Brahminical India during the 1930s laid the basis of her Aryan racial philosophy.

2

ARYAVARTA

Leaving aside Schliemann's Aryan swastikas, Maximiani Portas had long been attracted to the Orient by the poet Leconte de Lisle. Even in her early teens she had been thrilled by his evocation of the deified Aryan hero of India and the pride of the privileged godlike race:

"Rama, son of Dasharatha, whom the Brahmins honour,
Thou whose blood is pure, thou whose body is white,"
Said Lakshmana, "hail, O resplendent subduer
Of all the profane races!"[1]

Years later she would write that the music of these verses was destined, one day, after the failure of her great dreams in Greece, to drive her to the caste-ridden land as to the immemorial stronghold of natural order and hierarchy. While her delight in the icy idylls and scornful perfectionism of Leconte de Lisle go some way toward explaining her interest in Vedic India, the complex of factors that led her to search for the Aryan heritage in South Asia is deeply rooted in European myths of racial origin deriving from the Romantic period.

As if taking her cue from Sir Charles Eliot's image of India as an undisturbed pre-Christian pagan culture in the remote tropics, she claimed that she went to India "to seek gods and rites akin to those of ancient Greece, of ancient Rome, of ancient Britain and ancient Germany, that people of our race carried there, with the cult of the Sun, six thousand years ago, and to which living millions of all races still cling; and to witness, in the brahmanical élite of to-day, a striking instance of the miracle that racial segregation can work, and the triumph of an Aryan minority throughout the ages."[2] But her vision of Aryavarta, the traditional name of Aryan territory in India, was also strongly colored by her newfound enthusiasm for Hitler and German National Socialism. She went to India, she added, to see at first hand a civilization founded upon the idea of natural racial hierarchy. She imagined that Indian society could show how the world would appear around A.D. 8000 once the New Order of Nazism had prevailed for six thousand years.[3]

Now, in the early spring of 1932, Portas had her boat ticket for the land of her racial dreams. She was twenty-seven years old, had completed two degrees in the humanities and natural science, and written two substantial theses for her doctorate. She had traveled from France to Greece already several times, but now she was on the threshold of a new experience—the exotic world of Asia. In Lyons she bade her mother and college friends farewell and took a train down to Marseilles. The passenger liner was already waiting at the docks, and she embarked among a noisy throng of colonial administrators and their families, merchants, and missionaries bound for India and Southeast Asia. The long sea voyage took her across the Mediterranean and through the Suez Canal, down the Red Sea and across the Arabian Gulf, and she disembarked at Colombo in Ceylon. From the port she proceeded to Kandy, where she made offerings to Buddha in a temple and felt the distinctive allure of Oriental religion amid the incessant beat of drums. After a fortnight in Ceylon (Sri Lanka), she crossed the water from Talaimannar to Rameswaram over the sandbank shoals of Rama's Bridge between Ceylon and southern India.

Her arrival on the sacred island of Rameswaram in May 1932 coincided with the great spring festival celebrating the exploits of Rama described in the famous Hindu epic *Ramayana*, already familiar to her from the poetry of Leconte de Lisle. The main theme of the epic was the story of Prince Rama, the son of King Dasaratha of Ayodhya by Queen Kausalya. The second queen, Kaikeyi, wanted to secure the throne for her son Bharata, and Rama was driven into exile. Rama, his beloved wife Sita, and his half-brother Lakshmana share many adventures abroad, in the course of which Sita is abducted by Ravana, the demon king of Lanka (Ceylon). Rama and Lakshmana then mount a campaign against Ravana with the assistance of Hanuman, the king of the monkeys. After crossing the shallows of Rama's Bridge to Ceylon, the trio defeat Ravana's forces in battle and rescue Sita. The story ends happily with Rama and Bharata sharing the kingdom. The epic is generally held to be based on the kingdom of Kosala and its capital Ayodhya in the seventh century B.C. The campaign against Ravana reflects the contemporary penetration of the Aryan tribes into the Dravidian stronghold of South India and their victory over the darker races. The heroic legend was edited by Brahmins into a book of devotion that is so well known among Hindus that its hundreds of incidents form a repertoire of favorite folktales.

The rich and colorful spectacle of the Rameswaram spring festival offered Maximiani Portas her first encounter with the living world of Hindu myth and Aryan legend. In the tropical evening darkness she watched the pageant unfold before her eyes. Seven elephants with purple draperies hanging down from their backs were ridden by beautiful, dark young men who resembled bronze statues by the light of flaming torches. The elephants then began to follow the chariot of Rama and Sita as the procession circled the sacred tank. The spectators threw jasmine and other flowers into the passing chariot as a token of love and respect for Rama and his faithful consort. Surrounded on all sides by the rapt and enthusiastic crowds, chiefly Dravidians and Tamils of South India, Portas reflected on the devotion that these dark-skinned Indian races still showed toward the northern Aryan invaders of old, symbolized by the fair-skinned couple in their chariot. It gave her great encouragement to see dark people honoring the white people, even worshiping them as gods, thousands of years after the conquest. The Rameswaram ceremony appeared to Portas an allegory of Nazi dreams of Aryan world dominion.

Through her passage to India in search of the Aryan heritage Portas retraced the intellectual journey of many European philosophers and philologists who had begun to seek the origins of mankind in India from the mid-eighteenth century onward. During the Middle Ages and the Renaissance, European scholars had generally accepted the biblical account in the Book of Genesis that traced the descent of all the races initially from Adam and Eve in the Garden of Eden and then from Noah and his sons, Shem, Ham, and Japhet. Their descendants were typically identified as the Semites (Jews and Arabs), the Hamites (Egyptians and other inhabitants of North Africa), and the remaining human race including the Europeans was reckoned to be Japhetites. However, the discovery of the Americas and many previously unknown aboriginal peoples placed an increasing strain upon this biblical explanation. During the Enlightenment the *philosophes* expressed the anticlerical and antibiblical mood of a rational age by dissenting from the old Hebraic account of human origins in favor of a more exotic yet universal source. The location of this source in India provided a background to this quest for a new Adam. The subsequent development of this postbiblical anthropogeny gave rise in the nineteenth and twentieth centuries to the Aryan myth, which exercised a powerful and fatal influence on Nazi racial doctrine.

Both Voltaire and Kant, to take two leading figures of the Enlightenment, declared India the source of all arts and civilization. In a letter of 1775 Voltaire stated that he regarded the "dynasty of the Brahmins" as the nation that had taught the rest of the world: "I am convinced that everything has come down to us from the banks of the Ganges." Such ideas appealed to Kant, who suggested that mankind together with all science must have originated on the roof of the world in Tibet. The culture of the Indians, he asserted, came from Tibet, just as all European arts came from India. However, it was Johann Gottfried Herder (1744–1803), the court preacher at Goethe's Weimar and the pioneer of Romantic nationalism, who was most influential in introducing this Indophilia into the German-speaking world. Loyal to his Lutheran calling, he regarded the Bible as the most accurate copy of some "natural revelation" associated with the Indian birthplace of mankind. Full of admiration for India, he praised the Brahmin priests for educating their people to a degree of virtue and learning far beyond European standards.

In his major work *Ideen zur Philosophie der Geschichte der Menschheit* (Outlines of a philosophy of the history of mankind) (1784–1791), Herder strongly opposed the Noachian or Jewish genealogy:

> The pains that have been taken, to make of all the people of the Earth, according to this genealogy, descendants of the hebrews, and half-brothers of the jews, are contradictory not only to chronology and universal history. . . . [N]ations, languages and kingdoms were formed after the deluge, without waiting for envoys from a chaldean family. . . . Suffice

it, that the firm central point of the largest quarter of the Globe, the primitive mountains of Asia, prepared the first abode of the human race.
. . .

Herder exhorted his European readers to dismiss the Middle East— "these corners of Arabia and Judaea, these basins of the Nile and the Euphrates, these coasts of Phoenicia and Damascus"—as the cradle of mankind and instead to scale the summits of Asia.

These thinkers of the Enlightenment thus broke with the biblical tradition and located the birthplace of the entire human race east of Eden between the Indus and the Ganges. In retrospect, it appears that the idea of an Indian source of mankind played the role of an intermediary traditional mythology between the biblical genealogy of creation and the modern evolutionary genealogy of Darwin. In the late eighteenth century, philosophers were ready to reject Adam as a common father and the conventional Noachian genealogy in their search for new ancestors but still clung to the idea of their origin in the mysterious Orient. It now remained for the new science of linguistics to take these ideas a stage further by suggesting that it was not the whole human race but one particular race—a white ancestral European race— that had descended from the mountains of Asia to colonize and populate the West. Although English writers were the first to make these philological discoveries, it was German Romantic scholars who matched linguistic with racial groups and eventually gave a name to these ancestors by opposing the Aryans to the Hamites, the Mongols, and the Jews.[4]

Although the close relationships between some European languages had been noted by the beginning of the seventeenth century, the Irish scholar James Parsons was the first to conduct a survey of basic words in a larger number of languages. In his study *The Remains of Japhet, being historical enquiries into the affinity and origins of the European languages* (1767), he first demonstrated the similarity between Irish and Welsh with an extensive (thousand-word) comparison of their vocabularies. He then expanded his inquiry to the other languages of Eurasia by comparing the words for the numerals in Celtic (Irish, Welsh), Greek, Italic (Latin, Italian, Spanish, French), Germanic (German, Dutch, Swedish, Danish, Old English, English), Slavic (Polish, Russian), Indic (Bengali), and Iranian (Persian). The clear relationship between the corresponding words was further underscored by the evident lack of any link with the words for the same numbers in Turk-ish, Hebrew, Malay, and Chinese. By showing that the languages of Europe, Iran, and India had all derived from a common ancestor, Par-sons may be credited with the discovery of the Indo-European family of languages. However, his work was idiosyncratic in several impor-tant respects (for instance, he believed that Irish was the first language), so that this honor is usually reserved for Sir William Jones (1746–1794).[5]

The status of Hebrew as the original language of mankind had al-ready been challenged by German philologists at Göttingen before En-glish scholars suggested that the Hindu language of Sanskrit might be ancestor of the classical European languages. The study of Sanskrit had proceeded apace once the Brahmins of Bengal had been ordered, around 1780, to translate the ancient laws and sacred writings of India into English. After being appointed a justice of the High Court of Bengal in 1783, William Jones set about the study of Sanskrit and swiftly recognized its affinities with Greek and Latin. As founder of the Royal Asiatic Society, he was accorded widespread academic attention. In his third anniversary discourse to the Society on Indian culture in 1786, Jones made his famous pronouncement about the common origin of the Sanskrit, Greek, Latin, Gothic, and Celtic languages. He also noted close analogies between Graeco-Latin and Indian mythology, including the names of their pagan deities. His discovery was soon disseminated into cultivated society at the beginning of the nineteenth century, thanks in large part to Friedrich Schlegel (1772–1829), the brilliant author and critic.[6]

Friedrich Schlegel and his brother August Wilhelm had already dis-tinguished themselves as the founders of German Romanticism by the critical and poetic works they published at Jena between 1796 and 1801. Friedrich Schlegel was recognized as an accomplished scholar of classical literature before he was drawn toward a study of the Orient. After studying Sanskrit at Paris in 1802–1803, he gave a series of lectures on universal history at the University of Cologne from 1805 onward. He was convinced that all culture and religion possessed an Indian or-igin and even declared that Egyptian civilization was the work of Indian missionaries. The Egyptians had in their turn founded a colony in Ju-daea, and he noted that Moses had intentionally not passed on ideas about metempsychosis and the immortality of the soul to the Israelites because of the gross superstitions that had become attached to them.

August Wilhelm Schlegel (1767–1845) also continued the Romantic tradition of Indian scholarship by learning Sanskrit and later publishing editions of the *Bhagavad Gita* (in Latin) and the *Ramayana.*

In his highly influential essay *Über die Sprache und Weisheit der Inder* (On the language and wisdom of the Indians) (1808), Friedrich Schlegel paid fulsome tribute as a philologist to the beauty, antiquity, and philosophical clarity of Sanskrit. But in the final part of the book he aired his anthropological ideas about a new masterful race that had formed in northern India before marching down from the roof of the world to found empires and civilize the West. In his view all the famous nations of high cultural achievement sprang from one stock, and their colonies were all one people ultimately deriving from an Indian origin. Although he wondered why the inhabitants of fertile areas in Asia should have later migrated to the harsh northern climes of Scandinavia, he found an answer in Indian legends relating to the tradition of the miraculous and holy mountain of Meru in the Far North. Thus the Indian tribes had been driven northward not out of necessity but by "some supernatural idea of the high dignity and splendour of the North." The language and traditions of the Indians and the Nordics proved that they formed a single race.[7]

The new anthropogeny of the gifted white European races was complete by 1819, when Friedrich Schlegel applied the term *Aryan* to this as yet anonymous Indic-Nordic master race. The word had been derived from Herodotus's *Arioi* (an early name for the Medes and Persians) and recently used by French and German authors to designate these ancient peoples. However, Schlegel's new usage caught on as he linked the root *Ari* with *Ehre*, the German word for honor. Again, he was philologically quite correct because one also finds the same root with a similar meaning in the Slav and Celtic languages. However, the anthropological implications of the new word for the ancestral European race were much more exciting and flattering: as Aryans, the Germans and their ancient Indian ancestors were the people of honor, the aristocracy of the various races of mankind. It should be noted that Friedrich Schlegel was neither an extreme German nationalist nor an anti-Semite. He campaigned for the emancipation of the Jews in Germany and married the daughter of the distinguished Jewish philosopher Moses Mendelssohn. Nevertheless, his ideas in due course stimulated the boldest ideas about Aryan supremacy among German, French, and English scholars.

Throughout the first half of the nineteenth century famous and obscure German philosophers and philologists alike worked tirelessly to develop and refine the Aryan myth. Many more speculations were supplied by Julius von Klaproth (who coined the term *Indo-Germanic*), Georg Wilhelm Friedrich Hegel, Jacob Grimm, and Franz Bopp. In 1820 the geographer Karl Ritter described the Indian armies breaking through to the West across the Caucasus. As the originator of the famous dictionary, Grimm exercised a lasting influence on literary and historical textbooks. He described the arrival of the Greeks, Romans, Celts, and Germans in Europe in successive waves of immigration from Asia. However, the Aryans were not yet set against the Jews in these accounts. The outlines of the Aryan-Semitic dualism first became apparent in 1845, when Christian Lassen (1800–1876), the pupil and protégé of the Schlegel brothers, contrasted the Semites unfavorably with the Indo-Germans as unharmonious, egotistical, and exclusive. His emphasis on biology, the triumph of the strongest, the youthful and creative nature of the most recent species, and the superiority of the whites provided the basic ingredients of all subsequent thinking about the master race. Such notions were soon combined with a virulent anti-Semitism by the famous composer and author Richard Wagner (1813–1883), who enjoyed a fervent following in Germany and Austria.[8]

Through the lectures and books of the great philologist Max Müller (1823–1900) in Oxford and Ernest Renan (1823–1892) in France, the Aryan myth had become established dogma throughout European learned society by about 1860. From this time on most educated Europeans came to know that the European nations were of the Aryan race, which had come from the high plateaus of Asia. The common ancestors of the Indians, Persians, Greeks, Italians, Slavs, Germans, and Celts had dwelt in this region before migrating across Asia and Europe to found their respective ethnic groups, which in due course became the nations known to ancient and medieval history. The idea that the Europeans had an origin distinct from the Jews was also implicit and indeed survived any ensuing revisions of the Aryans' geographical origins. Linguistics, anthropology, and biology had combined with the cultural and political achievements of the European powers to underwrite their sense of confidence as world leaders. They were all Aryans and the Aryans were the superior race, the highest form of humanity.

From the mid-1870s onward the discoveries of archaeology and modern occultism each supplied further impetus to the development of the

Aryan myth through the identification of the swastika as a racial symbol. Already in 1872 Emile Burnouf, the anti-Semitic director of the
French archaeological school in Athens, had assimilated the swastika
into the Aryan myth. He claimed that the old Aryan symbol depicted
the laying of sacred fires in Vedic India and was later adapted into the
cross by Christianity. Burnouf collaborated closely with Heinrich
Schliemann during the latter's excavation of Troy at Hissarlik in 1871–
1875 and offered extensive commentary on the swastika found on hundreds of artifacts and terra-cotta whorls unearthed at the site. By noting
that the swastika had always been rejected by the Jews, Burnouf also
recruited the Aryan symbol for anti-Semitism. Schliemann also regarded the swastika as a footprint of his remote racial forebears, linking
the Trojans, Thracians, ancient Germans, and Vedic Indians in a common Aryan ancestry. The glamour of gold, silver, and Homeric legends
had enabled Schliemann to popularize the notion that the swastika was
a uniquely Aryan religious symbol whose spatial distribution mapped
the racial continuities of the ancient West and the mysterious East. The
swastika was henceforth launched as the Aryan symbol in the European
mind.

Schliemann's later books *Ilios* (1880) and *Troja* (1884) further documented the swastika and other links between the Homeric myths and
Vedic India, and the theme was soon taken up by others. In 1877 Ludvig Müller had already described the swastika as the emblem of the
supreme Aryan god, and in 1886 Michael Zmigrodzki, a Polish anti-
Semite, published a curious racist tract about the swastika entitled *Die
Mutter bei den Völkern des arischen Stammes*. He also mounted an
exhibition of more than three hundred drawings showing the swastika
on artifacts at the Paris Exposition of 1889. In the same year Zmigrodzki addressed two international congresses on the subject of the swastika, one of which was attended by Schliemann, Burnouf, Müller, and
other Aryanists and swastikaphiles from around the world. By the end
of that decade the swastika was thus well established as an Aryan racial
symbol.[9] Ernst Ludwig Krause (1839–1903), a popular German writer
on science, myth, and archaeology, first introduced the Aryan swastika
into the current of German *völkisch* nationalism with his seminal book
Tuisko-Land, der arischen Stämme und Götter Urheimat (1891), which
carried commentaries on the Vedas, the Edda, the Iliad, and the Odyssey.

The Aryans and their sacred symbol the swastika were further pop-

ularized by modern occultism, in particular by the Theosophy of Helena Petrovna Blavatsky (1831–1891). The Russian adventuress and
medium founded her Theosophical Society in New York in 1875, subsequently moving her operations to India in 1879. Initially inspired by
spiritualism, hermeticism, gnosticism, the Jewish cabbala, and freema-
sonry, Blavatsky hankered after an Eastern source of wisdom. Once in
India, she duly found this in the traditions of Hinduism and Buddhism.
While Western esoteric traditions are prominent in her first book, *Isis
Unveiled* (1877), the East dominates the mature Theosophy of *The
Secret Doctrine* (1888). Here she wrote of human evolution through
seven root races, the fifth and current one being the Aryan race. Familiar with the ideas of Burnouf and Schliemann, she attributed great
mystical significance to the swastika as "Thor's hammer," and incorporated the symbol in the seal of the Theosophical Society from 1881.[10]
Theosophy appeared to transcend both science and organized religion
and found many adherents in Europe once branches of the society were
established in England, France, and Germany in the 1880s. Despite the
universalism of Theosophy, its Aryans and swastika had a potent influence on mystical racism in Germany and Austria from the late 1890s
onward.[11]

But it was the location of the original Aryan homeland that continued to preoccupy scholars. Flushed with victory in the Franco-Prussian
War of 1870–1871, the Germans had evolved a highly chauvinistic
version of Aryan origins that favored the idea of a northern European
homeland. These nationalistic claims were strengthened by contemporary advances in racial anthropology. During the 1870s the blond, blue-
eyed Nordic racial type, previously considered the mark of a dreamy,
sentimental temperament, was identified with virility and conquest.[12]
A number of German writers turned the whole theory of Aryan migration backward with the suggestion that the Aryans originated in
Europe and migrated only later to Asia, a notion apparently supported
by the observation that the Brahmins of India were lighter than the
lower castes. Karl Penka claimed a Scandinavian origin for the Aryans
in his books *Origines Ariacae* (1883) and *Die Herkunft der Arier*
(1886). Already mentioned in the context of the swastika, Ernst Krause
proposed a northern Aryan homeland in his book *Tuisko-Land* (1891),
which launched the idea among the nationalists and *völkisch* racists of
Germany. Popular anthropologists like Ludwig Wilser and Ludwig
Woltmann, the racial mystics Guido von List and Jörg Lanz von Lie-

benfels, and the archaeologist Gustav Kossinna continued to discuss the
Nordic Aryans after the turn of the century, and this idea became a
basic tenet of Nazi racial doctrine as summarized by the party philosopher Alfred Rosenberg in *Der Mythus des 20. Jahrhunderts* (The
myth of the twentieth century) (1930).

Given the existence of entries for "Aryans" and "Indo-Europeans" in
standard encyclopedias and textbooks in France, England, and Germany
from the late 1860s onward, there is nothing remarkable about Maximiani Portas's adoption of the racial Manichaeanism based on an Aryan-Semitic dualism. However, her ideas about the original Aryan
homeland owed more to European romanticism and native Indian
scholarship than to the theories of German racist and nationalist authors. In this respect she was somewhat out of step with her Nazi
models; instead of seeking out the heirs of the pristine race in northern
Europe, she had traveled to India, "that easternmost and southernmost
home of the Aryan race." Her thinking was faultless, inasmuch as she
based her speculations on traditional theories concerning the Aryans
and their migrations. For example, Max Müller had believed that the
purity with which the Hindus had preserved the Aryan language and
religion showed that those Aryans who had migrated to India had been
the last to leave their highlands in Central Asia. Portas's enthusiasm
for the Aryan Indians was thus firmly grounded in the Aryan myth as
it had developed in Europe since the German Romantics.

Her ideas concerning the origins of the Aryans were drawn from the
books of Bâl Gangadhar (Lokmanya) Tilak (1856–1920), widely acclaimed as "the father of Indian unrest."[13] Tilak was born into an orthodox Chitpavan Brahmin family at Ratnagiri in Maharashtra. His
father was a schoolmaster and a good Sanskrit scholar, but in spite of
its aristocratic heritage the family belonged to the lower-middle class
at the time of Tilak's birth. After completing his education at Poona
University, Tilak spurned a career in government service and devoted
himself to the cause of national awakening. From the first, his ideas of
political emancipation were based on mass education and mobilization,
and he was revered as a leading spirit in the fight for Indian independence. He joined forces with other nationalists in starting the New English School, the Deccan Education Society, and Fergusson College in
1885. After disagreements and his disassociation from the Deccan Ed-

ucation Society, Tilak acquired control over the *Kesari* and the *Mahratta* newspapers of the society, through which he fostered a spirit of popular resistance to foreign rule.[14]

While Tilak's anti-British views were strongly nationalist and revolutionary, his social and religious views were conservative and pro-Brahmin. Besides his radical political activities Tilak was an accomplished scholar of ancient Hindu sacred literature. As an Indian nationalist, he was particularly interested in the Vedas as the earliest document of the Aryan Indians and the oldest writings in the history of mankind. By these means Tilak sought to articulate an Aryan myth that would not only reawaken Indian pride in the glorious past but also confer legitimacy on the traditional institutions of Brahminism and caste society. In his first book, *Orion, or Researches into the Antiquity of the Vedas* (1893), Tilak related the positions of the heavens mentioned in the Vedas to the precession of the equinoxes. These astronomical calculations thus enabled him to date the oldest Vedas to around 4500 B.C. During a brief term of imprisonment for sedition in 1897–1898, Tilak immersed himself in further Vedic study and duly published his major statement concerning the age and original location of Vedic civilization, *The Arctic Home in the Vedas* (1903).

On the basis of astronomical statements in the Vedas, Tilak's later chronology went even further back than the dates advanced in *Orion*. He concluded that the Aryan ancestors of the Vedic writers had lived in an Arctic home in interglacial times between 10,000 and 8000 B.C., enjoying a degree of civilization superior to that of both the Stone and Bronze Ages. Owing to the destruction of their homeland by the onset of the last Ice Age, the Aryans had migrated southward and roamed over northern Europe and Asia in search of lands suitable for new settlement in the period 8000–5000 B.C. Tilak believed that many Vedic hymns could be traced to the early part of the Orion period between 5000 and 3000 B.C., when the Aryan bards had not yet forgotten the traditions of their former Arctic home. During the period 3000–1400 B.C., when later Vedic texts including the *Brahmanas* were composed, the Arctic traditions were gradually misunderstood and lost. Regarding Aryan prowess, Tilak concluded that "the vitality and superiority of the Aryan races, as disclosed by their conquest, by extermination or assimilation, of the non-Aryan races with whom they came in contact . . . is intelligible only on the assumption of a high degree of civilisation in their original Arctic home."[15]

Tilak's ideas of Aryan Arctic origins, together with the conventional Aryan myth, deeply influenced Portas's view of India, its culture, and its peoples. She imagined the Aryan invasions of India as having occurred over a longer period during the fourth and third millennia B.C. However, in common with European scholars, she preferred to view the Aryans as gifted barbarians whose military skills in horsemanship and use of wheeled chariots enabled them to dominate the Dravidians and other dark-skinned races they encountered in the more advanced Indus civilization in northwest India. From the Vedas it was possible to reconstruct a great deal about these light-skinned proto-Nordic invaders. After entering northern India through the passes in the Hindu Kush mountains, the Aryans had settled the Punjab and then gradually penetrated along the river courses throughout the Gangetic plain of northern India. They lived initially as seminomadic pastoralists on the produce of cattle. The cow was thus a very precious commodity and often an object of veneration. The Vedic hymns describe the Aryans as a vigorous warrior aristocracy more interested in fighting than in agriculture. Great prestige and pleasure was attached to battle, chariot racing, drinking the intoxicating *soma*, music-making, and gambling with dice.[16]

The Vedic hymns also show how important a role religion played in the life of the Aryans. The forces of nature were typically invested with divine powers and personified as male or female gods. As Sir William Jones had noted, several of their names betray common Indo-European linguistic origins. Indra was a weather and storm god, also the power of virility and generation. Later he became a mighty war god, a heroic ideal, and the protector of the Aryan race. There were several solar deities, including Mitra (identical to the ancient Iranian god Mithra), Surya (Sun), and Savitri (a female deity to whom Hindu prayers at sunrise are still offered). Varuna (compare the Roman god Uranus) was a patriarchal god presiding over the heavens. Dyaus (compare the Greek god Zeus) was a father god of declining importance; Soma the god of the divine drink *soma*; and Yama the god of death. The foremost god was perhaps the fire god Agni (whose name recalls *igneus*, the Latin word for fire) on account of the central importance of fire in domestic life and in sacrifices, a major feature of ancient Aryan life. So great was the reverence for Agni that the fire on the home hearth was never allowed to go out.

Portas was above all interested in the caste system of Hinduism, which she regarded as the Aryan archetype of racial laws intended to govern the segregation of different races and to maintain the pure blood of the light-skinned and fair-complexioned Aryans. When the Aryans first invaded India, they were already divided into three social classes: the warriors, or aristocracy; the priests; and the common people. The Aryans spoke contemptuously of the dark-skinned, flat-nosed folk of Dravidian and aboriginal stock whom they had conquered, calling them Daysus (meaning "squat creatures," "slaves," or even "apes"). A more exclusive development of the caste system followed this encounter; it involved both fear of the Daysus and anxiety that assimilation with them would lead to a loss of Aryan identity. The Sanskrit word for caste is *varna*, which actually means color, and this provided the basis of the original four-caste system comprising the *kshatriyas* (warriors and aristocracy), the *brahmans* (priests), and the *vaishyas* (cultivators); and the *sudras*, the Daysus and those of mixed Aryo-Daysu origin. Portas venerated the Aryan race for its racial purity as the zenith of physical perfection and for its outstanding qualities of beauty, intelligence, willpower, and thoroughness. She regarded the survival of the light-skinned minority of Brahmins among an enormous population of many different Indian races after sixty centuries as a living tribute to the value of the Aryan caste system.

Maximiani Portas's subsequent exploration of India and Hinduism was inspired by her quest for the Aryan heritage. From Rameswaram she journeyed northward. After ascending the famous Rock of Trichinopoly several hundred feet above the town, she was spellbound by the sight of the famous Golden Temple amid the jungle on a nearby hill. In the other direction she noticed the ugly modern building of the Jesuit Hospital. Then and there she resolved to do all in her power to maintain the Hindu traditions against Christianity and all other philosophies of equality. Maximiani henceforth regarded India as her home. With the exception of a brief period in the spring of 1934, when she returned to Lyons to pass her oral examination for her doctorate, she lived and worked in India. After extensive travels throughout India in the period from 1932 until the middle of 1935, she lived from July to December 1935 at Rabindrath Tagore's ashram in Shantiniketan at Bolpur in Bengal, renowned for its cosmopolitan membership. The negligible cost of living at the ashram outweighed her aversion to its liberal spirit and the presence of émigré German Jews. Here she learned Hindi and perfected her command of Bengali. She then taught English history and

Indian history at Jerandan College not far from Delhi and worked in a similar capacity at Mathura, the holy city of Krishna during 1936. Ever more involved in the life and customs of Hinduism, she adopted a Hindu name, Savitri Devi, in honor of the female solar deity, by which we will henceforth refer to her in this account.

Savitri Devi came to know India well and loved it. She was indeed an unusual visitor in the 1930s. Unlike the British and French officials, the busy merchants, the zealous missionaries, and a mere handful of sight-seeing tourists, she had come as a pilgrim to admire and learn about India's proud past and its living religion. She richly evokes the colorful diversity of India in *L'Etang aux lotus* (The lotus pond) (1940), a book recording her early impressions of the country in the years 1934 to 1936. In the course of long train journeys to Benares, Lahore, and Peshawar, she was often rewarded by new Indian friends, interesting conversations, and invitations to their hometowns. She was invariably touched by their kindness, their dignity, intelligence, and harmonious spirit. She piously approached the sacred town of Brindaban, where legend describes how the god Krishna spent his pastoral youth surrounded by music, poetry, and amorous adventures with the milkmaids. She described the festival atmosphere of Mathura, Krishna's birthplace, as the crowds of pilgrims thronged its temples in memory of the divine avatar. She visited the great temples in Udaipur, Puri, and Benares on the holy river Ganges. Everywhere she went, she admired the timeless beauty of India and the spiritual poise of its many peoples.

By the end of 1936 she had settled in Calcutta, the capital of Bengal. In the great teeming metropolis she was particularly struck by the extraordinary contrasts of European colonial life and sophisticated Bengali culture. She described the English memsahibs smartly dressed for tennis walking on Chowringhee Road, the busy major thoroughfare of European Calcutta with its smart hotels, restaurants, cinemas, and hairdressers. But images of old, timeless India always strayed into the picture, often in the form of a wandering cow gazing into the shop windows or resting on the tramlines and stopping the traffic. Just around the corner stood the famous "Bengal Stores" that catered exclusively to Indian tastes. Its customers were elegant Bengali women, in groups of two and three accompanied by their husbands, from the wealthy native suburbs of Tollygunge with its cool lakes, Alipur and Ballygunge. These well-educated women in colorful saris made their purchases from among the fabrics and perfumes, before taking tea to the sound of Indian music. Savitri Devi marveled at their style and simplicity. In India she felt she had discovered a country that could be modern without being ugly.[17]

On Park Street and in other native quarters Savitri Devi encountered the other face of Calcutta, its grinding poverty amid the baking heat, dust, and squalor. The limbless dying on the filthy pavements, naked children, a blind man asking for alms at the windows of a halted bus. Beggars, bony cows, and thin dogs thronged the far northern districts of Shambazar and Baghbazar, the rundown congested areas around the Sealdah railway terminus, Bowbazar Street, College Street, Harrison Road, and beyond the bus station. But even here the population was unbroken in spirit, avid for beautiful things, and friendly. Savitri Devi described how she wandered through a maze of narrow alleys past old low houses, painted yellow or pink, to visit a Bengali family in Shambazar. Although their dwelling was poor and decrepit, the bookshelves held a yellowing Sanskrit edition of the *Ramayana* and classics of Indian literature and history. Returning around midnight, she passed by a fruit and cake vendor who, by the light of a flame, was reading aloud to two or three men the great *Mahabharata* epic. The Bengali love of learning and story, still spread by this traditional means among the illiterate, deeply impressed her. India might be poor, but, in her view, its ancient Aryan spirit was indomitable.[18]

From her base in Calcutta she imagined the prehistoric Aryan tribes' slow progress with their wooden-wheeled wagons down through the Punjab, the "land of the seven rivers," then along the courses of the Ganges and Jumna until the whole area between the Himalayas and the Vindhyas from sea to sea was settled and recognized as Aryavarta or Aryan territory. But this was not just an ancient idyll. She was often asked by Europeans what she thought of British rule in India, to which she often wanted to counter what they thought of Roman rule in Europe. From her point of view, the legacy of Christianity in the West had proven much more enduring than that of colonial rule might ever be in India.[19] For Savitri Devi, Hinduism was the custodian of the Aryan and Vedic heritage down through the centuries, the very essence of India. In her opinion, Hinduism was the sole surviving example of that Indo-European paganism once common to all the Aryan nations: "If those of Indo-European race regard the conquest of pagan Europe by Christianity as a decadence, then the whole of Hindu India can be likened to a last fortress of very ancient ideals, of very old and beautiful religious and metaphysical conceptions, which have already passed away in Europe. Hinduism is thus the last flourishing and fecund branch on an immense tree which has been cut down and mutilated for two thousand years."[20]

Savitri Devi had left Europe to find the last living Aryan culture and found it in Hindu India. Whenever she recalled the spectacle of honors paid to the fair-skinned Aryan gods of old on the island of Rameswaram, a festival she revisited in May 1935, she thought that India of all places should be receptive to the new paganism of Nazism.[21] At Shantiniketan she had met Margaret Spiegel (Amala Bhen), an émigré Berlin Jew working as Tagore's secretary. Spiegel was appalled by Savitri Devi and considered her a far worse Nazi than the provincial racists she had known in the Third Reich. Savitri Devi's global pan-Aryan doctrine and her recognition of Hinduism as an Aryan legacy certainly placed her apart from the narrow nationalism of most German Nazis.[22] Years before in Palestine she had resolved to honor the pagan gods and fight the Judaeo-Christian legacy of the West. Her first concern now was the defense of Hinduism as the bastion of Aryandom against all encroachments by Christianity and Islam. In late 1937 she fulfilled her desire for practical engagement in this struggle by joining the Hindu Mission in Calcutta as a traveling lecturer in the states of Bengal, Bihar, and Assam. In the words of Camillo Giuriati, the Italian consul of Calcutta, she had become "the missionary of Aryan Heathendom."[23]

3

HINDU NATIONALISM

Savitri Devi regarded Hinduism as the only living Aryan heritage in the modern world. In her eyes, Hinduism was a powerful ally in her campaign to confront and oppose the Judaeo-Christian heritage and its casteless, egalitarian challenge to the Aryan tradition. But her Aryan-Nazi championship of Hinduism also interacted with domestic political movements in India between the wars. These movements were concerned with varieties of Hindu nationalism, conceived as an upper-caste strategy to unify and strengthen Indian society against the threat of other cultures (Islam and Christianity), while seeking to emulate the confidence and authority of the British. These movements were strongest in northern India, where the Muslim threat was more acutely perceived, and originated in Maharashtra, where Brahmin prestige had been challenged by backward caste movements from the 1870s onward. When Savitri Devi became politically active in the late 1930s, such Hindu nationalist movements as the Hindu Mahasabha and the Rashtriya Swayamsevak Sangh (RSS—National Volunteer Union) were growing rapidly in an urgent response to Muslim ascendancy.

Both these movements had begun in the early 1920s against a background of massive communalization of Indian political life. The collapse of the Congress-Khilafat (Muslim) alliance after Gandhi's unilateral withdrawal of the Non-Cooperation movement in 1922 was followed by a great wave of riots, polarizing the Hindu and Muslim communities into conflicting camps. The same period saw the first organization of the Dalits (Untouchables or Scheduled Castes) as an anti-Brahmin movement in Maharashtra under Dr. B. R. Ambedkar. The Arya Samaj, a Hindu reforming sect of the mid-nineteenth century, championed the

Aryans of the Vedic era, and the Hindu Sabha had already begun to channel these ideas into proto-Hindu nationalism in the Punjab by 1910. However, only with the launch in 1923 of the "Hindutva" idea by V. D. Savarkar, also from Maharashtra, did this ideology crystallize into an ethnic nationalism coupled with Brahminical authority. His idea inspired Dr. K. B. Hedgewar, a fellow Maharashtrian, to found the RSS, a youth organization intended to reinvigorate the nation through an awareness of India's glorious past, Hindu piety, paramilitary training, and sports.[1]

At this time Hinduism in India was also directly affected by the political institutions of British rule. The principle of communal representation became general in the award of 1932, which made provision for Muslim representation in state legislatures by quotas based on the numbers of each religious group in the population. The new Hindu political organizations sought to address this problem of declining Hindu influence by seeking conversions among non-Hindus and the return to the fold of former apostates through Hindu Missions. After her arrival in 1932, Savitri Devi had sought such a Hindu agency in South India, notably without success due to the greater integration of Islam in this region. The situation was altogether different in Bengal, where the political balance was more acute. In early 1937 she presented herself to Srimat Swami Satyananda, the president of the Hindu Mission in Calcutta, and asked if she might offer her services to the Mission.

When Satyananda asked about her own religious beliefs, Savitri Devi declared she was an Aryan pagan and regretted the conversion of Europe to Christianity. She wanted to prevent the sole remaining country honoring Aryan gods from falling under the spiritual influence of the Jews. She also added that she was a devotee of Adolf Hitler, who was leading the only movement in this Aryan pagan spirit against the Judaeo-Christian civilization of the West. Satyananda was impressed by the young Greek woman with intense eyes and an outspoken manner. The Hindu Mission could certainly use such an ardent and educated fighter fluent in both Bengali and Hindi. In fact, Satyananda shared many Hindus' admiration for Hitler on account of his Aryan mythology and use of the swastika, the traditional sign of fortune and health. He told her that he considered Hitler an incarnation of Vishnu, an expression of the force preserving cosmic order. In his eyes the disciples of Hitler were the Hindus' spiritual brothers. With this meeting of minds, Satyananda engaged Savitri Devi as a Hindu Mission lecturer. Her duties involved speaking at the Mission headquarters in Calcutta and also traveling to give lectures throughout Bengal and the neighboring states of Bihar and Assam.[2]

By the late 1930s Savitri Devi was living in the "Ganesh Mansion" at 220 Lower Circular Road, a major thoroughfare running along the southern and eastern perimeters of the inner city. From here she had only half an hour's walk to the headquarters of the Hindu Mission in Kalighat. Her route passed by St. Paul's Cathedral with its soaring tower, the white marble walls and dome of the Victoria Memorial, the racecourse and polo ground, and beyond this the wide green expanse of the Maidan park and the bastions of Fort William. The smart Bengali residential suburb of Kalighat farther south made a proud native contrast to these splendid monuments of British India in their spacious settings. Across Tolly's Nala, a minor waterway running through Kalighat to the River Hooghly, lay the Italian Renaissance Belvedere residence of the British lieutenant governor in Bengal, and the Horticultural Gardens, various government offices, law courts, and the jails. The Hindu Mission occupied two houses at 31/2–3 and 32/B Haris Chatterji Street on the right bank of Tolly's Nala. Farther south stood the famous Kali Temple, dedicated to the angry incarnation of Shakti, the goddess of power. This sanctuary attracted a large number of pilgrims daily. Whenever Savitri Devi visited the temple, she received as a *prasad* (blessing) a blood-red vermillion paste, the symbol of Kali, to wear on her forehead.

By mid-1937 she was deeply involved with the Hindu Mission, which ran an active program of lectures and meetings from its headquarters at Kalighat throughout Bengal, Bihar, and Assam. Her work gave her an unparalleled opportunity to learn more about Hinduism, to observe its customs and beliefs across a large region, and to make the personal acquaintance of interesting and influential figures in Indian political life. Through the Hindu Mission she came into contact with other Hindu nationalist groups, including the youth movement of Dr. Balakrishna Shivaram Moonje, Dr. Hedgewar's Rashtriya Swayamsevak Sangh (RSS), and the Hindu Mahasabha, whose president was the veteran Indian patriot V. D. Savarkar. His career of anti-British revolutionary extremism and his writings on Indian history, Hindu identity, and destiny exercised an important influence on Savitri Devi and the evolution of her Hindu-Aryan ideology.

Vinayak Damodar Savarkar (1883–1966) was born into a middle-class Chitpavan Brahmin family at the village of Bhagur near Nasik in the Maratha province of Maharashtra in western India. He was an early convert to the cause of Indian independence. Savarkar admired the Chaphekar brothers who had murdered a British administrator at Poona in 1897 and gone to their execution singing verses from the *Bhagavad Gita*; deeply impressed, he took an oath before his family goddess to fight for India's freedom. By 1899 he had begun his career of anti-British conspiracy with the founding of secret societies and went on to make patriotic speeches and organize demonstrations over the partition of Bengal in 1905. A high academic achiever, he won a scholarship in 1906 that enabled him to study in London, where he became a leading figure at the India House. Here he continued his revolutionary activities, raising political consciousness among other expatriate Indian students and learning how to make bombs. Savarkar published his first book, *The War of Indian Independence* (1908), to commemorate the fiftieth anniversary of the Indian Mutiny but it was promptly suppressed by the British Government.

Meanwhile, a member of Savarkar's group was convicted of assassinating Sir Curzon Wyllie in London, after his own brother Ganesh was sentenced to transportation in 1909 for terrorist activities. In 1910 the collector of Nasik was shot in revenge for the brother's sentence, and Savarkar was arrested in London for complicity in the murder. Extradited to India, he was convicted of treason and of being an accessory to murder and sentenced to two consecutive life-transportations. He served ten years in jail on the Andaman Islands, from 1911 to 1921, and three further years in prisons at Yervada, Nasik, and Ratnagiri. Savarkar used the period of his confinement for writing and became a prolific author, publishing thirty-eight books in the course of his lifetime. These included poetry, essays, and an autobiography in Marathi; the treatise on the Indian Mutiny and an account of his transportation and prison sketches in the Andamans were published in English.[3]

In Ratnagiri prison Savarkar wrote his famous short work *Hindutva* (1923), which set out his view of Indian history from a Hindu point of view and his conception of Hinduness. A preface posed the question "Who is a Hindu?" and stated, "A Hindu means a person, who regards this Land of Bharat Varsha, from the Indus to the Seas as his Father-Land as well as his Holy-Land." The work was inspired by a mythical spirit, bold generalization, and heroic quotation, which commended it to Savitri Devi and other Aryan enthusiasts. Tracing the origins of the Hindu nation, Savarkar eloquently recalled the prehistoric colonization of the Aryans:

> The intrepid Aryans made [India] their home and lighted their first sacrificial fire on the banks of the Sindhu, the Indus. . . . [L]ong before the ancient Egyptians, and Babylonians had built their magnificent civilization, the holy waters of the Indus were daily witnessing the lucid and curling columns of the scented sacrificial smokes and the valleys resounding the chants of Vedic hymns—the spiritual ferver that animated their souls. The adventurous valour that propelled their intrepid enterprizes, the sublime heights to which their thoughts rose—all these had marked them out as a people destined to lay the foundation of a great and enduring civilization.[4]

Savarkar's broad canvas of Indian history found a particular focus in the zenith and decline of the Mughal Empire between 1560 and 1760. The rise of Maratha power, first in Maharashtra, later throughout India, challenged and finally destroyed the Mughal Empire, ending the long period of Muslim rule in India. Savarkar regarded this Maratha ascendancy as the most important movement of Hindu liberation in Indian history: it laid the basis of a self-conscious Hindu and national identity in the entire country. His flattering view of the importance of the Marathas as the pioneers of Hindudom in modern India doubtless owed much to his own Maratha ancestry and upbringing in Maharashtra. The Maratha challenge to the impressive and long-standing edifice of Mughal authority also struck him as an inspiring precedent and prelude to his own campaign to drive out his British enemies, the founders of another secure and magnificent Indian empire. At the same time, the recent Muslim tensions and challenges to Brahmin authority in the province were an obvious factor in his ideology.

The sudden rise of the Marathas is one of the mysteries of Indian history. This race of small, sturdy individuals renowned for their hardiness, perseverance, and industry lacked the grace and style of the Rajputs and other Indian tribes. The majority were Sudras or members of the cultivator class, and their leader (*peshwa*) was usually drawn from the small minority of an extremely intelligent and exclusive Brahmin class. The Marathas first entered history through their leader Sivaji (1627–1680), who began his career as a robber chief in the Bijapur and soon controlled a sizeable territory in defiance of the Mughal emperor Aurangzeb. Sivaji killed the Muslim army chief Afzal Khan at a parley, and the Marathas destroyed his forces in 1659. The rich Mughal port of Surat was sacked by Sivaji in 1664. Now forced to take this local rebel seriously, Aurangzeb appointed his son, Prince Muazzam, to command the army in the Deccan plain against the Marathas. Associated with the prince in this campaign was the rajah Jai Singh of Jaipur, who made common cause with Sivaji and encouraged him to accept a treaty and surrender to imperial authority as an expedient in 1666.[5] With deep approval, Savarkar quoted Sivaji's words of Hindu championship and martial resolve: "We are Hindus. The Mahamedans have subjugated the entire Deccan. They have defiled our sacred places! In fact they have desecrated our religion. We will therefore protect our religion and for that we would even lose our lives. We will acquire new kingdoms by our prowess and that bread we will eat."[6]

Periods of peace alternated with active hostilities, Maratha power increasing all the while. Continued successes involving the extortion of tribute from nominal Mughal provinces led Sivaji to assume the dignity of an independent king in a coronation at Raigarh in 1674. By the time of his death he had consolidated a small independent kingdom in western India. Although Sivaji's achievement certainly rested on military prowess, his intense devotion to Hinduism was a vital factor in arousing the defiant nationalism of the Marathas against the Mughal power. He thus welded his people, both caste-conscious Brahmins and independent farmers, into a new nation proud of its identity and Hindu religion.[7] Savarkar overlooked Sivaji's robber state and asserted that Maratha ascendancy was no parochial movement, "The Hindu Empire . . . was the great ideal which had fired the imagination and goaded the actions of Shivaji while he was but within his teens" and commented that "the rise of Hindu power under Shivaji had electrified the Hindu mind all over India. The oppressed looked upon him as an Avatar and a Savior."[8]

Savarkar traced the subsequent expansion of Maratha power across India in the generations of Baji Rao and Nanasaheb. During the rule of the second *peshwa* Baji Rao (1720–1740), the Marathas succeeded in making themselves masters of Gujurat, Malwa, and Bundelkhand and briefly invaded the outskirts of Delhi in 1737. The powerless and corrupt state of the Mughal Empire invited foreign intervention, first from the Persians in 1739, then from the Afghans. By 1758 the Marathas had occupied the Punjab and it seemed that they were destined to become the rulers of all India. Their frontier extended in the North to the River Indus and the Himalayas and in the South almost as far as the tip of the peninsula. Sadashiv Bhao, the cousin of the third *peshwa* Balaji Rao, was an outstanding military leader and the real power in the Maratha government. In 1760 he renewed the invasion of Upper India and occupied Delhi, where the triumphant Marathas celebrated the eclipse of Mughal rule by hammering the imperial throne to pieces.[9]

However, in January 1761 Maratha power was broken at the mighty third battle of Panipat outside Delhi against the Afghans, in which more than 200,000 Hindus and most Maratha leaders were slaughtered. But the Afghan advantage was quickly lost through mutiny and the Mughal Empire was now defunct.[10] Savarkar therefore exalted the Marathas as the founders of a Hindu national state. In his view, this battle marked the definitive close of the Mughal period and left the Marathas, though seriously weakened, as the dominant regional power in India until the advent of the British Empire in 1818: "The day of Panipat rose, the Hindus lost the battle—and won the war. . . . [T]he triumphant Hindu banner that our Marathas had carried . . . was taken up by our Sikhs. . . . In this prolonged furious conflict our people became intensely conscious of ourselves as Hindus and were welded into a nation to an extent un-known in our history."[11]

Following this review of the Maratha period as the era of pan-Hindu liberation, *Hindutva* was devoted to a description and celebration of Hinduness. Savarkar defined a Hindu as an Indian national, with references to the geographical unity of the subcontinent, the bonds of blood, and the maintenance of its purity by the caste system. "The Hindus are not merely the citizens of the Indian state," he asserted, "they are united not only by the bonds of love they bear to common motherland but also by the bonds of a common blood. . . . All Hindus claim to have in their veins the blood of the mighty race incorporated with and descended from the Vedic fathers" and "[N]o word can give a full expression to this racial unity of our people as the epithet Hindu does. . . . [W]e are all Hindus and own a common blood."[12] However, besides their shared ancestry, Savarkar claimed that Hindus were culturally united by Hindu civilization through a common history, a common literature, a common art and architecture, a common law and jurisprudence, common fairs and festivals, rites and rituals, ceremonies and sacraments. India was not only a Hindu's fatherland but also his Holy Land, for it was the land of the Vedas, Hindu mythology, god-men, ideas, and heroes.[13]

Savarkar's "Hindutva" idea thus assimilates territorial-cultural determinants into a concept of nationalism that stresses the ethnic and racial substance of the Hindu nation. It is most probable that he emphasized this racial criterion in order to minimize the importance of internal divisions in Hindu society, which he as a Brahmin wanted to preserve. He evidently rejected a liberal concept of the nation-state based on a social contract between individuals within a state's administrative borders. Here his thought was in keeping with German political theory gleaned from reading the Swiss jurist Johann Kaspar Bluntschli (1808–1881) during his years of imprisonment. Significantly, Bluntschli's concept of German ethnic nationalism influenced both Savarkar and the second leader of the RSS, M. S. Golwalkar, in their exposition of Hindu nationalism.[14]

Between 1924 and 1937 Savarkar was not permitted to leave the Ratnagiri district. Once this restriction was lifted, he resumed political activity, translating his philosophy of "Hindutva" into extreme Hindu nationalism. He was immediately elected president of the All India Hindu Mahasabha at its nineteenth session held at Ahmedabad in 1937 and presided over its next five annual sessions. Although the Hindu Mahasabha had been founded as a social organization in 1915, it now became a vigorous lobby group for Hindu interests under Savarkar's leadership. In his presidential speech of 1937, Savarkar described the Mahasabha as a pan-Hindu organization with the task of "the maintenance, protection and promotion of the Hindu race, culture and civilization for the advance and glory of Hindu Rashtra . . . a national body representing the Hindu Nation as a whole" and cast a watchful eye at the antinational designs of the Muslims in India.[15]

At the twentieth session of the Hindu Mahasabha held at Nagpur in 1938, Savarkar attacked the Indian National Congress. In his view, its secular Indian patriotism had denied the Hinduness of the Indian majority but still failed to embrace the Muslims, who jealously defended their religious community. The Congress was but a hostage of Muslim intransigence, constantly seeking to appease the Muslims to the disadvantage of the Hindu majority. Savarkar railed at the British for denying the Hindus political representation in proportion to their population through the Communal Award of 1932—in his view an unjust system of weightages and preferences—and for breaking up the Hindu electorate into such constituencies as to prevent the growth of Hindu political solidarity. He protested against the operation of quotas favoring Muslims in the government services (as high as 60 percent in Bengal, for example), and the curtailment of Hindu recruitment to the army and police with the result that the Muslim minority was predominant in these forces. Besides these political grievances, Savarkar drew a grim picture of Hindus subject to religious and racial persecution in the Muslim states of Hyderabad and Bhopal, and as the hapless victims of riots and tribal frontier raids.[16] These grievances and the fear of permanent political subserviency had indeed haunted the thinking and emotions of many caste Hindus throughout the 1930s.

Savarkar concluded that the Indian National Congress had failed the Hindus; its Indian patriotism was a secular sham, and only the Hindu Mahasabha could properly represent the Indian Hindu nation. Savarkar exhorted his followers to abandon the false ideas that had prevailed since the birth of the Congress in the 1880s. Hindu nationalism was the only effective form of Indian nationalism. After a brief review of the Maratha era of Hindu nationalism and the foundation of a Hindu empire, Savarkar demanded that the self-conscious Hindu nation must again be revived and resurrected.[17] At this 1938 session of the Mahasabha it was clear that Savarkar was advocating Hindu radicalism as the only effective response to Muslim provocation and ascendancy in national affairs. His extreme Hindu nationalism now tended toward a Hindu communalism that paralleled Muslim defensiveness and thus accentuated the polarization of Hindu-Muslim enmity.

Savitri Devi's involvement with the Hindu Mission in Calcutta drew her into the vortex of this Hindu nationalist movement in the late 1930s. In her writings she shared V. D. Savarkar's political concerns about Hindu disadvantage and Muslim ascendancy. She endorsed his demand for a revival of Hindu national consciousness as the only real form of Indian patriotism. She agreed with the thesis of *Hindutva* that Hindu nationalism must derive its strength from a sense of shared history, culture, and an awareness of India as one's Holy Land. And in return she was recognized as a valuable supporter by the nationalists themselves. Ganesh Savarkar praised her in a cordial foreword he wrote for her first book on Hinduism: "She has one advantage over the usual worker from within the Hindu fold. She was Greek by nationality. It is owing partly to her appreciation of Hindu art, thought and 'dharma,' and partly to deeper reasons that she was drawn to our society and that she adopted what we call 'Hindutva' for the rest of her life. But, naturally, being a European, she could, though from within, study the condition of the Hindus in a detached manner."[18] Such recognition placed her in that tiny minority of elective Hindus, who have gained acceptance as compatriots.

Her new book, *A Warning to the Hindus* (1939), was published under the auspices of the Hindu Mission after she had worked there for some eighteen months. The book was evidently highly regarded by the mission, for it was also published in six Indian languages, including Bengali, Hindi, and Marathi. The first chapter, "Indian Nationalism and Hindu Consciousness" echoes V. D. Savarkar's rallying cry of "Hindutva" with her main thesis that Hinduism is the national religion of India and that there is no real India besides Hindu India. She was similarly contemptuous of Congress's secular patriotism and asserted that "there is no such thing as an Indian civilization which is neither Hindu nor Musulman. . . . [T]he only civilization for all India is Hindu civilization. The only culture for all India is Hindu culture. Indian national consciousness is nothing else but Hindu national consciousness," and again "[A]s nothing is more necessary to India, to-day, than a strong national consciousness and national pride . . . nothing is more necessary, to-day, than to revive, to exalt, to cultivate intelligent Hinduism through the length and breadth of India."[19]

Her work at the Hindu Mission had familiarized her with the grievances of Hindus and their sense of embattlement in the increasingly Muslim culture of some provinces. In a chapter entitled "The Defence of Hindudom: A Danger Signal," she produced statistics on the relative numerical strengths of Hindus and Muslims in various Indian states. She conceded that the Muslim minority was still negligible in the Far South (3 percent), Orissa (2 percent) and Bihar (10 percent), the United Provinces (13 percent), the Central Provinces (5 percent) and West Bengal (6 percent). However, on turning her attention to the Punjab, "the cradle of Aryan culture in India," and Bengal, her own adopted province, she saw cause for grave concern. Estimating the Hindu population of Bengal at 22 million and the Muslim population at 28 million, with a further 2 million in the border district of Assam, she found that the Muslim population of Bengal was practically half the entire Muslim population of British India. She commented that this Muslim population of Bengal alone was already more than double that of Turkey and that the Muslim population of just one of the Bengal districts (Mymensingh) was more than half that of all Arabia.[20]

Already, she complained, one could walk through miles of Bengali countryside and not meet a single Hindu who was consciously cultivating the religion of his forefathers with worship, devotions at a family shrine, observances and the celebration of festival days. She dwelt fondly on the now all too rare encounters with learned Brahmins in Bengali villages, marveling at their refinement and culture, their pleasure in philosophical debate, and their ready Sanskrit quotations from Holy Scriptures. "They have the sweet temper and amiable manners of people who have been aristocrats since the beginning of the world" and "by coming into contact with them, one feels like discovering an untouched spot of ancient India."[21] But they now seemed a tiny threatened minority, while Muslims became ever more numerous in rural areas.

She was relieved to observe that the proportion of Hindus was greater in towns than in villages and took solace in the company of educated Hindus, who were numerous and kept Hindu tradition and Hindu culture alive in their homes. "While sitting with them, you feel you are in India; in fact, you *are* in India still," she reflected, while noting that the masses were getting day by day more Mohammedanized. Indeed, the threat of Muslim submergence and cultural alienation was becoming ever more apparent: "There are quarters in Dacca and Chittagong, where the number of bearded men that you cross in the streets, wearing a red 'tupi' upon their head, makes you feel as if you were in Cairo or in Bagdad, not in India."[22]

She considered that the usual upper-caste Hindu response to this sense of decline was complacent, namely, that it was "quality" rather than "quantity" that mattered, that the existence of a small minority of educated Hindus was worth more than a mass of ignorant Hindus. She argued that it was not the tenets of Hinduism that were in danger; they would always hold true irrespective of the numbers of Hindus. It was the Hindus, as a nation, who were in danger of extinction, at least in some parts of India. She defended Hindudom, not Hinduism. She recalled that the truth in Plato's writings was still true, but that it did not keep ancient Greek society and civilization from passing away. Similarly, "[T]he value of Hinduism will not save Hindudom, if Hindudom is not strong, numerically and politically."[23]

But why was the numerical strength of Hindudom and the whole notion of "Hindutva" so important to her? The relative numbers of Hindu and Muslim populations in the various Indian states, the need for a strong national consciousness and national pride in India, what significance could these issues possess for her, a Greek national who had first arrived in India only half a decade earlier? The answer to these questions is the elaboration of her Aryan cult, which is also to be found in the pages of *A Warning to the Hindus*. The chapter entitled "Indian Paganism: The Last Living Expression of Aryan Beauty" provided a philosophical interlude between those more prosaic sections of the book devoted to Indian nationalism, population censuses, the threat of Mohammedanization, and the need for a radical Hindu revival in the style of V. D. Savarkar. This cult of Aryanism alone represents those deeper reasons, mentioned by Ganesh Savarkar, that drew her to Hindu society and led to her lifelong adoption of "Hindutva."

Savitri Devi had come to India in 1932 to find a living equivalent of the old Aryan cults of Europe. Once she had stepped outside the bounds of Christian and secular civilization, she beheld "a cult, one of the immemorial Pagan cults, surviving in the midst of the modern world." She loved the Hindus as one of the few modern civilized people who were openly pagan and revered their country since "[India] remains the last great country of Aryan civilization, and, to a great extent, of Aryan tongue and race, where a living and beautiful Paganism is the religion both of the masses and of the intelligentzia." Her quest for the lost Aryan world, once wistfully admired in the dead culture of classical Greece, had at last found an object in a living culture. A golden age had become the present for her in exotic India and she could exclaim with delight: "We like this word 'Paganism' applied to the Hindu cults. It is sweet to the ears of more than one of the fallen Aryans of Europe, accustomed to refer to 'Pagan Greece,' and to 'Pagan Beauty,' as the most perfect expression of their own genius in the past."[24]

Savitri Devi celebrated Hinduism for its open cult of visible beauty. This beauty, this ritual, this ceremony, she believed, had once been current in the Aryan cults of Europe, but now this cult could be found only "in its last sunny home: Hindu India." Her own experience of this cult of beauty shines through her radiant description of Indian festivals, rich with vivid colors, sumptuous magnificence, and exotic splendor:

> Just go to Madura or to Rameswaram, nowadays, and see a real Hindu procession there, with elephants bearing immemorial signs of sandal and vermillion upon their foreheads, and draperies of silk and gold flowing over their backs, down to the ground; with flutes and drums, and torches reflecting their light upon the half-naked bronze bodies, as beautiful as

living Greek statues; with chariots of flowers, slowly going around the
sacred tank. Just see the pious crowd (hundreds and thousands of pilgrims,
gathered from all parts of India), throwing flowers, as the chariots pass.
And above all this, above the calm waters, the beautiful crowd, the mighty
pillars, the huge pyramidal towers, shining in the moon-light . . . above
all this, behold the one, simple, phosphorescent sky.

Just watch an ordinary scene of Hindu life: a line of young women
walking into a temple, on a festival day. Draped in bright coloured sarees,
sparkling with jewels, one by one they come, the graceful daughters of
India, with flowers in their hair, with flowers and offerings in their hands.
In the background: thatched huts, among the high coconut trees and
green rice-fields all around,—the beauty of the Indian countryside. One
by one they come, . . . like the Athenian maidens of old, whose image we
see upon the frize of the Parthenon.[25]

The religion of beauty was not confined to the forms and colors of
the popular Hindu cults. Savitri Devi deeply admired Hinduism's conception of God, in both his creative and destructive aspects, as the expression of a broad artistic outlook on life and on the universe. She
dismissed Christianity and other creedal religions for their exclusive
concentration on man: "[T]heir centre of interest is man, the background, man's short history, man's misery, man's craving for happiness; the scope, man's salvation." In Hinduism this anthropocentric
view had no place. The center of interest was the eternal universe of
existence, in which man was only a detail. The dancing succession of
birth and death and rebirth in all things, over and over again, was a
form of play, which in its millions of manifestations was simply beautiful. She approved of the Hindu idea that the fate of all species and
individuals is to grow more conscious of the beauty of that play and
eventually to experience their own identity with the force (the Godhead) playing with them. This force is adored and worshiped solely
because it offers a beautiful if amoral view of existence.[26] For Savitri
Devi, this philosophy represented the esoteric heart of the Aryan cult.

The Aryan cult she had admired in Greece had died centuries ago.
Here in Hindu India she had rediscovered that lost Aryan world. However, her work at the Hindu Mission and exposure to the ideas of V.
D. Savarkar and the Hindu Mahasabha suggested that this last living
example of Aryan culture in the world was itself under threat. Hence
her alliance with the radical Hindu nationalists, her anxious scrutiny
of population censuses, and her appeal for a devotional nationalism of

home and hearth to revive the memory of Sivaji and other heroes of Indian history.

Savitri Devi saw ominous parallels between the fate of pagan classical Greece and the endangered Aryan cult of India. She compared the experience of beleaguered Hindus in Muslim-dominated provinces to that of Greek pagans in their own country during the early Middle Ages. She recalled the oppression of the last pagans by the Christians: works of art destroyed, festivities stopped, schools of philosophy shut down, wise men exiled. She characterized the period from Emperor Constantine I until the accession of Emperor Julian (A.D. circa 331–363) in terms of "the growing tyranny exercised by the Christians . . . upon the declining minority of Pagans, in the towns and villages of Greece, Asia-Minor, Egypt, Italy."²⁷

This alarmist comparison between late ancient Greece and present-day India was extended to indicate the dreadful possibility that Hindu India might itself become a dead civilization. In the context of a threatened Hindu world, her memories of the sun-bleached ruins of Athens and the Attic peninsula were no longer just relics of a golden age but omens for India: "Greece is covered with gorgeous ruins. Upon steep promontories, there are still rows of white columns, looking over the blue sea, full of isles. There are blocks of sculptured marble, and old statues to be found even in the market place. But living life all around, runs on different lines. The national Gods have become objects of admiration in museums. . . . But nobody worships them. There are no Panathenian processions, in pomp and glory, going up the Acropolis today."²⁸

She warned that Hindu complacency and inaction were a clear sign of weakness, that Hindudom was yielding every day to hostile forces, losing its numerical advantage, its political rights in the country, and its place as a nation. The fate of pagan Greece could easily overtake the Hindus and become the fate of pagan India tomorrow. She painted a desolate picture of India without Hindus: "A swarm of mosques will be built here and there, in the place of minor shrines. Mohammedan life and European life combined, will make unrecognisable India look much like modern Egypt. Cultured Indians will look upon their national Gods, as Christian Europeans look upon Greek 'mythology.' And the Ganges will still be flowing. But there will be no ritual bathing in its waters, no pilgrims, going up and down its 'ghats,' no garlands of flowers thrown into it as an offering. India . . . will no longer be 'our' India."[29]

Savitri Devi followed the Hindu nationalists in her recommendation of measures for a revival of Hindudom. In her chapter devoted to social reforms, she identified the major causes of numerical losses in Hindudom as the denial of elementary social rights to the minority of Hindus; the strictness of social rules within the Hindu fold, leading to the easy outcasting of transgressors; and the refusal of the Hindu fold to accept those who wished to return, let alone those who wanted to convert to Hinduism. Again she drew a parallel with the ancient world. The triumph of Christianity was largely attributable to the rigidity of the Graeco-Roman social order. Although ancient Greek and Roman society was not as complicated and caste-ridden as Hindudom, there was a wide gulf between the freeman and the slave. The universal appeal of Christianity to all men exploded such division and hierarchy. Echoing the fierce antichristian invective of Friedrich Nietzsche (1844–1900), she regarded the victory of Christianity as a widespread revolt of the slaves and barbarians against the existing social order of the Roman Empire. Mindful of this historical Aryan failure in Europe, Savitri Devi advised the relaxation of the caste system with its rights and privileges, in order to develop a Hindu populism. Here she was reflecting the ideas of V. D. Savarkar, who regarded the caste system as a brake on the development of Hindu solidarity and nationalism.[30]

She foresaw naturally that the upper-caste Hindus would fiercely defend their rights and their exclusiveness but asked what good such reactionary attitudes would achieve if all was swept away with the extinction of Hinduism. She pointed out that the noble families of ancient Greece and Rome had been lost, and no single modern Greek or Roman could now be sure that there were neither slaves nor barbarians among his ancestors. Their defense of family privilege had not addressed the universal challenge of Christianity and, in consequence, the vigor and endurance of the old Aryan cult in Europe was lost. Unless the Hindus now made a desperate effort to overcome the disadvantages of Hindu society, there would be no future for all Hindus, let alone for the precious privileges of the Hindu elite.[31]

Her recommendations were both social and national, rehearsing key aspects of the "Hindutva" agenda. Hindudom should unite into one firm, invincible bloc, trained in the art of self-defense; it was vital to keep all Hindus, without distinction of caste or creed, within that bloc; and it was important to bring within that bloc as many converts from Islam and Christianity as possible by attracting them to Hinduism as their own national cult. Caste privilege and prejudices should be given up in order to ensure a united Hindu consciousness. Moreover, all Hindus should consider the Hindu heritage of art, literature, and scripture their own as a matter of national pride and self-assertion. Women should play an important part in fostering a family education in devotional nationalism with domestic shrines for Sivaji and other national heroes. Her emphasis on unity over caste echoed Savarkar's strategy of protecting Brahminism in an inclusive form of ethnic nationalism. But her wish for a patriotic bloc trained in the art of self-defense was inspired by a certain divergence between the Mahasabha and the Rashtriya Swayamsevak Sangh (RSS–National Volunteer Union) in the late 1930s.

As early as 1925 Dr. Hedgewar had founded the RSS to foster "Hindutva" activism among the Maharashtrian youth. Born into an orthodox Deshastha Brahmin family in Nagpur, Keshavrao Baliram Hedgewar (1889–1940) qualified as a medical doctor but devoted his whole life to the struggle for Indian political freedom. By 1910 he had been initiated into the national struggle by Balakrishna Shivaram Moonje (1872–1948), a former aide of B. G. Tilak and leader of the Hindu Sabha in Nagpur. Hedgewar learned terrorist techniques from the Bengali secret societies, after joining the inner circle of Anushilan Samiti (Society of Practice) during his college years. Back at Nagpur in 1916–1919, he organized anti-British activities through the Kranti Dal (Party of the Revolution) and participated in Tilak's Home Rule Campaign of February 1918. He brought to all his political activities a deep religious sense. After reading Savarkar's *Hindutva* and meeting the author in March 1925, he founded the RSS, a Hindu nationalist sect that has proved a vital factor in Hindu politics right up to the Bharatiya Janata Party (BJP) of the 1990s.[32]

How could a vast country like India be so easily ruled by a small group of colonial administrators? Recognizing that Indian subjection was due to lack of unity, vitality, and physical strength, Hedgewar promoted Hindu self-consciousness, high morale, and athletic prowess through the RSS, founded at Nagpur on 27 September 1925. The date of its inauguration was chosen because it was the date of the festival commemorating Rama's defeat of Ravana in the epic. Hindu religious ceremonial played a large part in this youth movement with its own ritual calendar and obeisance to the saffron flag of Rama, which was said to have served as Sivaji's battle standard. *Swayamsevaks* (volunteers) wore a uniform of black forage cap, khaki (later white) shirt, and khaki shorts. The shirt and shorts were adopted in conscious emulation of the British police. The paramilitary style extended to sports and weapons training with the *lathi* (bamboo staff), sword, javelin, and dagger. The combination of native Hindu observance with a tough image of British authority was intended to build character and an awareness of India's glorious past. Initially, the movement restricted itself to young boys aged twelve to fifteen years in Maharashtra. Its public tasks involved protecting Hindu pilgrims at festivals and confronting Muslim prohibitions on music before a mosque.[33]

B. S. Moonje was a cofounder of the RSS, and Ganesh Savarkar, Savitri Devi's patron, helped the organization expand in western Maharashtra by merging his own Tarun Hindu Sabha (Hindu Youth) and Mukteshwar Dal (Liberation Organization) into the RSS.[34] In 1927 Hedgewar instituted the Officers' Training Camp (OTC) in order to build a corps of *pracharaks* (preachers), who formed the leadership of the RSS. Celibate and leading an austere life of devotion to the cause (even today), members of this elite acted as military-group leaders and gurus to the young Hindu men. Lacking trained cadres of its own, the Hindu Mahasabha regarded the RSS as a valuable asset for youth politics. At its 1932 Delhi session the Mahasabha commended its activities and emphasized the need to spread its network all over the country. The RSS *shakha* (local branch) network expanded from 18 in the Nagpur area in 1928 to about 125 (with 12,000 volunteers) throughout Maharashtra in 1933. By the late 1930s, with sharpening Hindu-Muslim conflict in North India, the RSS had covered many provinces with some 40,000 volunteers in 400 *shakhas* in 1938, rising to 60,000 in 500 branches by 1939.[35]

Nehru and other commentators have seen the RSS as an Indian version of fascism. By the late 1930s the Hindu nationalists were taking note of European fascism. Savarkar approved the German occupation of the Sudetenland on the grounds of common blood, and the Nazi Party paper, the *Völkischer Beobachter*, carried a feature on him.[36] When Madhav Sadashiv Golwalkar, shortly to succeed Hedgewar as RSS leader, published his book *We, or Our Nationhood Defined* (1939), the RSS message of ethnic nationalism was unequivocal. Golwalkar rejected Congress's liberal concept of nationhood and quoted Bluntschli at length. The *Anschluß* of Austria and annexation of the Sudetenland were "logical," conforming with "the true Nation concept."[37] Race was the most important ingredient of nationality for Golwalkar, who was deeply impressed by Hitler's ideology:

> German national pride has now become the topic of the day. To keep up the purity of the Race and its culture, Germany shocked the world by her purging the country of the semitic races—the Jews. Race pride at its highest has been manifested here. Germany has also shown how well nigh impossible it is for Races and cultures, having differences going to the root, to be assimilated into one united whole, a good lesson for us in Hindusthan to learn and profit by.[38]

In contrast to his mentor Hedgewar, Golwalkar advocated a strongly racial concept of the Hindu nation and urged Hindus to regard themselves at war with both the Muslims and the British.

The RSS was the crucible of Hindu national identity by the time Savitri Devi was penning her book. But Hedgewar was primarily concerned to build up Hindu solidarity and saw a Hindu state only as a long-term goal. He was reluctant to deploy the RSS in political action as the troops of the Mahasabha.[39] This explains why Golwalkar and Savitri Devi urged its further militarization along fascist lines. During 1938 and 1939 violent anti-Hindu riots became more frequent in Muslim-dominated provinces, and many Hindus were apprehensive about security. V. D. Savarkar dwelt on these riots in his presidential addresses to the Hindu Mahasabha in both years. Savitri Devi also referred to the riots and expressed anxiety about the future maintenance of order in an independent India without the British presence. Satyananda, her mission boss in Calcutta, had already called for young Hindu men to organize in pledge-bound military cadres.[40]

Savitri Devi applauded Satyananda's idea, seeing military organization as an ideal means of educating the Hindus in a new mentality of unity, brotherhood, and cooperation. She agreed that the Hindus should be rid of their long-suffering image and reputation for unlimited forbearance. For her, the national cult of India was rather a cult of strength and youth, the cult of the fair Aryan warriors, worshipers of Dawn, who settled in India ages ago. All members of the new military cadres should take an oath that they would place the welfare of Hindudom above any considerations of personal welfare; that they would treat any Hindu as they would treat a man of their own caste; that they were responsible for the defense of the wider Hindu community throughout India; that they would unconditionally obey their leader. Savitri Devi was certain that such militant Hinduism could most effectively forge the new Hindu nationalism, since "military life creates a new society, with a new type of relationship, a new brotherhood: the brotherhood of those who share the same hardships and the same dangers, who obey the same orders, and fight on the same side."[41]

Just as the decline of Hindudom threatened the extinction of this last surviving Aryan cult, so the promise of its military and nationalist revival conjured the vision of a global Aryan renaissance. Savitri Devi invoked the memory of Emperor Julian "the Apostate" (reigned A.D. 361–363), who renounced Christianity and attempted a revival of paganism and the Olympian gods in the Roman Empire. She dreamed of a martial and powerful India turning the clock back some fifteen hundred years and even reintroducing the old Aryan cult of paganism anew in Europe:

> Hinduism, once, used to extend over what is now Afghanistan, over Java, over Cambodia. . . . Powerful Hindu India could reconquer these lands and give them back the pride of their Indian civilisation. She could make Greater India once more a cultural reality, and a political one too. . . . She could teach the fallen Aryans of the West the meaning of their forgotten Paganism; she could rebuild the cults of Nature, the cults of Youth and Strength, wherever they have been destroyed; she could achieve on a world-scale what Emperor Julian tried to do. . . . And the victorious Hindus could erect a statue to Julian, somewhere in conquered Europe, on the border of the sea; a statue with an inscription, both in Sanskrit and in Greek: What thou hast dreamt, We have achieved.[42]

Her apocalypse of a global Aryan revival by means of Indian imperialism envisaged the total eclipse of Christianity and secular humanism. A new Aryan-Hindu-classical pagan order would arise in the West. Her Aryan ideal formed the link between her admiration of ancient Greece and her hopes of Hindu India. She would later write she had done her best for the Aryan cause in "the two old hallowed centres of Aryan culture: Greece and India."[43] *A Warning to the Hindus* had drawn frequent parallels between the decline of pagan Greece and the vulnerability of Hinduism in modern India. At the same time, hopes of a resurrected Hindu Indian empire presaged an Aryan Europe. It was therefore only fitting that the book should link Julian and India in a dedication of hopeful prophecy: "Dedicated to the Divine Julian, Emperor of the Greeks and Romans. May future India make his impossible dream a living reality, from one Ocean to the Other."[44]

The year 1939 had seen massive demonstrations of Hindu nationalists in the Muslim Nizam state of Hyderabad. This Nizam Civil Resistance movement led by the Arya Samaj and the Hindu Mahasabha fielded more than fifteen thousand supporters. Punjabis, Madrasis, Sindhis, Bengalis, Beharis, Marathas, Sikhs, Jains, Brahmins, and Bhangis, rich and poor, the Hindus joined in marches and protests for a six-month period under a common Hindu banner. The orange pan-Hindu Mahasabha flag with its immemorial Vedic symbols of green swastika, lotus stem, and curved sword beneath the holy word *AUM* flew triumphantly over the massed ranks of demonstrators throughout the Nizam state. V. D. Savarkar saw the movement as a Hindu crusade and paid a fulsome tribute to all participants in his presidential address to the Mahasabha later that year.[45]

Perhaps such scenes of huge demonstrations marching under the swastika of the pan-Hindu flag encouraged Savitri Devi to see the modern Hindus as the victorious soldiers of a future Aryan world empire, which would fulfill Emperor Julian's dream of a pagan revival in the West. And yet, India was still part of the British Empire in 1939; even she must at times have doubted the truth of this vision. Already she was searching for another, more forceful agent of Aryan revival. The Hellenes of Greece, the Hindus of India, both were fighters in the Aryan cause. But neither nation had the power to challenge the Western democracies and their colonial world order. The rhetoric of *A Warning to the Hindus* might serve to foment Hindu nationalism, but her hopes for a global racial renaissance were now increasingly linked to the Third Reich in Germany.

Savitri Devi's alliance with the Hindu movements was chiefly due to Hindutva nationalism's intimate involvement with Brahminical culture. Its concept of ethnicity was rooted in upper-caste racism, and this helps explain why both the Mahasabha and the RSS were unable to tap more mass support before the war. The subsequent success of Hindu nationalism after the Second World War does not form part of Savitri Devi's story. But it has remained a powerful and enduring factor in Indian politics right up to the present day. Following Indian independence in 1947, the RSS with about 600,000 volunteers nationwide entered national politics. Briefly banned after Gandhi's murder, Golwalkar's RSS network successfully forged a coalition with the new Jana Sangh in 1951, which became the Bharatiya Janata Party (BJP) in 1980. In the early 1990s, with Muslim confrontation and the bid to restore upper-caste authority, the BJP reenacted the urgency of the situation in the 1930s. New plans for a magnificent Rama temple in the holy city of Ayodhya were mooted. The demolition of the great Babri Masjid mosque on the proposed site by RSS extremists on 6 December 1992, an image flashed worldwide by news agencies, was but another climax in the long history of Hindutva politics.[46]

4

THE NAZI BRAHMIN

Since the mid-1930s observers of the international scene could note that Italy, Japan, and Germany had each embarked on campaigns to extend their spheres of influence and to revise the balance of power in their favor. Italy attacked Abyssinia in October 1935, in order to create an East African empire including the Italian colonies of Eritrea and Somalia. In March 1936 Germany had occupied the Rhineland in a flagrant challenge of the Versailles Treaty; France and Britain stood by; the League of Nations merely expressed condemnation. Germany's prominent military support for Franco in the Spanish Civil War, the creation of the Axis with Italy in autumn 1936, followed by the Anti-Comintern Pact with Japan in November all served to confirm the impression that the Third Reich was a new power to be reckoned with.

Between 1935 and 1938 there was considerable escalation in the use of military force in the world and a corresponding decline in the authority of the League of Nations. A war was already being fought in the Far East, following the Japanese attack on China in 1937 and the subsequent occupation of Peking and the eastern provinces. In Europe Germany was putting great pressure on its neighbors with German-speaking populations, leading to the *Anschluß* of Austria in March 1938 and the resultant encirclement of the Sudetenland provinces of Czechoslovakia. The Munich Conference of September 1938, attended by the German and Italian dictators, and the British and French prime ministers, ratified the cession of the Sudetenland to Germany, stripping Czechoslovakia of its mountainous border defenses and preparing the way for an invasion of Prague and the establishment of the German protectorate of Bohemia and Moravia in March 1939. Hitler had effectively forced Britain and France to agree to the dismemberment of Czechoslovakia, the state they themselves had created in late 1918 and sanctioned at the Versailles Peace Conference. Nazi Germany had clearly emerged from the Munich Conference as the most powerful state in Europe.

As a rival and potential opponent of Britain, the Third Reich was of interest to extreme Indian nationalists in their quest for independence. However, it was a major drawback to them that the Nazi view of India was generally disparaging. In *Mein Kampf* (1925) Hitler made no secret of his contempt for anticolonial movements. He characterized Indian freedom fighters as "Asiatic jugglers" and denied any parallel between Germany's desire to shake off the postwar Versailles system and anticolonial rebellion in India or Arab nationalist movements. For him, the oppressed nations were simply racially inferior.[1] Moreover, his racialist ideas were subject to considerations of foreign and colonial policy. As long as he hoped for an arrangement with Britain regarding Germany's continental expansion, Hitler thought that it was best that India should remain under existing British control. Even later, when his policy toward Britain became hostile, Hitler did not modify this view. He believed that India must stay under white man's dominion; considered British rule to be exemplary; and feared only its possible replacement by Soviet Russia. In his many later wartime references to India, he frequently cited British rule in India as the model for Germany's future domination of eastern *Lebensraum* in Russia.[2] Alfred Rosenberg, the chief Nazi ideologue, shared these racial and political views on India. He was also contemptuous of the Indians as racially unconscious "poor bastards" and refused to regard them as proto-Aryans. Any Nordic blood in the tropics, he believed, had long since been dissipated among the huge numbers of the dark-skinned races. Like Hitler, he thought British rule in India must be supported.[3]

Much Indian public opinion was hostile toward Nazism owing to this negative racial view. There had been widespread indignation at racialist attacks against Asians in the Nazi media and at physical assaults against the small Indian community in Germany. Although a cell for Nazi members had been founded in India in July 1932, growing into a territorial group (*Landesgruppe*) by 1937, there was also the active Anti-Nazi League that successfully encouraged the boycott of German goods by publicizing the racist statements of Nazi leaders. In December 1938 there was official condemnation of Nazi Germany with an anti-German declaration by the Congress, mainly in response to the nationwide attacks on Jewish shops and property in early November known as *Kristallnacht*. Both diplomatic and commercial pressures were brought to bear upon the Reich government to tone down its disparaging views on India, but no flexibility was forthcoming since the Nazi leadership considered the preservation of good relations with Britain to be paramount. When the Indian nationalist leader Subhas Chandra Bose spent several months in Germany between July 1933 and the spring of 1936 and again in the autumn of 1937, his efforts to achieve a better Indo-German understanding were fruitless at a governmental level; both Hitler and Ribbentrop declined to meet him before the war.[4]

But Bose and many extreme nationalists still had hopes of Nazi Germany. In their profound hostility toward British rule, they were eager to explore any prospect of finding anti-British allies among the dictatorships in Europe. In their zeal they either completely overlooked the evidence of anti-Indian Nazi racism or thought it a mere cover for diplomatic policies still working toward a misguided arrangement with Britain, which would surely be rejected in due course. After the German invasion of Prague in March 1939, Indian opinion on Germany polarized sharply into two camps: those who would be loyal to Britain in the event of a war between Britain and Germany and those who would not. The Hindu Mahasabha adopted a particularly strong pro-German position, assuming a close congruence between the Aryan cult of Nazism and Hindu nationalism. As one Mahasabha spokesman declared:

> Germany's solemn idea of the revival of Aryan culture, the glorification of the Swastika, her patronage of Vedic learning and the ardent championship of the tradition of Indo-Germanic civilization are welcomed by the religious and sensible Hindus of India with a jubilant hope. . . . Germany's crusade against the enemies of Aryan culture will bring all the Aryan nations of the world to their senses and awaken the Indian Hindus for the restoration of their lost glory.[5]

These pro-Nazi views of the Mahasabha would have impressed Savitri Devi in early 1939 when she was close to the Mahasabha and in the final stages of writing *A Warning to the Hindus*. However, she had already made earlier pro-Nazi contacts in Calcutta. She had already met Subhas Chandra Bose, probably at some stage in 1937, when the latter had returned to Indian political life after some five years' absence due to travel in Germany, Austria, and Italy and intermittent detention by the British authorities. She admired Bose's uncompromising Indian nationalism but swiftly understood that he was more an Indian politician than a dedicated Nazi. His interest in the Third Reich was largely tactical, based on the old maxim that my enemy's enemy is my friend: that closer links between India and Hitler's Germany could help nationalists in some future bid for independence from British rule. In common with most educated Indian nationalists he was impressed by India's Vedic past, but these interests were principally a means of bolstering Indian self-esteem and fostering patriotic pride in a great precolonial civilization. In these respects his views would have appeared politically helpful to Savitri Devi, even if she could not recognize in Bose a Nazi ideological comrade.

She was to meet just such an admirer of Aryan racism and Adolf Hitler in early January 1938, when a Greek acquaintance in Calcutta gave her an introduction to Asit Krishna Mukherji, a Hindu publisher with strong pro-German sympathies. He was the editor and proprietor of *The New Mercury*, a fortnightly National Socialist magazine published with the support of the German consulate in Calcutta from 1935 until 1937, when it was suppressed by the British government. She had already noticed this publication, which was the only Nazi paper in India, during her earlier travels around Bengal and read its contents with great interest. Mukherji's editorial line was unabashedly pro-German and pro-Nazi, yet he also stood for a pan-Aryan racism with a strong Indian element. The articles in the magazine were written by Mukherji, his coeditor Vinaya Datta, and others. Their subjects ranged from Hitler's views on the nation and architecture, and translated excerpts of *Mein Kampf* to studies on the original Aryans, the origin of the swastika, and the Arctic homeland of the Aryans.

A. K. Mukherji assiduously cultivated cordial relations with the German consulate at 3 Lansdowne Road in Calcutta and was on excellent terms with the consul, Baron Edwart von Selzam (1897–1980); the consul-general, Baron Wernher von Ow-Wachendorf; and his successor Count von Podewils-Durnitz. In return Mukherji received for his publication a stream of news and other features highly favorable to Hitler and the Third Reich. On the eve of his departure for a new assignment in 1938, Baron von Selzam wrote in a secret communiqué to all German legations in the Far East that no one had rendered services to the Third Reich in Asia comparable to those of Sri Asit Krishna Mukherji's.[6]

At their first meeting on 9 January, Savitri Devi and A. K. Mukherji made a strong impression on each other. Mukherji came from an old Brahmin family, whose ancestors had come from North India to Bengal in the twelfth century at the invitation of King Balamicen, who had converted the country from Buddhism back to Hinduism and wished to reintroduce the caste system. Under Buddhism the Bengali population was a mixture of aborigines and Dravidians, and it had therefore been necessary to import a new ruling caste of priests from the northern Hindu states. As a scion of such ancient Aryan stock, Mukherji was noticeably fair and light-skinned. His family comprised six brothers and two sisters, and following the early death of his father, his elder brother Asoka took responsibility for their affairs. Asoka decided that Asit Krishna should complete his education in Europe in view of his scholarly distinction at school. Mukherji attended London University, subsequently taking a doctorate in history with a thesis on the "Third Rome," the millenarian conception of Moscow and the Russian Empire as the successor of Byzantium. These interests in Russia and wider questions of religious and cultural influence provided the starting point of Mukherji's odyssey through the ideologies of the modern world.[7]

Like many other Indian nationalists, he was initially attracted to Russia as a potential ally against Britain. Following his graduation from London University, he spent two years studying and traveling in the Soviet Union. The Soviet authorities were eager to recruit Indian supporters and feted Mukherji with privileges and special visits to showpiece achievements in order to gain a promising communist sympathizer and agent for political work in India. But Mukherji was unimpressed by the proletarian paradise and its materialist ideology. On returning to India, he turned down numerous offers of work from communist newspaper editors. Once this became known, he was approached by liberal and anticommunist publishers, eager to secure the services of an educated Indian who had seen the Soviet Union at first hand and rejected its system. But Mukherji was having none of it. Unknown to all, he was profoundly convinced that economic interpretations of society were flawed. In his opinion, it mattered little whether capitalism was organized for the benefit of the individual, as in the Western democracies, or for the state, as in the Soviet Union. His view of history and politics was colored by a racial perspective: states rose and fell in accordance with the vigor of their racial stocks. He thus surprised everybody when he commenced publishing *The New Mercury* with its self-proclaimed support of Nazi Germany and Aryan racism.

Mukherji admired the growing might and influence of the Third Reich. He was deeply impressed by the Aryan ideology of Nazi Germany, with its cult of Nordic racial superiority, anti-Semitism, and race laws. He approved of the German emphasis on the Hellenic ideal of physical strength and beauty, so well displayed in the Olympic Games held in Berlin in the summer of 1936. He recognized the Nazi flag—a black swastika upon a white circle on a red background—as a close relative of the pan-Hindu flag with its ancient Aryan symbols of swastika, lotus, and sword. Likewise, he saw the parallels between the martial spirit of the Third Reich and the old Hindu warrior tradition of the Marathas and other Indian races, between K. B. Hedgewar's Rashtriya Swayamsevak Sangh (RSS) boys in their khaki shorts and the uniformed Hitler Youth. When M. S. Golwalkar succeeded Hedgewar as leader of the RSS in 1940, Mukherji was surely pleased to note the latter's open admiration of Nazi Germany. Just as the Hindu nationalists were protesting against colonial rule, Germany was also on the march in defense of Aryandom and had already challenged Britain and France, its sworn enemies, for an end to the ignominious Versailles settlement and more, for the leading position in Europe.

Savitri Devi's encounter with Mukherji was a pivotal event in her life. She had at long last found someone with pan-Aryan convictions who shared her belief in the Aryan revival of India. She was astonished at his knowledge of European and particularly Byzantine history (a topic dear to her own heart) but recognized him as a master and teacher in matters relating to Nazism and the Third Reich. At their very first meeting Mukherji asked what she thought of Dietrich Eckart, the bohemian poet, famous playwright, and racist publisher who had acted as Hitler's mentor and introduced him to influential and moneyed circles in Munich after the First World War. Dietrich Eckart (1868–1923) had also frequented the Thule Society, a clandestine German nationalist group founded in early 1918 by the mysterious Rudolf von Sebottendorff to propagate Aryan racism in the Bavarian capital. Mukherji saw the Thule Society with its pan-Aryan ideas as the secret initiatory society behind the open political movement of National Socialism.[8] Savitri Devi knew nothing about Eckart or the Thule Society and was dazzled by this educated Brahmin's knowledge concerning the esoteric inspi-

ration of the Hitler movement. The two became firm friends and com-
rades-in-arms for the Nazi cause in India.

The meeting with Mukherji also provided a strong impetus for Savitri Devi's return to Europe. As she had declared in 1937 to the president of the Hindu Mission, she was a devotee of Hitler. During the
early September days of each year she spent in India during the 1930s,
she had fervently listened to the crackling radio broadcasts from the
Nazi Party rallies in Nuremberg. Thus she had shared the overwhelming enthusiasm of the German crowds for their adored Führer
amid the waving flags and vast tribunes. Mukherji knew and understood her passion but was convinced that she could achieve more for
Nazism in Germany than in her Hindu Mission work. He urged her
to work for Hitler and Aryan rebirth at the German center: "What
have you been doing in India, all these years, with your ideas and your
potentialities? Wasting your time and energy. Go back to Europe,
where duty calls you!—go and help the rebirth of Aryan Heathendom
where there are still Aryans strong and wide-awake; go to him who is
truly life and resurrection: the Leader of the Third Reich. *Go at once;
next year will be too late.*"9

But Savitri Devi considered her work in India to be more pioneering;
there seemed no need for haste in view of waxing German power and
its territorial expansion. However, with the outbreak of war between
Britain and Germany in September 1939, the situation quickly changed.
All pro-German activities in British India were proscribed, and she
could no longer risk lacing her Hindu Mission lectures with praise of
Hitler and Nazism. Mukherji's early advice now seemed highly appro-
priate, and she considered various ways whereby she could join the
German war effort by making Nazi broadcasts in French, Greek, and
Bengali back in Europe. A direct journey from India to a belligerent
state was out of the question. However, because Italy had not yet entered the war, a voyage to Naples seemed to offer prospects of entering
Germany. She had planned to sail from Bombay on an Italian vessel
in late June 1940, but the unexpected Italian declaration of war against
the Allies on 10 June left the ship stranded at Bombay.10 Now she was
trapped and powerless in India. In later years, after the defeat of Nazi
Germany, she would often bitterly reproach herself for having failed
to take Mukherji's advice.11

After September 1939 Savitri Devi's position in Calcutta had become problematic. The holder of a Greek passport, she was known to the British authorities as a Hindu Mission lecturer with Nazi sympathies. As a suspected alien, she ran a clear risk of deportation or detention. But as a British passport holder, she would still be able to travel without restrictions. In early 1940 Mukherji therefore proposed that they marry, in order that she become the wife of a British subject and so return to Europe.[12] It was, she claims, not a romantic match but one based on their cordial friendship and shared ideals. The date set for the wedding coincided with news of the British evacuation from Dunkirk and the imminent fall of France. Resplendent in her best gold-and-scarlet sari, Savitri Devi was married to Asit Krishna Mukherji in a Hindu ceremony on 9 June 1940 in Calcutta. Her hopes of a later passage to Italy and broadcasting for the Reich were rudely dashed the following day when Italy entered the war, eager for the spoils of France. She was now to remain in India for the duration of the war.

Their marital home was an apartment at 1 Wellesley Street, an inner city road running parallel to Chowringhee Road, while Mukherji's office was located in the center of smart white Calcutta at 8 Esplanade East. The Esplanade itself was the thoroughfare running from west to east in front of Government House, the residence of the governor of Bengal between the wars. This imposing Georgian mansion had been commissioned at exorbitant cost by Lord Wellesley (1760–1842), the elder brother of the Duke of Wellington, on the model of Lord Curzon's ancestral home, Keddleston Hall in Derbyshire, and was completed in 1805. Until 1911, when Delhi superseded Calcutta as the administrative capital of India, this had been the residence of the governor-general (later the viceroy) during the Raj, and thus the focus of sumptuous festivities and splendid military displays. Just across the Esplanade stretched the cool green expanse of the Maidan park crossed by graceful avenues of mature trees, with views of the Ochterlony Monument, the Eden Gardens, and Fort William in the distance. Other grand representative buildings in the Esplanade area included the Old Town Hall in Grecian style and the Imperial Library. Across from Mukherji's office lay the Curzon Gardens, while further to the southeast ran Chowringhee Road, the most fashionable precinct of Calcutta, where shops, hotels, and restaurants occupied the old palaces and mansions dating from the eighteenth and nineteenth centuries. A brief memoir provides a portrait of Savitri Devi in early wartime Calcutta: "Walking down

Chowringhee Avenue [sic] under my bright-coloured parasol, feeling happy; boasting of Germany's lightning victories and talking of the coming world New Order in Indian tea-parties."[13]

With the notable exception of extremist pro-German nationalists, India remained loyal to Britain in its war against Germany. However, because the war was represented as a war of democratic and freedom-loving peoples against Nazi tyranny and the German appetite for conquest, Indian politicians were quick to demand assurances from the British government regarding the future of their country. It was expected that Allied war aims would also provide for Indian independence and self-government once the war was over. International hostilities thus tended to rally the Indian Congress in support of its goal of self-determination and this had the effect of defusing communal strife between Hindus and Muslims. The Hindu Mission took a softer line after the outbreak of war, and in the summer of 1940 Savitri Devi penned another Mission publication intended to join the two great religious groups in a spirit of nationalist reconciliation. During a visit to South India in July 1940 she was inspired by the words inscribed upon the tomb of Sultan Tippu (1753–1799), the Muslim ruler of Mysore, near Seringapatam. Its prayer for perfect peace reminded her how India's religious conflicts had long prevented its political unity. In her book *The Non-Hindu Indians and Indian Unity* (1940) she wrote that India must forget social prejudice and communal hatred in order to achieve national independence.

Both Asit Krishna Mukherji and Savitri Devi undertook clandestine war work on behalf of the Axis powers in Calcutta. When Savitri Devi met Mukherji in early 1938, *The New Mercury* had already been closed down by the British government. Although the magazine appeared under the auspices of the German consulate, Mukherji was the editor and as a British subject he could claim no diplomatic immunity. With a fine sense for diplomatic and political allegiances, Mukherji began publishing a new magazine called *The Eastern Economist* in collaboration with the Japanese legation in Calcutta at 5–6 Esplanade Mansions, not far from his office. Mukherji was also on calling terms with K. Yonezawa and T. Yoshida, successive Japanese consul-generals between 1937 and 1940. Although this pro-Japanese editorial activity offered less scope for his pan-Aryan articles and Teutonic enthusiasm, he was at least working with a close ally of Germany in the Anti-Comintern Pact and its future military partner. Savitri Devi claimed that Mukherji knew

Subhas Chandra Bose, the firebrand Bengali Congress nationalist leader, who escaped from India in early 1941 and reached Germany where he set up the "Free India Center" in Berlin and recruited for an Indian Legion from among captured Indian POWs in the Third Reich. She also stated that Mukherji used his position with the Japanese legation to put Bose in contact with the Japanese authorities, with whom he collaborated between 1943 and 1945 in organizing the Indian National Army (INA) in Burma.[14] Bose's long and notorious career in Indian nationalist politics, his vehement opposition to the British, and his readiness to seek allies among Britain's enemies in order to achieve independence for India are the subject of the next chapter.

During the first two years of the war, domestic life continued at the Mukherji household in Wellesley Street much as before. Savitri Devi and Mukherji typically spent their evenings reading and discussing Vedic traditions, racial ideology, and Hitler's *Mein Kampf*. Alongside her work with the Hindu Mission, she spent some time at a club learning about Indian cuisine and practicing yoga, which she had originally been taught in 1936 by a Brahmin at Lahore. Although the Indian Congress was loudly demanding assurances from the British government concerning self-rule in the context of a war fought by the democracies against the dictatorships, the streets of Calcutta were unchanged from peacetime. The Bengalis were not among the "martial races" recognized by the British and thus not usually subject to recruitment for the Indian Army. However, once Britain moved to secure its position in the Middle East by sending troops to Persia and Iraq in 1941, large numbers of the Indian Army were deployed and recruitment was stepped up. However, it was not until the entry of Japan into the war in December 1941 that Calcutta was put on a proper wartime footing. Once the Japanese forces had overrun Thailand, the city was within range of Japanese bombers and there were sporadic airraid alerts.

From late 1941 onward considerable numbers of British and American servicemen were stationed in Calcutta. Their presence and this closer involvement of the city in hostilities enabled the Mukherjis to play their small part in military espionage activities. Every Wednesday Savitri Devi invited Allied officers from the East and West Club in Chowringhee Terrace to come and meet her husband at their home.[15] Bottles of whisky provided by a relative lightened the mood and loosened the tongues of their Allied guests. The Americans in particular were delighted by Mukherji. No doubt flattered by an invitation to a

Brahmin's home, they were interested to learn something about Hindu lore and astrology from this knowledgeable and engaging Indian. As Mukherji ingeniously laced his discussions of the war with derogatory references to Hermann Goering and other Nazi leaders, they never once suspected his pro-German sympathies and Nazi convictions. One American Jew, Savitri Devi recalled with relish, was a particularly good source of indiscretions concerning strategic information and military plans. Whatever useful information Mukherji gleaned from his American guests was then passed to four Indians who regularly crossed the Burmese frontier every fortnight to reach Japanese intelligence officers. As a result of this information several top-secret Allied aerodromes in Burma were blown up and some Allied units were encircled and captured. Burma fell to the Japanese in the spring of 1942.

From May 1942 onward Savitri Devi spent most of her time working on a book about the religion of the coming New Order based on her studies of the solar cult of the Egyptian pharaoh Akhnaton.[16] The outbreak of the "Quit India" movement in summer 1942 had sparked anti-British riots and again raised the hopes of the pro-German nationalist factions. Up until the end of 1942, when the Axis military expansion had reached its greatest extent, Asit Krishna Mukherji and Savitri Devi exulted in the heady expectation of British India's defeat. In this respect, their vision of the Axis conquest and partition of the world reflected the division of Eurasia agreed between Germany, Italy, and Japan in the Secret Military Convention at Berlin on 18 January 1942. She had already formed a vivid mental picture of the mechanized Wehrmacht divisions, armored corps and infantry, noisily rattling through the resounding rock walls of the Khyber Pass following the Nazi conquest of the Soviet Union, Iran, and Afghanistan. The victorious German army would thus follow in the historic footsteps of the first Aryan invasions of southern Asia and the later incursion of the Greeks under Alexander the Great. Both she and her husband imagined the German and Japanese forces meeting in Delhi and the tumultuous victory celebrations that would be held in Hitler's honor at the Red Fort in the former heart of British rule.

The retreat of German forces in the Soviet Union during 1943 suggested that the Indian invasion might be postponed for some time. However, Savitri Devi's confidence in an ultimate Axis victory over the Allies, while unshaken by major German defeats at Stalingrad and in the North African desert in late 1942, received an enormous boost from the renewed assault by Japanese and Bose's INA forces across the Indo-Burmese frontier in March 1944. As soon as the news of the Japanese breakthrough into the Imphal plain reached them in Calcutta, the Mukherjis were again convinced that an Axis invasion was now close at hand. Once the INA had entered India, they hoped there would be a general rising against the British. Between March and June 1944 the Japanese and INA launched attacks on Imphal and Kohima in eastern Assam and the INA tricolor flag was even raised on some briefly held Indian territory. However, the Japanese supply lines across the difficult country of hills and rivers were inadequate, and the invading forces were compelled to retreat by the summer months. The rest of 1944 saw the steady advance of British forces across Burma. The Mukherjis' hopes of a renewed Japanese offensive withered.

This was the beginning of the end for Savitri Devi's bold hopes of an Aryan revival in India on the back of Nazi triumph. By the beginning of autumn 1944 the German position in Europe had greatly deteriorated. Following the successful Anglo-American landings in Normandy in June 1944, Germany found itself once again fighting on both east and west, as in the First World War. The Red Army continued to press the German armies back across Eastern and Central Europe, taking Romania in August and Bulgaria in September 1944. At the same time the Poles rose against their German occupiers, and by the end of October 1944 Soviet forces had broken into the German Reich in East Prussia. Unable to bear hearing further news of German retreats and defeats, Savitri Devi decided to leave Calcutta. In October 1944 she took her Akhnaton manuscript and traveled down into South India, hoping somehow to evade the announcement of Germany's final defeat in anonymity and unfamiliar surroundings. One day she happened to see a man on a train reading a newspaper with the headline "Berlin is an inferno." She recoiled as if receiving a physical blow. Now she avoided newspapers, kept to small towns and frequented only temples and native Hindu company on her lonely trail across India in a desperate attempt to avoid learning of the inevitable collapse of the Third Reich.

But of course she could not escape. At the end of May 1945 she found herself in Sringeri, a small town on the Western Ghats overlooking the Malabar Coast. The town is celebrated as the birthplace of Shankara, who in the eighth century drove Buddhism from India, developed the Vedanta philosophy, and revived the Hindu caste system.

It seemed to her a cruel irony that it was here she should overhear two Muslims talking in a café about the German surrender three weeks earlier. Despondent, she made her way back to Calcutta at the end of July. During her absence Mukherji had been working on a book of his own, *A History of Japan*, which was published in August 1945. Back home in the flat on Wellesley Street she heard from her husband that Germany was to be divided into four zones of Allied occupation. However, Mukherji tried to comfort her by saying that the Hindu cycle of the ages must continue and that the present dark age would end in due course. As a Hindu Brahmin, Mukherji took a long philosophical view, but she was devastated by the fall of her idol and the betrayal of the Nazi Aryan revival.

In October 1945 Savitri Devi joined in the annual festival of Kali, the dark blue goddess representing the consort and strength behind Shiva, the Hindu god of destruction. At the great Kalighat temple, not far from the Hindu Mission where she had earlier worked for a Hindu-Aryan revival, she beheld the familiar figure of the goddess, holding in two of her arms a sword and a severed head, while her other two arms were raised in a blessing. According to Hindu belief, Kali is the author of earthquakes, volcanoes, and all that is destructive. Savitri Devi threw herself into the festival in a mood of frantic desperation, imploring the goddess to avenge the defeated Reich and the defendants in the Nuremberg trials that had just begun. She decided that she could now no longer remain in India so far away from these momentous events in the wake of Nazi defeat. She wanted to take part in whatever resistance might exist against the Allied victors in occupied Germany. She gave her twenty or so beloved cats into the care of a friend and prepared for her departure into an uncertain future. Asit Krihna Mukherji had meanwhile begun to practice as a Hindu astrologer in the absence of journalistic prospects owing to his pro-Nazi reputation. It was a sad parting from her husband at Calcutta in November 1945. More than thirteen years had elapsed since she had witnessed the Rameswaram festival on her arrival in India and her hopes of a global Aryan renaissance had been in the ascendant. Now her career as an underground die-hard neo-Nazi was beginning.

5

THE DUCE OF BENGAL

Mysterious Indian agents and their involvement in Western affairs have always offered rich material for European adventure stories. Wilkie Collins's *The Moonstone* (1868) described stealthy Hindus in Victorian London; Somerset Maugham included in *Ashenden* (1928) the tale of an Indian spy working for the Germans in Switzerland during the First World War. The extraordinary career of Subhas Chandra Bose, the Indian nationalist leader with whom the Mukherji couple had political contact, shows how life can often surpass literature in terms of idealistic ambition, dramatic incident, and tragedy. The Mukherjis' espionage for the Japanese in Burma was but one cell in the extensive network of Bose's clandestine efforts to supplant British rule in India, if necessary by treason with Britain's enemies Germany and Japan during the Second World War. The story of this remarkable man's struggle for Indian independence throws valuable light on the Mukherjis and their world in wartime Calcutta.

Subhas Chandra Bose was born in 1897 in Cuttack, the sixth son of a respected Bengali lawyer who acted as government pleader and was later appointed to the Bengali Legislative Council in Calcutta.[1] The Boses were a large family and several of the sons attended college in Calcutta, where a home was established in Elgin Road in 1909. Subhas attended a secondary school in Cuttack, where he was strongly influenced by his headmaster, who taught Indian religion and literature, laying emphasis on an Indian cultural revival. During his teens Bose was also deeply impressed by the modern Hindu teachings of Ramakrishna (1836–1886) and his disciple, Vivekananda (1863–1902), who said that the West was spiritually backward and needed India's religious guidance, while India had lagged in material achievements and needed the West's energy, technical skill, and organization. At this time Bose became very conscious of his Indian heritage; he changed to Bengali dress and was less attracted to English ways than was his father.[2]

In 1913 Bose entered Presidency College in Calcutta University to study philosophy. The period of his studies saw a further ripening of his Indian consciousness against a background of widespread undergraduate admiration for Aurobindo Ghose (1872–1950) and the Swadeshi movement in Bengal between 1905 and 1910. Aurobindo had been associated with Bâl Gangadhar Tilak, the nationalist leader and author of learned books about Aryan origins, in the minority Extremist group within the Congress, which, in contrast to the majority Moderates of the Congress, openly called for a rapid end to British rule. When the government under Lord Curzon decided on the partition of Bengal in 1905, the Swadeshi movement erupted with a boycott of British goods, protests, and demonstrations. Aurobindo returned to Calcutta and led the Extremist Party within the Congress for the next five years. He developed the idea of passive resistance, called for immediate independence, and saw Indian liberation in religious terms, believing that India had a special spiritual mission to fulfill. In 1910 he retired from active politics and set up an ashram in Pondicherry, where he remained for the rest of his life. Although the Extremist group had left the political scene by 1913, Aurobindo was a popular hero among the students, the more so because the Congress was dominated by the Moderates loyal to the Raj through the years of the First World War.[3]

Bose was particularly attracted by Aurobindo's combination of the sacred and the secular, which formed a bridge between his earlier interest in Vivekananda and the cultural and political revival of his motherland. In the long summer vacation of 1914 Bose and a close friend traveled in northern India seeking spiritual truth and contact with gurus. To this same friend Bose wrote later about Aryan power and creativity while contemplating the revival of the Hindu race. A sharpening of his political awareness occurred during his third year at Calcutta University, when he was suspended in February 1916 for the physical assault of an Anglo-Indian professor renowned for chauvinist and disparaging remarks about the Indians. He was allowed to resume his studies at another college in the university from July 1917 and graduated with a First in the summer of 1919. Bose was also a zealous recruit in the University Volunteer Corps, which he joined in 1917, gaining a valued sense of physical prowess and military competence.[4]

Bose's father now offered him the opportunity of going to England to continue his studies and to sit for the India Civil Service (ICS) examination, which promised admission to the exalted administrative elite of the Raj. Bose faced a dilemma. He dearly wanted to study in England, again proving his equality with the British, but was uncertain that he wanted to serve the Raj as a career. He sailed for England in September 1919, began studying for the Tripos at Cambridge and also passed the ICS exam in August 1920, but then took the unprecedented step of resigning from the ICS while still at Cambridge in April 1921. Bose had finally decided that his future career lay in the service of his country, not as a privileged civil servant loyal to the old British order but as a politician in the nationalist Congress movement in Bengal under the leadership of Chitta Ranjan Das. Once he had completed his course at Cambridge, Bose returned home in June 1921.[5]

During the 1920s and 1930s Bose achieved high prominence and senior office in the Congress movement, both in Bengal and later on the national stage. In common with other nationalist leaders, he was also subject to repeated terms of imprisonment under repressive government regulations. In the early 1920s there was often a strong note of socialism and a concern for the working classes in his newspaper articles, which contrasted with the bourgeois nationalism of Congress moderates. In April 1924 he was appointed chief executive officer of the Calcutta Corporation, where he pursued a policy of communal rapprochement between Hindus and Muslims in line with C. R. Das's Bengal Pact. Bose always subscribed to the territorial patriotism of the Indian National Congress and knew that communal sectarianism was a political handicap in the mixed province of Bengal. Following a long term of imprisonment, Bose took a seat on the Bengal Legislative Council and was elected president of the Bengal Provincial Congress Committee in 1927. He also served as president of many youth and student conferences, headed a number of trades unions, and was president of the All-India Trades Union Congress in 1930–1931. In August 1930 Bose was elected mayor of Calcutta. In his inaugural speech, he spoke of a "synthesis of socialism and fascism," whereby he wished to combine the justice, equality, and love of socialism with the efficiency and order of fascism in an Indian context.[6]

In January 1932 all Congress organizations were declared unlawful. Together with many other Congress members, Bose was arrested. He was sentenced to a further term of imprisonment and not released until February 1933 on the condition that he leave India. In the eyes of the government, he was a radical revolutionary nationalist and considered much less dangerous outside the country. In this enforced exile from India, Bose now embarked on a long period in Europe, which he used to meet many European politicians, discussing the problems and issues of municipal and national government. He was also a busy ambassador, presenting the case for Indian independence in speeches and articles, establishing Indian cultural and student exchange organizations in several countries, and writing his first book, *The Indian Struggle 1920–1934*.

In March 1933 he arrived in Vienna, which became a preferred base for his subsequent stay in Europe. From there he visited Czechoslovakia, where he met the foreign minister, Dr. Eduard Beneš, and then Poland. In July 1933 he reached Berlin and met several senior officials in the Foreign Ministry and the director of the German Academy at Munich. In December 1933 he went to Rome, where he had a couple of cordial meetings with Mussolini and received encouragement in his struggle for Indian independence. A second tour of Europe took Bose back to Germany in March 1934, where he again met officials to protest negative German views of India and racial insults in the Nazi press and speeches. He argued that German-Indian relations would swiftly improve if these hostile statements and the racial legislation were dropped. Bose's desire for friendly relations with Germany as a potential ally evidently outweighed his disgust at Nazi racism. Following some further travels in Italy, Hungary, the Balkans, and Turkey, Bose returned in June 1934 to Vienna, where he worked on his book until the late autumn.[7]

The Indian Struggle recorded Bose's view of the recent political history of India. While praising Gandhi for many positive attributes, Bose highlighted the divisions of Congress during the 1920s as a clash between an older, reformist group of nationalists, backed by capitalists and owing loyalty to Gandhi on the one hand, and those radical, militant nationalists with whom he identified himself on the other. In this analysis, Bose seemed to view Gandhi, the Gandhian reformers and moderates, and the government of India collectively as oppressive forces and a brake on the genuine protagonists of nationalism and in-

Above: Savitri Devi in Indian dress, c.
1935. (Courtesy of Edizioni di Ar, Padua)
Right: Savitri Devi in Calcutta, c. 1939.
(Courtesy of Beryl Cheetham)

Vinayak Damodar Savarkar

अभ्युदय-निःश्रेयस्-निदर्शक
खड्ग-कुण्डलिनी-चिन्हांकित

हिंदुध्वज

PAN HINDU NATIONAL FLAG.

Left: Pan Hindu National Flag
Below: Shiva in the Dance of Destruction

The Dream of Netaji (oleograph, c. 1944). Indian National Army recruitment poster featuring Subhas Chandra Bose and his troops astride the subcontinent with the (Japanese?) rising sun over the Himalayas. (Courtesy of Dr. Christopher Pinney, Canberra)

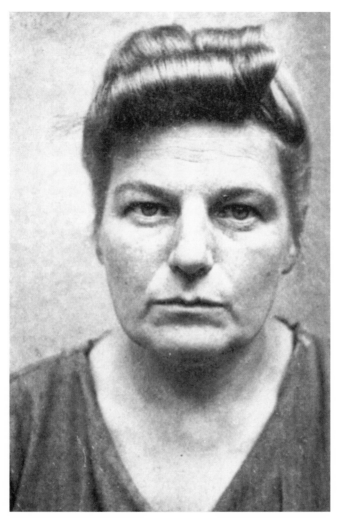

Hertha Ehlert, Belsen Trial photo, 1945. (Courtesy of T. & T. Clark Ltd, Edinburgh)

Savitri Devi's own cover art of *Defiance* (1950) (the fascist heroine salutes the rubble of Germany). (Courtesy of Muriel Gantry)

Cover art for *Pilgrimage* (1958) (rising sun over the Externsteine and German reconstruction).

Left: BNP camp, Narford, May 1961; l. to r.: two German comrades, Savitri Devi, and Robert Lyons of the National States' Rights Party. (Courtesy of Beryl Cheetham)

Below: NSM and WUNS Cotswold Camp, Guiting Wood, August 1962; Lincoln Rockwell, third from left, Savitri Devi, center, Colin Jordan and John Tyndall, fifth and third from right. (Courtesy of New Order, Milwaukee)

L. to r.: Uschi Rudel, Hans-Ulrich Rudel, John Tyndall, Beryl Cheetham, Savitri Devi, and Joe Jones, Munich, September 1968. (Courtesy of Beryl Cheetham)

Above: Savitri Devi, Fred Borth,
Wolfgang Kirschstein, and Beryl
Cheetham, Austrian-German
border, Salzburg, September 1968.
(Courtesy of Beryl Cheetham)
Right: Ernst Zündel in the 1960s.

Above: Miguel Serrano, Rudolf Hess rally in Santiago de Chile, September 1993.
Left: Savitri Devi in New Delhi, November 1978. (Courtesy of Samisdat Publishers Ltd, Toronto)

Savitri Devi's funerary urn and wreath at the New Order memorial service held at the American Nazi Party shrine in Arlington, April 1983. Her Evita-style portrait was decked with a funeral sash worn by Adolf Hitler. (Courtesy of New Order, Milwaukee)

dependence, who included himself, his political allies, and the Indian masses. Bose could only shake his head at the reverence in which the masses actually did hold Gandhi and accused many members of the Congress of a blind loyalty toward their leader. Bose declared that India needed a strong, energetic, and military kind of leader in its bitter struggle against British domination, and he gave Hitler, Mussolini, and Stalin as examples. As in his mayoral speech of 1930, Bose proposed a combination of communism and fascism as an effective ideology for the new India.[8]

After a short stay in India for his father's funeral, Bose had to resume his European exile and returned in January 1935 to Italy, where he saw Mussolini and presented him with a copy of his new book. Having suffered from illness persisting since his first imprisonment, he underwent surgery to remove his gallbladder in Vienna and spent the rest of the year convalescing. He continued to write articles dealing with the situation in Europe. In these pieces he condemned the Italian invasion of Abyssinia and speculated on the possibility of internecine conflicts between the older imperialist powers and the new dictatorships of Germany and Italy, and on the opportunities such a war could bring to India. In early 1936 Bose again visited Beneš in Prague and went on to Berlin, where he protested Nazi racism and anti-Indian propaganda in an address to the Indian students' organization. He called for a boycott of German goods in India in order that German business interests might lobby the Nazi regime to soften its line on India. Again, he failed to meet any senior German leaders and left to tour Belgium and France and to meet leaders in Ireland; he felt a particularly strong affinity with the Irish due to their long struggle against British rule. In France he attended an anti-imperialist conference and made a forceful speech, linking India's fight for independence with the struggle against Western and Japanese imperialism. In late March he sailed from Italy for India, having spent nearly three years in Europe.[9]

Detained on arrival in Bombay, Bose was not released until March 1937. For more than five years he had been effectively removed from the Indian political scene by imprisonment, exile, and detention. After being feted by a huge crowd on All-Bengal Subhas Day convened in April to welcome him back to public life, Bose spent several months recuperating in the hills at Dalhousie. In October he briefly attended Congress committee meetings in Calcutta and took his seat as an alderman on the Calcutta Corporation, but a relapse sent him back to

Europe for more convalescence. He now worked in the spa resort Bad-gastein on his autobiography, *An Indian Pilgrim*, in November and December, when it became known that he would succeed Jawaharlal Nehru as the next president of Congress. With his new office in pros-pect, Bose next visited Britain for the first time since his Cambridge days in 1921 and met leaders of the national government, the Labour Party, intellectuals, and the Indian community. In his speeches and conversations Bose stressed his socialist views and disowned fascism, earlier admired as an aggressive form of nationalism, as another ex-pression of imperialism.[10]

Returning to India, Subhas Chandra Bose now reached the peak of his career in Congress politics. As president of Congress at its session at Haripura in February 1938, Bose made his most important speech, in which he linked capitalism and imperialism, quoted from Lenin, and praised the British Communist Party. Addressing himself to the future of an independent India, he called for socialist reconstruction involving planning, land reform, and the state ownership of industry. These pol-icies clearly identified him with the left wing of Congress. However, Bose found himself isolated in the new Working Committee, which was dominated by moderate right-wing Gandhians, while the Gandhian framework was preserved with the former secretariat remaining based at Allhabad. The Gandhians were opposed to Bose over several vital issues: they were bourgeois nationalists close to wealthy Indian capi-talists and the middle classes; they favored a reformist route to independence rather than Bose's preference for confrontation with the Raj; and they were suspicious of his dealings with the dictatorships, which they regarded as greater evils than British imperialism.[11]

During 1938 Bose continued to reach out to foreign powers in his drive to advance Indian independence. Through Asit Krishna Mukherji he met Mr. Ohisa, a senior Japanese Foreign Ministry official in Cal-cutta, and two years later in 1940, he sent an emissary to Japan to meet the émigré Indian revolutionary Rash Beshari Bose (no relation) and Japanese officials. In December 1938, in Bombay, Subhas Chandra Bose met Nazi officials, including Dr. Oswald Urchs, the leader of the NSDAP (German Nazi Party) organization in India. Bose stood again for the presidency of the Congress against the wishes of the Gandhians and was reelected with broad left-wing support in January 1939. Once more he was denied support by the Gandhians in the Working Com-mittee and he resigned in April 1939. Bose then founded his own "Forward Bloc" party within the Congress, and organized protests at Congress resolutions, which resulted in his being disqualified as president of the Bengal Provincial Congress Committee. It was quite clear that the Gandhian clique in Congress also wanted to destroy his own power base in Bengal. With the outbreak of war in September 1939, their differences in foreign policy became more apparent, as Gandhi, Nehru, and their followers stood with the Allies against the Axis powers, while Bose and the radicals were prepared to exploit the war situation for India's advantage.[12]

By the end of 1940 Bose had recognized that he had failed to convert Gandhi and the mainstream Congress members to his point of view. He began making plans to leave India and to seek help abroad. Between 1938 and 1940 he had already sent out feelers to Germany, Japan, and the Soviet Union. However, in early 1941 only Germany was at war with Britain. Although he had received a much warmer reception in Italy during the 1930s, Bose knew that Germany was by far the superior in military might. Nazi Germany had to be his destination. Who else in India other than his family knew of his plans? Some have claimed that V. D. Savarkar, leader of the Hindu Mahasabha, who had plotted abroad before the First World War, encouraged him to take this course of action. Despite his long-standing aversion to communalist movements, Bose had indeed briefly sought an alliance with the Mahasabha in 1940 as his own leftist support crumbled.[13] Asit Krishna Mukherji, a passionate admirer of the Third Reich, would have known of Bose's earlier interest in fascist Italy and Nazi Germany, and it is possible that he urged Bose to go over to the Germans.

Although under house arrest during January 1941 at his home in Elgin Road, Bose managed to elude the police in the night of 16/17 January and traveled secretly from Calcutta to Kabul, where he received assistance from the Italian and German legations. Journeying on by car and rail to Moscow, he reached Berlin by early April. From the outset Bose sought to elicit from the Axis powers a declaration of Indian independence as one of their war aims. He initially proposed to the Germans that a Free Indian Government should be established in Berlin, financed by a loan to be repaid at the end of the war. The chief activities of this government would be propaganda through radio broadcasts to India and the organization of strikes, sabotage, and revolts in India in conjunction with the arrival of a military force of some fifty thousand soldiers to destroy the British Raj. At a meeting with Joachim von

Ribbentrop, the German foreign minister, in late April in Vienna, Bose reiterated his wish for a German declaration for a free India and also suggested that Indian POWs in German or Italian captivity could be used as the invading liberation forces.[14]

Bose's proposals interacted with German strategic thinking in several ways. In the first place, Hitler had no sympathy with the notion of non-European provisional governments in Berlin.[15] But the idea of a nationalist rising in India seemed interesting in the context of the pro-Axis coup in Iraq in late March. There was support in the German Navy and Foreign Office for an Axis thrust from the eastern Mediterranean through Vichy Syria and Iraq to Iran, in order to seize oil reserves, to put further pressure on Britain at the gate of India, and to beckon to Japan.[16] Throughout May 1941 Bose was exultant at the German readiness to issue a declaration for a free India. However, the failure of Germany to support Iraq and Syria adequately against Allied invasion postponed any realization of an Axis strategy for the Middle East. The declaration on India was shelved, in any event, for as long as Bose remained in Germany. Military planners now devoted themselves first and foremost to Hitler's overriding obsession with his anti-Bolshevik crusade. Operation Barbarossa for the invasion of the Soviet Union was launched in June 1941.[17]

The invasion struck a major blow at Bose's plans in Europe. The Soviet Union was widely admired in India as an anti-imperialist power and thus an ally of India against Britain. The German attack now placed Nazi Germany in the camp of imperialist aggressors. But Bose was persistent and in early July he emphasized to the Foreign Office that a declaration on India was even more pressing to clarify German intentions to Indians now apprehensive about the prospect of approaching German armies. But the Germans thought such a declaration would be premature with no prospect of Axis military action in the Middle East until the subjugation of the Soviet Union was complete.[18] Bose was demoralized by the complications created by the invasion and may already at this time have thought he would be better off in Asia.[19]

However, the Germans did accept Bose's proposals for radio propaganda and the raising of an Indian military force. The German Foreign Office was keen to foster Indian nationalist propaganda as a means of discouraging Indian youth from fighting in the Indian Army for British interests, especially in North Africa and the Middle East.[20] During the summer of 1941 Bose recruited a number of Indians in Axis-controlled

Europe for the purposes of journalism and broadcasting. In November 1941 the Free India Center (*Zentralstelle Freies Indien*) was formally instituted on the Lichtensteinallee in the Tiergarten district of Berlin. The center made broadcasts to India in more than half a dozen Indian languages and also prepared magazines and books on nationalist topics. These nationalist broadcasts, produced entirely by Indians with no German censorship, were a great success and became much more popular than the more sober BBC programs among Indian audiences.[21]

By early 1942 the Wehrmacht had begun training Indian POWs at two camps in Germany. These trainees for an Indian Legion were drawn from POWs originally captured by the Italians in North Africa and eventually numbered some three thousand. Bose's recruiting speech included the words "Hitler is your friend, a friend of the Aryans, and you will march to India as your motherland's liberators." An oath of loyalty to Adolf Hitler with reference to Subhas Chandra Bose was established and the title "Netaji" (Leader) was adopted for Bose. The Indian Legionnaires wore German uniforms with eagle-and-swastika badges, in which they recognized their own religious symbol. The German High Command anticipated that the Indian Legion would be used for commando-type operations in the Middle East, and eventually in Afghanistan and in the North-West Frontier Province of India.[22]

The international situation was dramatically changed by Japan's entry into the war with its attack on Pearl Harbor on 7 December 1941 followed by swift moves against the Philippines, Hong Kong, Malaya, and the Dutch East Indies in Southeast Asia. Within a matter of days the British were at war with Japan, and the United States was at war with Germany and Italy as well as Japan. India now assumed some importance in Japanese strategy. Since October 1941 the Japanese had been putting out feelers toward the Indian community in Thailand. Major Fujiwara Iwaichi, a gifted intelligence officer, developed contacts with Pritam and Amar Singh, leading Sikhs of the Indian Independence League (IIL) in Bangkok. When the Japanese invasion of Malaya began, Fujiwara and members of the IIL mounted a propaganda offensive among captured Indian troops, which numbered more than sixty thousand at the fall of Singapore in February 1942. Already in mid-December Fujiwara had met a captured Indian Army officer, Captain Mohan Singh, who offered to raise a liberation army from Indian POWs. The Japanese government gave cautious encouragement to these developments through Rash Behari Bose, the elderly émigré Indian revolutionary living in Tokyo, who convened several conferences of the Indian nationalists in March at Singapore and Tokyo and again in June 1942 at Bangkok, where it was decided to raise the Indian National Army (INA).[23]

Throughout 1941 Subhas Chandra Bose had repeatedly tried without success to obtain a declaration for a free India from Germany and Italy. With the entry of Japan into the worldwide conflict, he now began to look eastward for new opportunities of action on behalf of Indian nationalism. On 17 December he had met the Japanese ambassador Oshima in Berlin and asked for his transfer to Southeast Asia, where he would organize the Indian independence movement under Japanese protection.[24] Captain Mohan Singh had long spoken of Bose to Fujiwara as an essential leader, and in January 1942 the Indian nationalists in Bangkok requested that Bose be brought in from Europe as their leader. Ribbentrop hastily approved of Bose's transfer to East Asia, but without first obtaining Japanese approval.[25] Although there were further delays and misunderstandings between Germany and Japan regarding their policy on a free-India declaration and Bose's transfer, the latter was agreed in principle in April 1942.

Subhas Chandra Bose had now spent almost a year in Germany, posing as an Italian under the cover identity of "Mazzotta." He had refused to go public in the Axis media or make any broadcasts himself through the Free India Center until the Axis powers issued a declaration on India. However, the fall of Singapore on 15 February 1942 represented such an enormous blow to British prestige in Asia that Bose decided to speak out. In his first broadcast on 27 February Bose declared that it heralded "the collapse of the British Empire . . . and the dawn of a new era in Indian history." The German Foreign Office also believed that the fall of Singapore signaled an opportune moment for an Axis declaration on India. But this momentum was soon lost due to a lack of information on Japanese intentions at this critical juncture. Most important, Hitler himself was consistently reluctant to give any encouragement to a declaration on free India. Not only did he admire British rule in India and see it as a model for the German domination of Russia but he always felt ambiguous about fighting the English—a fraternal Germanic people—and still held out hopes of a settlement with Britain and its empire.[26]

The Axis powers had attempted to achieve some measure of strategic cooperation following Japan's entry into the war. The Secret Military Convention of 18 January 1942 between Germany, Italy, and Japan proposed that the demarcation line of the German and Japanese operational zones should lie along the 70° east longitude, thus passing across western Siberia, through Afghanistan and down the River Indus to the Indian Ocean, leaving most of India in the Japanese sphere. Both the German and Japanese navies were eager to cooperate in a joint strategy to achieve mastery of the Middle East and the Indian Ocean. However, this truly global approach foundered owing to Hitler's view that the conquest of the Soviet Union was the sole precondition for regaining the strategic initiative. The campaign there was also now taking much longer than expected. The Japanese, for their part, were divided over their future plans. Some Japanese planners considered an attack on the Soviet Union and an advance into Siberia as far as Omsk, but Japanese naval successes in Southeast Asia tended to sideline the army's ambitions in the Soviet Far East. Ultimately, neither Germany nor Japan was able or willing to exploit the political opportunities in the Arab and Indian world.[27]

Bose was granted his one and only meeting with Hitler on 27 May 1942. Bose addressed the Führer as "an old revolutionary," which recalled both Hitler's days of struggle in the Weimar Republic and his own against the British Raj. Hitler soon launched into a long monologue, declaring his preference for military might over mere propaganda. The German armies were still fighting north of the Caucasus and therefore not yet in a position to support Arab rebellions, let alone an Indian uprising. The time for a declaration would come only once it could be endorsed by immediate military support. Moreover, the Japanese would be in a position to offer this help far sooner than Germany. Hitler finally shifted the responsibility for Bose and the Indian declaration onto the Japanese by offering him submarine transport to East Asia.[28]

Bose was profoundly disillusioned by this final rejection. Having first sought German support for a free India on his arrival at Berlin in April 1941, the intervening fourteen months had brought him only limited success in the establishment of the Free India Center and the Indian Legion. No formal guarantee of Indian independence had been forthcoming from Germany. Bose undoubtedly felt that he had wasted his time by going to Germany in the first place. However, because only Germany and Italy had been at war with Britain in April 1941, he had made his choice. With Japan on the Axis side since December 1941, Bose felt that he was losing further time remaining in Europe during 1942. Moreover, while the strategic options for Axis cooperation over India were at their most favorable, Germany and Japan seemed neither to trust each other nor to understand each other's objectives.

Bose's desire to reach Asia mounted following the outbreak of the "Quit India" movement with widespread rebellion and disturbances in India in August 1942. Initially, he hoped to travel by air with the help of the Italians, who had in July completed the first nonstop flight between Europe and the Far East. Bose made his farewells in Berlin and went to Rome in October, but the flight was delayed, rescheduled, and later canceled. Eventually, an agreement between Tokyo and Berlin was reached that Bose would travel by submarine. On 8 February 1943 Bose and a companion from the Free India Center boarded the German submarine U-180 at Kiel. Their voyage took them around the British Isles and southward down the Atlantic. On 24 April contact was made with the Japanese submarine I-29 in the Indian Ocean at a point 25° south latitude 60° east longitude east of Madagascar. The two Indians were transferred by dinghy in rough seas from one submarine to the other. The exchange was an apposite symbol of the fragile link between the two Axis powers in a global context. On 6 May Bose arrived at the Japanese naval base of Sabang off the northern coast of Sumatra and flew on to Tokyo, where he arrived in mid-May.[29]

Bose had waited long for this opportunity to fight for Indian independence in East Asia. Ever since his days as a student volunteer in 1917 and leading the Bengal Volunteers as the military guard of the Calcutta Congress in 1928, he had dreamed of commanding a national army of liberation against the British. He made a powerful impression on members of the Japanese ruling military group and received firm backing from Prime Minister Tojo for a free India. A new lease of life for the Indian National Army (INA) began with Bose's arrival at Singapore in June 1943. The "first" INA had fallen into disarray by the end of 1942 owing to fundamental disagreements between Captain Mohan Singh and the overbearing Japanese authorities. The pro-Japanese Rash Behari Bose was able to retain only eight thousand men. The leadership of the IIL and command of the INA now passed cordially from the old émigré revolutionary to his younger namesake, who was received with acclaim by the Indians of Southeast Asia. Subhas Chandra Bose's "second" INA soon reached a strength of more than forty thousand men and three divisions, including a women's regiment. In October 1943 Bose also announced the Free India Provisional Government, based at Singapore, which was recognized by Germany, Japan, and their allies.[30]

Bose wanted a full combat role for the INA in the major Japanese assault across the Indo-Burmese border in March 1944. He believed that once the INA had entered India, there would be a general rising against the British. Between March and June 1944 the INA fought extremely bravely in the Japanese attacks on Imphal and Kohima in eastern Assam, and succeeded in planting the Indian tricolor on some briefly held Indian territory. But overextended supply lines across the dense and hilly jungle and superior British forces under General Slim forced the Japanese and the INA to retreat. Throughout the rest of 1944 and the first part of 1945, the British continued to push the Japanese back through Burma. Bose and the INA remained loyal to the Japanese until the bitter end, taking part in the defense of Malaya. As the Japanese began considering their terms of surrender following the atomic bomb attacks on Hiroshima and Nagasaki on 6 and 9 August, Bose decided to reach out to the Soviet Union as a power not too friendly with the British. He planned to take members of his cabinet to Manchuria and there to make contact with the advancing Soviet army. On 17 August he boarded a bomber at Saigon bound for Dairen, which crashed the next day on taking off from Taipei in Formosa. Subhas Chandra Bose, the samurai of Indian independence, died of his injuries on 18 August 1945 in an army hospital.[31]

How likely is Savitri Devi's claim that her husband knew Bose and introduced him to the Japanese authorities? Since Bose did not set foot in India in the period between his escape via Kabul to Berlin in January 1941 and his arrival at Tokyo in May 1943, any *personal* introduction can only have been made by A. K. Mukherji in the interval from January 1938 when Bose returned from Europe to assume the presidency of Congress to July 1940 when he was arrested. We have already noted Bose's overtures to German and Japanese officials during 1938 in India, and it is therefore possible that A. K. Mukherji effected an introduction in the latter case. Moreover, while Bose was in the political wilderness following his resignation from the presidency of the Congress in April 1939, he did explore an alliance with both Jinnah of the Muslim League and V. D. Savarkar of the Hindu Mahasabha. Contact with Savarkar, who may himself have advised Bose to go to Germany, could imply an association with Mukherji. But because Japan was not at war with Britain until December 1941, it seems unlikely that anyone in India could have introduced him to the Japanese authorities for the purposes of raising the INA. For this he had his own contacts in Berlin.

Although both Bose and Mukherji were radical nationalists, they would have disagreed about ideology. Bose was always consumed with the struggle for Indian independence and interested in Germany and later Japan only as strategic allies in his campaign against British rule. In the early 1920s his political views were inspired by a left-wing, anti-imperialist ideology in opposition to the reformist bourgeois Gandhians in the Congress. Although he extolled a "synthesis of fascism and socialism" in 1930, he had distanced himself from the imperialist aggression of Germany and Italy by the end of the 1930s. His admiration for fascism essentially concerned its cult of nationalism, which he wished to emulate in India. Last, Bose always held true to the secular, territorial nationalism of Congress and was opposed to any communalism dividing Muslims and Hindus in Bengal and India.

Bose's heroic reputation in India remains a legend. His figure was touched by the popular Hindu belief that all great leaders, but especially national heroes who challenge enemies, are manifestations of the avatar. This divine immanence is scarcely reconciled with mortal status. Thus it was hardly known, still less believed, that Bose had secretly married an Austrian woman, Emilie Schenkl, his companion in Europe until 1943. Many Indians today do not believe that Bose perished in the plane crash at Taipei. Stories of his reappearance in India, or the likelihood of his being in the Soviet Union or China have always circulated as an oral tradition and in the press. One persistent myth in 1959–1964 identified him as the sadhu at an ashram in North Bengal. As late as 1970 the Indian government set up a second inquiry into his "disappearance." It is still widely rumored that he escaped, was hidden in the Soviet Union, or secretly lives in some redoubt within the Himalayas. An avatar is immortal and thus Bose cannot age. He is simply awaiting the moment when he will reappear at the head of his troops to liberate his Indian people from hardship or international crisis.[32]

A. K. Mukherji and Savitri Devi looked elsewhere for redemption. They harked back to the Aryan origins of the Hindus and wanted a Hindu India, in which Muslims would be second-class citizens. Their enthusiasm for Adolf Hitler and German National Socialism revolved around the Aryan mystique of Nazism and was absolute and unconditional. Bose had witnessed Nazi contempt for Indians in Germany and also knew that Hitler and Alfred Rosenberg disqualified the Indians as proto-Aryans in their writings. Mukherji and Savitri Devi ignored these points; their conception of the Third Reich was fundamentally utopian. Last, Bose had actually met Hitler and been disappointed in his efforts to secure a German guarantee of Indian independence. He even challenged Hitler about the derogatory passages about Indians in *Mein Kampf*. Savitri Devi's attitude toward Hitler was fundamentally one of religious adoration: for her Hitler was the avatar.

6

AKHNATON AND ANIMAL RIGHTS

"You cannot 'de-nazify' Nature!" protested Savitri Devi, when confronted by Allied policy toward the defeated Germans.[1] Her superhuman ideal of the proud, hard Aryan type was essentially rooted in a view of nature that was pantheistic, romantic, and rhapsodic. Some years before she wrote her outspoken Nazi books, she authored eulogies of nature that address the contemporary interests of Greens, anarchists, and the New Age. Her potential appeal to these modern dissidents lies in a cult of nature that rejects the centrality of man and man's material convenience. Her book on the solar cult of the Egyptian pharaoh Akhnaton involved a utopian rejection of all politics that promote man's interests at a cost to the beauty and abundance of nature. Her spirited defense of animal rights was rooted in a total rejection of Judaism, Christianity, and Islam, which she believed raised man to false theological status and cut him off from the rest of creation.

Her Akhnaton book, A Son of God (1946), was written in wartime India between May 1942 and January 1945, while her eulogy of animal rights, Impeachment of Man (1959), was written in the immediate aftermath of the German surrender, begun in Calcutta in July 1945 and completed after her return to Lyons in March 1946. Mindful as she was of the general opprobrium attaching to the Third Reich in the postwar years, these books make only coded references to her idol Hitler and National Socialism. Free of any obvious Nazi taint, both books have been recently republished for new audiences interested in mysticism and the occult, Green issues, vegetarianism, and the New Age. However, because her Nazi ideas are rooted in a misanthropic cult of nature and animal worship, her rediscovery by mystical, left-wing, and

Green readers poses a clear danger of Nazi entryism within new ideological alliances. Both these books are examined here; the current revival of interest in her ideas is reserved for the final chapter.

In the spring of 1942 Savitri Devi had every confidence in a forthcoming Axis victory and the partition of Eurasia between Germany and Japan. In this exultant mood she directed her thoughts toward the kind of religion that might accompany the new Nazi world order.[2] In common with German theorists of "blood and soil," she conceived of this religion as allied to life and nature in bold, vitalist terms eschewing any notions of a transcendent God derived from the Judaeo-Christian tradition. However, given her earlier inspiration from the Aryan myth, Hellenism, and radical Hindu nationalism, one must wonder what lay behind her newfound enthusiasm for the sun cult of Akhnaton, king of Egypt in the fourteenth century B.C. Who was Akhnaton and what was his significance for a Nazi religion of nature?

The Egyptian pharaoh Akhnaton (circa 1395–1366 B.C.) is best known for his radical religious reforms, his beautiful consort Queen Nefertiti, and the founding of a new capital city called Akhetaton, which was intended to serve as the center of a new solar world order. He was born at Thebes, the son of the pharaoh Amenhotep III and Queen Tiy, and succeeded his father in 1383 B.C. as Amenhotep IV, the tenth pharaoh of the Eighteenth Dynasty, which had opened the magnificent New Kingdom in ancient Egypt. By this time Thebes had become the southern capital of the New Kingdom; its huge temples and palaces, towers and pylons, paved courts, and long ceremonial avenues reflected the wealth and power of the ruling Ahmoside dynasty after its victory over the alien Hyksos rulers in the sixteenth century B.C. Thebes was also the holy city of the sun god Amon, who traversed the sky in the solar bark from dawn to sunset. The social and economic life of Egypt revolved around the worship of Amon, who was served by a rich and powerful priesthood. The reign of Amenhotep III recorded the zenith of Thebes's power and prestige as the center of the civilized world.

All this was to change as a result of Akhnaton's reforming zeal. Early in his reign Amenhotep IV was inspired to worship solar energy as the ultimate power and parent of all earthly things. He introduced the reformed sun cult of Aton (the Disk), from which he rigorously excluded Amon and all other gods as mere idols. Although he began by building a temple to Aton in Thebes, the ubiquity of Amon's name and image in the capital soon drove the king to extreme measures. Once he had changed his name from Amenhotep (meaning "Amon is at rest or pleased") to Akhnaton (meaning "Joy of the Sun"), he sailed down the Nile in 1375 B.C. to found his new capital Akhetaton ("City of the Horizon of the Disk") as the center of his new sun cult. For the next decade Egypt underwent a religious revolution and political upheaval. Akhnaton proscribed any reference to the plural "gods." He caused all inscriptions and images of Amon in the kingdom to be defaced or destroyed, and dispossessed the powerful Amon priesthood of its great wealth and estates. The former revenues of the priesthood now passed directly to the pharaonate, thus greatly strengthening royal power against the professional priesthoods. Furthermore, Akhnaton emphasized the absolute divinity of his royal person by identifying himself with the solar energy of the Disk.

The new city was hastily built on the east bank of the river within a semicircle of enclosing cliffs, and its boundaries were marked with stelae bearing carved reliefs. Here Akhnaton and Nefertiti removed their court, together with a population of some eighty thousand persons. Henceforth the burning sun was worshiped with offerings of flowers, fruit, and animals at altars under an open sky in colonnaded courtyards, which distinguished the new monotheistic cult of Aton. Numerous reliefs showed Akhnaton and his queen Nefertiti with their children, attended by their followers, adoring the rayed Disk of the sun and its life-giving beams. This art was also remarkable for its naturalness and vitality; the informality and joyful zest of its subjects bore witness to a new era. The royal figures were often sculpted in a style reminiscent of the Fourth and Fifth Dynasty in the Old Kingdom (2705–2230 B.C.), which suggests that Akhnaton might have invoked the ancient sun cult of Ra practiced at On (Heliopolis) to support his reforms.

Akhnaton's new solar world order was a theocracy in which the king was identical with one God—the Aton—and ruled as its divine representative on earth. But the celebration of an immanent deity on earth incurred a high material cost. The construction of the new capital Akhetaton, together with new temples to Aton in Memphis and Heliopolis and elsewhere in the Egyptian Empire, drained the land of its labor and resources and ruined the economy. Because tax collection was no longer in the hands of local priesthoods, the king relied on the army, a novel practice that led to corruption and mismanagement. There were also uprisings against Egyptian rule in Syria and Palestine, which the king neither could nor would suppress. Last, plague was raging through the land and claimed members of the royal family and possibly Akhnaton himself, who died in 1366 B.C. The Amon priesthoods were swift to lead a religious restoration: the neglect of Amon was blamed for all Egypt's woes; Akhetaton was swiftly abandoned; the images of the royal family and Akhnaton were defaced, their tombs desecrated; their memory was expunged from the chronicles. The reign of Tutankhamen saw the return of the traditional ways and drew a veil of oblivion over Akhnaton and his brief era.

So complete was this anathema that Akhnaton was forgotten for nearly three thousand years. The site of Akhetaton lay some 190 miles south of modern Cairo at Tell-el-Amarna on the east bank of the Nile and was first rediscovered by European travelers and amateur archaeologists in the 1820s. These early visitors were intrigued by the unique nature of the reliefs on the tombs at Tell-el-Amarna. These large compositions were devoted to the activities of a royal family, consisting of a king and queen and several of their infant daughters. Almost every scene showed above the royal family an image of the sun as a disk shooting forth a dozen or more rays, each ending in a ministering hand. This rayed disk was clearly a symbol of veneration and had a close connection with the royal couple. Its hands brought the *ankh*, or sign of life, to their nostrils, or appeared to offer support to their limbs and bodies.

Until the royal couple had been identified as Akhnaton and Nefertiti, the people in the reliefs were known by scholars as "Disk worshipers." Since the figures of the king and queen, together with their names and that of the disk god, had been evidently defaced by iconoclasts in practically all the accessible reliefs, it was supposed that the "Disk worshipers" were regarded by their successors as heretics. Their names were not only excised on these tombs but also omitted from all lists of pharaohs known at the time. The riddle of the Tell-el-Amarna tombs attracted systematic exploration by Sir Flinders Petrie in the last two decades of the nineteenth century. Further work was undertaken by the Egypt Exploration Society under the direction of successive field directors, including Leonard Woolley and John Pendlebury, from 1920 into the mid-1930s.[3]

The mystery of Akhnaton's disappearance from history and the poignancy of his fate guaranteed him an active afterlife in the modern imagination. Interpretations of Akhnaton and his sun cult began with Sir Flinders Petrie's *Tell el-Amarna* (1894) and then *A History of Egypt* (1899), in which he paid a magnificent tribute to Akhnaton as a great religious reformer who anticipated modern scientific knowledge; James Breasted identified him as the world's first idealist and individual in his *History of Egypt* (1906); and Arthur Weigall admired the young king, seeing him as a precursor of Christianity in the pagan world.[4] The interest in Akhnaton received fresh impetus from the excavations following the First World War. Arthur Weigall's popular prewar book, *The Life and Times of Akhnaton*, was published in a third and revised edition in 1922; James Baikie updated his earlier classic, *The Story of the Pharaohs*, and published *The Amarna Age* (1926) as a "study of the crisis of the ancient world"; Ethel Bristowe wrote an accessible book about the Amarna discoveries and a best-seller about Akhnaton entitled *Naphuria* (1936). Sigmund Freud went so far as to suggest that Jewish monotheism was derived from Akhnaton's sun worship in his widely read work *Moses and Monotheism* (1939).

Within a few decades, the figure of Akhnaton had risen from complete obscurity to familiarity, even fame. The story of an Egyptian pharaoh, a progressive and a heretic, whose memory had been erased for several thousand years, held a certain appeal in the interwar period marked by the quest for new ideals and authority. Although Savitri Devi had visited Egypt during a brief visit to the Middle East from India in 1937, she could just as easily have encountered the widespread reputation of Akhnaton in Europe or India.[5] She was in quest of a universal religion that could link East and West in the celebration of this world and nature rather than a transcendent deity; above all, a religion that was fit for the new Aryan order. She accordingly constructed her own highly positive interpretation of Akhnaton and his sun cult on the basis of the wide range of specialist and general books that had been published on the heretical pharaoh from Petrie up until the Second World War. The fruits of this research were a short booklet *Akhnaton's Eternal Message* (1940) and *Joy of the Sun* (1942), an account of Akhnaton's life for children, which were both published in Calcutta; her major study of Akhnaton's life and philosophy appeared after the war in London as *A Son of God* (1946).

Savitri Devi's description of ancient Egypt was richly evocative. She swiftly drew her readers into a resplendent world of powerful pharaohs, cultural brilliance, and sumptuous luxury. Her glowing prose bore el-

oquent witness to the beauty, wealth, and prestige of Thebes, the birthplace of Akhnaton:

> On the western bank of the Nile, upon a site which to this day retains
> its loveliness, was built the Charuk palace, the residence of the Pharaoh
> Amenhotep the Third. . . . From the terraces of the palace one beheld to
> the east, beyond the Nile and its palm-groves, white walls contrasted with
> dark shadows, flat roofs of different levels, flights of steps, broad avenues
> and gardens and monumental gates: all that glory that was Thebes. In
> the foreground, the towering pylons of the great temple of Amon
> emerged above the outer walls of the sacred enclosure that stretched over
> miles. And the gilded tops of innumerable obelisks glittered in the daz-
> zling light or glowed like red-hot embers in the purple of sunset. One
> could distinguish many other temples dedicated to all the gods of Upper
> and Lower Egypt, temples with doors of bronze and gates of granite. . . .
> To the west, the eye wandered over the vastness of the desert. It is in
> that palace that Akhnaton was born.[6]

The bathos of this last sentence set the tone of *A Son of God*: this
work was the gospel of a new religion, complete with a pious account
of the life of its founder.

Her account of Akhnaton began with an imaginative reconstruction
of the young prince's birth and upbringing. Savitri Devi regarded
Queen Tiy, Akhnaton's mother, as the greatest and most lasting influence on the royal prince. She claimed that the queen worshiped Aton—
the Disk—the oldest sun-god of Egypt, whose seat was at On (Heliopolis) in Lower Egypt. Although the priesthood at On was trying to
revive the cult of Aton, Aton was still only a secondary god among
many at this time. Queen Tiy was no monotheist but she must have
taught her child to render homage to the sun at sunrise and sunset and
so prepared him to love the sun as a living and loving god who brought
light, warmth, and vitality to all things on earth. Savitri Devi pictured
the young prince's wonder at the reflection of the sun on his mother's
face, the joyous singing of the birds at first light, the opening of water-
flowers in the sunshine, and the delight of birds, beasts, and butterflies
that feel the sun's caress. These early impressions of childhood laid the
emotional and psychological basis of Akhnaton's receptivity to the idea
of the sun's divinity.[7]

Savitri Devi also speculated about the influence of Aryan ideas on
Akhnaton's religious development. These were attributable to the Mittanians, a Hurrian people ruled by an Aryan aristocracy who worshiped

Mithra, Indra, Varuna, and other well-known Vedic gods. The Mittanians inhabited the land of Nahrina, the watershed of the River Euphrates, which placed them on the northeastern flank of the Egyptian world at this time. Alliances with foreign princesses were not uncommon in the Eighteenth Dynasty, and Thotmose IV, Akhnaton's grandfather, had taken Mutemuya, the daughter of Artama, king of Mitanni, as his chief wife. Amenhotep III, Akhnaton's father, had married, besides his chief queen Tiy, at least two Mitannian princesses, with whom Akhnaton was familiar. While allowing that the young prince may have gleaned from these ladies some notion of the Aryan sun god Surya that anticipated his worship of Aton, Savitri Devi thought the similarity of these deities was due to the fact that Akhnaton was himself partly Aryan (as the grandson of Mutemuya).[8]

A list of the king's titles on the earliest known inscription of his reign combined traditional titles with new appellations relating to his new religious ideas. This text described him as "the High-priest of Ra-Horakhti of the Two Horizons rejoicing in his horizon in his name 'Shu-which-is-in-the-Disk.' "[9] Savitri Devi suggested that, while Akhnaton had earlier associated the divine attributes of the sun with the material Disk, he had by this time conceived a more subtle idea of godhead by considering the "Heat" or "Heat-and-Light" (Shu) inherent in the Disk. Savitri Devi approvingly quoted Sir Flinders Petrie's conclusion that the young pharaoh had discovered the principle of equivalence of heat, light and other forms of energy, which is the basis of modern physics. She suggested further that Akhnaton, by identifying the energy of the sun with the material Disk, had anticipated the equation of energy and matter in the modern theory of relativity.[10] The radiant energy he and his followers adored in the sun also animated the flying birds, the running beasts, and all human achievement.

This religion of the Disk was no cold abstraction, Savitri Devi claimed, but a religion of love. This was not a personal love, such as that of a parent for his or her offspring, nor that of a tribal deity for his chosen people. The love of a God that has brought forth millions and millions of lives from himself is a love that expresses itself in two modes: the active, productive principle and the passive, receptive principle. This love is a bond of physical and logical unity between energies in nature. This love is also a relation of intention, not a personal love of a god made in the human image, but as a sign of God's beneficence toward all living things; as a tendency toward well-being that nature encourages and assists; as an inexhaustible and indiscriminate goodness underlying the whole of creation.[11]

The energy of the sun bestowed its benefits upon all things. This universality was particularly important to Savitri Devi, who decried the existence of gods made in the human image. She compared this universality favorably with the "childish" partiality of man-made gods toward their authors. Savitri Devi did not accept a demarcation line between man and the rest of the living world. She criticized monotheistic creeds from Judaism onward for positing a god who gave special rights to man to use all other creatures for his own benefit. In her opinion, the concern of Jehovah with his chosen people, the Jews, typified the limitations of a tribal or local deity. Christianity, she maintained, was no more than a globalized tribal religion; the Christians had raised Jesus Christ to the deity of an extended tribe, namely, mankind, which was no more than one species among many others in the endless variety of nature. She detested Christianity and other creedal religions for making man, and not life, the center of their creation myths and the basis of their scale of values. Savitri Devi celebrated an impartial immanent deity in all nature.[12]

If nature offered such an abundance of wonders, man had no need of myths and supernatural explanations of existence. Savitri Devi saw Akhnaton's cult as "pagan" in the same sense as she admired ancient Greek and Hindu notions of beauty and reality. In her view, all three philosophies expressed joy in the visible created world; they each regarded healthy sentient life as "the actual masterpiece of universal Energy and the supreme beauty." According to her "pantheistic monism," the single cosmos of nature composed of divine matter-energy was itself an immanent deity. There was no other supernatural or transcendent reality beyond the natural world. Denying any dualism or transcendence, she celebrated this pagan religion of nature as the authentic Aryan worldview, age-old, still surviving in India, and destined to become the philosophy of a new Nazi order.

In the final chapter of *A Son of God*, Savitri Devi considered the history of the Western world since Akhnaton's reign. From her standpoint in the present, the young pharaoh's gospel shone like a beacon across the intervening centuries of gloom. "With Tutankhamen [Akhnaton's successor] began for the Western World an era of spiritual regression which is lasting still."[13] With this apparent paradox she set out to expose Christianity and its secular legacies as the bane of the

West. In particular, she sought to demonstrate that the history of Western thought witnessed an ever-widening gap between its recognized religions and rational thought, as well as an increasing divorce between such religions and life, especially public life. She regarded this gap, essentially one between religion and science, between the church and secular society, as the cause of intellectual conflict and moral unrest throughout the history of Western culture.

The earliest evidence of this mental unease occurred in ancient Greece. After the false dawn of scientific imagination in Akhnaton's reign, rational thought was reintroduced to the West by the *physiologoi* of Ionia in the sixth century B.C. This time such ideas took root. Generations of Greek philosophers from Pythagoras to Plato developed the deduction of ideas and the rational explanation of facts, combined with logic, mystical insight, and mathematics. These thinkers thereby rose above the narrow religious outlook of their age. However, the Greek world still remained loyal to its rich mythology and traditional gods, which resisted the challenge of reason. Indeed, there was widespread conflict; Socrates was put to death "for not believing in the gods in whom the city believed." Savitri Devi also drew attention to the incongruity of the rumbustious antics of the all-too-human Greek gods with the high intellectual achievement of classical Greek philosophy.[14]

She saw Christianity as "the next great wave in the history of Western consciousness" but had few words to say in its favor. There was scarcely "a greater contrast between the clear Hellenic genius and the spirit of the creed destined to overrun Hellas, Europe, and finally America and Australia. As preached by St. Paul, it was an irrational and unaesthetic creed, fed on miracles, bent on asceticism, strongly stressing the power of evil, ashamed of the body and afraid of life." But she did concede that its God was a universal God and a God of love. Nevertheless, in her view this Christian God still retained some characteristics of Jehovah, the tribal deity of the Jews. It was a God who gave man, alone among all living creatures, an immortal soul, which was infinitely precious in His eyes, for He loved man in the same partial way that old Jehovah loved the Jewish nation. For Savitri Devi it was a democratic God who hated the rich, the high-born, and those who put their trust in human reason rather than accepting the authority of His Gospel.[15]

The universalism of Christianity was a major advance over the older popular and national religions. But Savitri Devi caviled at the love and

mercy at the heart of Christian teaching as but a wan reflection of the
universal love implicit in the Buddhism and Jainism of India. She held
that Christianity appealed to the intellectually uncritical, the emotionally unbalanced, and the socially oppressed or neglected. Parroting
Nietzsche's maxims, she claimed that Christianity offered redemption
to the barbarians, women, and slaves—"the majority of mankind"—
and this ensured its triumph in the Roman Empire. In the medieval
and modern period Christianity continued as a religion of plebeian salvation, first throughout Europe and later to the subject peoples of its
colonial empires.

Savitri Devi maintained that the Aryan world could not indefinitely
forget its classical heritage, centuries of rational thought, nor "that
avowed ideal of visible beauty, of strength, of cleanliness—of healthy
earthly life . . . of the ancients." The Renaissance witnessed the rediscovery of Greek metaphysics and polytheism in European philosophy,
literature, and the arts. The celebration of man as a creative individual,
even the coequal of God, the enjoyment of song and pleasure, the
deification of the human body in painting, sculpture, and life all indi-
cated the dissolution of the Christian medieval order and the emergence
of a new independent spirit. The scientific revolution and the Enlightenment in the seventeenth and eighteenth centuries continued the historical process of Western man's emancipation from the authority of
Christian dogma. Ever true to her own Greek origins, Savitri Devi
regarded this intellectual development as "the tardy reaction of the bold
critical spirit of classical Hellas against judeo-scholastic authority . . .
the triumph of Euclid over Moses."[16]

Rationalism and the scientific worldview now coexisted with Christianity in the modern West. Intellectual discourse and scientific investigation were no longer subject to theological authority. Morality was
more a matter of legality and social sanction than the expression of a
divine imperative such as the Ten Commandments. While Savitri Devi
welcomed this decline of Christian religious authority, she detected a
profound ambiguity in modern Western values and beliefs. Although
reason and science were triumphant in the intellectual domain, man
still adhered to the charitable and democratic ideals of Christianity.
Shorn of their transcendent meaning in a secular society, these ideals
now simply expressed a man-centered conception of the world and
moral behavior. Man no longer believed in his own immortal soul but
spoke of the sanctity of human life. Man no longer believed that God

had created the world for man, but he exploited and even destroyed the natural world as if it were his own.

The Western world was in a state of spiritual and moral crisis. Despite the triumph of a rational worldview, man still hankered after a simple faith. He regretted the absence of scientific evidence for Christian beliefs. As for the moral teachings of Christianity, these had value as social regulations but did not necessitate a belief in God. But if man had lost his faith in God, he had not found one in science. Science did indeed offer intellectual certainty about the physical world, but the laws of thermodynamics and the periodic table of elements were hardly objects of worship and veneration. During the Enlightenment man had actually tried to create new religions. However, the cult of the Goddess Reason in the French Revolution and Auguste Comte's cult of Humanity had failed to inspire men. Savitri Devi concluded that "science, without the advantages of religion, is no more able to satisfy us than religion without a basis of scientific certitude."[17]

In her view, the religion of man, that is, secular humanism, was an unstable hybrid of rationalism and Christian ethics devoid of a belief in God. In a coded reference, she paid tribute to the Nazi religion of race and nation, now defeated and reviled:

> And the bold ideologists who, in recent years, in Europe, have endeavoured to wipe out altogether the spirit if not the name of Christianity and to raise the Nation—based on the precise physiological idea of race—as the object of man's ultimate devotion, those ideologists, we say, may seem wiser and more honest than their humanitarian antagonists.[18]

If Christianity and secular humanism failed to serve the interests of life, she declared that it would be better to brush aside two thousand years of errors and return to the pagan gods. However, she did recognize that the secular religions of racism and nationalism represented a narrower moral ideal than the universal ideals of Christianity and humanism and that it was perhaps retrograde to return to the worship of local and national gods. Nevertheless, she banished these doubts from her mind by asserting that the religion of race was the true expression of the religion of life in the minds of its best exponents.[19]

These intimations of her latent admiration for Hitler and Nazism remained a mere undertone in *A Son of God*. At this time it seems that her principal targets were Christianity and secular humanism; nationalism and racism were chiefly invoked to prove hypocrisy or bad faith in the dominant Western religious tradition. Savitri Devi claimed that the Western world was yearning for a religion based on rationality, for a love extended to all living things, and a conception of international relations that renounced war and aggression. The twentieth century was witnessing a growing desire for some "all-embracing truth, intellectual *and* spiritual, in the light of which the revelations of experience and faith, the dictates of reason and of intuition—of science *and* religion—would find their place as partial aspects of a harmoniously organic whole."[20] In her opinion, this romantic ideal was realized by Akhnaton's religion of the Disk. Its revival could provide the basis of a new spiritual order grounded in the philosophical traditions of India and Greece and thus unite East and West.

In the second half of 1944 Savitri Devi corresponded with Aldous Huxley in California about the religion of the Disk. Huxley thought this a rather naive affair and declared his own admiration for Eastern religions, particularly Zen, which gave man experience of the divine through a sense of timelessness. Savitri Devi agreed that men could grow to timelessness along various religious paths. However, having experienced it herself for the past six years, she was sure that some could reach the "peace which is beyond all understanding" and which is connected with the consciousness of timelessness through direct, vital communication with the young Prophet of the Sun. So she wrote in the preface to her book, describing herself as "one who, despite obvious unworthiness, dares to call herself, after three thousand three hundred years, his loving disciple."[21]

By any standards, *A Son of God* is an extraordinary work of idealism informed by a selective command of secondary sources, incisive reasoning, and an original mind. But it is also flawed by a prejudiced hatred of Christianity and a contempt for the mass of humanity. Besides these antihuman sentiments, a major weakness of the religion of the Disk lies in its nebulous and romantic idealism: a general affirmation of life and energy, devoid of priorities, is no guide for human conduct whatsoever in a complex world. Savitri Devi once described her philosophy as "true to the earth" with a nod toward Friedrich Nietzsche. However, if she applauded the latter's superhuman morality beyond good and evil and shared his contempt of Christianity for seeking the protection and advantage of the weak and humble, she did not want a superman above nature. Nature and life were the center of her scheme. The injunction to live in accordance with nature was the single commandment of the religion of the Disk. Man should understand nature as a rational, beautiful, and loving order and not seek to superimpose upon it his own needs or ideas of right. Any philosophical or moral notions reflecting this "supernatural" worldview led to error.

The religion of the Disk is quite simply a romantic religion of nature, presented in the up-to-date scientific notions of matter-energy and traditional cosmology. Here Savitri Devi saw some correspondence with the amoral nature worship and biological monism of Nazi ideology. Her object of reverence was the cosmic dance of nature, wherein man occupied a marginal and unimportant role. From the towering perspective of cosmic impersonality, the lack of human imperatives and proscriptions might not seem to matter much, nor even man's survival as a species. The religion of the Disk actually transcended man, treating him as but one species among the millions on our biodiverse planet. In her opinion, Nazism was also a religion of integral truth, transcending man and based on a universal love of all nature, destined to supplant Christianity and humanism. She simply regarded the sun cult of Akhnaton as a cult of life and thought that her wartime writings on the subject would help to prepare the religious background of the dawning National Socialist world order, "of which the prototype is none else but the eternal Order of Nature."[22]

Begun in July 1945 after her return to Calcutta in the bitter knowledge of Germany's defeat, *Impeachment of Man* initially pursues her relentless criticism of man-centered creeds to the detriment of "life" and nature in general. Once again she inveighs against the partiality and moral limitations of Judaism, Christianity, and Islam for celebrating only man's immortal soul and redemption, while considering animals and the rest of nature as mere spoil. The East again finds her favor. Thanks to the immemorial Indian belief in reincarnation, the life-centered creeds of Hinduism, Buddhism, and Jainism presuppose an unbroken continuity throughout the whole scheme of existence and an organic unity among all species. No one can know whether the mangy dog or the lame horse does not house the soul of a former friend or relative. However, since these religions ultimately aspire to a release from the cycle of rebirths, all individual existence is regarded as a sorrow. She regrets that this oriental pessimism does not actively foster the good treatment of animals.[23]

Animals are her chief concern here. Much of this essay is devoted to sentimental images of neglected and ill-treated domestic animals, interspersed with outrage at slaughterhouses and vivisection laboratories. The raising and killing of livestock for meat and their breeding to ensure a constant supply of fresh milk and tender young flesh are condemned wholesale. The trapping and killing of animals for their furs, feathers, and tusks, merely for the gratification of female vanity in fashion, are held up to scorn. Any kind of hunting for sport and use of animals for spectator sports she roundly rejects. She even welcomes the advancing mechanization of the world inasmuch as this will reduce the use of beasts of burden. With interim care these can be sustained until they are self-sufficient for a life in the wild. Even the keeping of pets, which live well in countries like England and Germany, where "Aryans" have a more developed appreciation of animals, is ultimately found to be a purely selfish indulgence on the part of humans. All too often, she bemoans, pets are regarded as a nuisance once they are old, inconvenient, or produce young.

Her aim in this book is much more radical than a mere attack on Christianity and an exaltation of nature. She effectively demands an end to man's exploitation of animals and living nature in any form whatsoever. Meat eating, the wearing of furs and feathers, hunting, bullfighting and circus performances, the use of animals in medical and scientific tests, even as beasts of burden are all categorically rejected as unworthy. Man is a superior animal, she concedes, by virtue of his reason and language, but so why should he, a noncarnivore by nature, prey on the rest of the animal kingdom in a manner no better than a ferocious brute? Again she adduces the moral limitation of the man-centered creeds of the West as the root cause of this lack of compassion for animals and their welfare. She complains that science and secularism, even after dismissing all metaphysics, still cling to the superstition of man-centered values: the "dignity of all men." Their goal remains the domination of the world in the hands of man, for man's benefit alone.[24]

"The history of animal life has been . . . the history of one long and increasingly hopeless struggle against the pretension of man to have the whole earth to himself."[25] With this charge, Savitri Devi unconsciously unveils her basic motive behind the sentimental vision of a world of animals living for their own benefit. Her real target is mankind, or at least the universal humanity that disposes so freely over the natural realm as a result of his self-serving religions and morality. The liberal, international ideology of human solidarity against the partial doctrines of racism, nationalism, and fascism is the anvil upon which she wields this hammer of animal rights. In her preface she writes that she was inspired to write this work by the hatred she felt for the hypocrisy and cowardice of the West's outrage at Germany's "crimes against humanity" while still tolerating all this ill-treatment and exploitation of animals. This "false ideal" of human brotherhood against a naturally hierarchized mankind and "healthy race-consciousness" (her coded references to Nazi ideology) is her real enemy.[26]

Indications of her misanthropic contempt for humanity in contrast to nature abound in this small volume. With an eloquence that matches the pessimism of Deep Ecology today, she documents the vicious, erosive encroachment of mankind upon the natural realm. She recalls that there were lions in ancient Greece and even wolves in seventeenth-century England, but man has taken their place and built his cities, spreading "the network of his ever-grabbling organised life."[27]

> As mankind expanded, forest-areas decreased in surface or vanished away altogether. . . . The forests of France and of the British Isles where stately priests and virgins worshipped the Principle of Eternal Life in the sacred Oak, gradually fell under the merciless axe. . . . The United States of America were a land of forests as late as the middle of the nineteenth century. . . . And there, in the place of the murdered trees . . . roads and railways, towns with endless suburbs, villages rapidly growing into towns, and vast expanses of cultivated land; more and more cultivated land to feed more and more people who might as well never have been born.[28]

People as a plague. People merely conceived in terms of quantity and their expansion at the expense of all other creation. She contends that far too much is made of human life as a bare physical fact: the fight against disease, to prolong life, to save as many human beings from death.[29] She is in revolt against the whole utilitarian ethos of the West, which seeks the greatest good of the greatest number. In her view, people are simply not equal. She is convinced that this emphasis upon universal welfare at the expense of nature will ultimately degrade the planet into a crowded polluted slum. She seeks a qualitative improvement of the world, by which she understands the creation of a hardy, physical breed of superior Aryans inhabiting an aesthetic world of natural beauty. For her, racism is an ecological imperative to conserve the good in nature.

The full violence of her misanthropy is most apparent whenever the Third Reich's crimes are condemned by a liberal West that sees nothing objectionable in its own exploitation of animals. Such a "civilisation," she declares, does not deserve to live. She waxes lyrical in her hopes of the West's destruction so that a new elite of nature-loving supermen might again rise and rule upon its ruins for ever. Indeed, she would rather see all mankind destroyed if there was no hope for nature. She expresses fears that a pacified mankind might colonize the whole earth without limiting its own numbers. Aghast at this prospect, she imagines deliverance in international rivalries and war, which, aided with atomic weapons of mass destruction, might annihilate man together with nature for all time.[30] The depth of Savitri Devi's hatred for conventional humanity was matched only by the cloying sweetness of her love of animals, especially dogs, cats, and domestic mammals.

The dramatic sight of the great volcano Hekla in full eruption captured all that Savitri Devi felt about the violence of nature and its power to sweep away the paltry works and beliefs of man. While in Iceland she witnessed this major event on 5 April 1947. Entranced, she watched the seven craters of the erupting volcano as they flamed and smoked, while shooting out great white-hot rocks in flashes of pink light against the bright nocturnal sky. Gaping mouths of fire flickered in the dark crust of the molten lava stream that poured downhill. The unceasing tremor of the earth and roaring beat of the burning mountain seemed to repeat the sacred primeval vocal "Aum." "Ravished in religious rapture," she walked up to the lava stream singing a hymn to Shiva, the lord of the cosmic dance of creation and destruction. In her exultant rhapsody of nature's chaotic power the deep tones of "Aum! Aum!" fused with the great roar of "*Sieg Heil!*" from Germany's millions in the Third Reich. Later in prison and at her trial in postwar Germany, she would recall Hekla's eruption as a vision of future revenge: the crash of Christian civilization, the resounding Horst Wessel Song, the triumphant swastika flag above the flames and smoke.[31]

She continued writing *Impeachment of Man* throughout her return voyage to Europe and subsequent visits to London and Lyons in the winter of 1945–1946. Daily confronted by the victorious Allied world, she privately indulged her Nazi loyalties alongside fantasies of a violent overthrow of the liberal democratic West. This small book, whose text never once mentions the words "Hitler" or "National Socialism," may be regarded as her renewed declaration of war against the West, cloaked in the ideology of nature worship and a "life-centred creed." Any ecologically minded person casually reading the book today would note with approval her eloquent defense of the rain forests, her fears of soil erosion, overpopulation, and planetary degradation. It all seems quite in tune with current Green thinking, except perhaps for the viciousness with which she attacks mankind. Only a hint of Nazism, easily overlooked, remains. The work is introduced by a quotation from Josef Goebbels on the Führer's views on vegetarianism, and another from Alfred Rosenberg at the time of his Nuremberg trial: "Thou shalt love God in all living things, animal and plants."[32] An avowal of pantheistic divinity combined with the practical rejection of Christian universalism: this remains the essence of Nazism's mixture of power worship and violence with sentimentality. It is the theology of Savitri Devi.

7

THE HITLER AVATAR

The organic growth of religious custom and belief throughout the Indian subcontinent from its origins in the Vedas of the Aryan invaders over a period of four thousand years held great appeal for Savitri Devi. Hinduism appeared to her as a great rambling and unreformed paganism true to its ancient sources and untouched by the imposed monotheism and priesthoods of the Judaeo-Christian tradition. It has already been shown how greatly she revered the Aryans as the most youthful, strong, and beautiful race, the highest expression of nature in the historical world. Given the Vedic origins of Hinduism, it is unsurprising that she should have felt an instinctive affinity for the pagan cults of India. But where did Savitri Devi find her particular inspiration in the immense variety of Hinduism and its long historical development, and more especially, how did Adolf Hitler fit into her Hindu-Aryan philosophy?

The Vedic deities and caste system of the Aryans, the *Ramayana* and *Mahabharata* epics, the *Bhagavad Gita*, the concept of the avatar, and Vaishnavite Hinduism as practiced in contemporary India formed the essential corpus of Hindu doctrine and scripture familiar to Savitri Devi by the end of the 1930s. From 1937 until the early 1940s, her work on behalf of the Hindu Mission involved her lecturing widely on popular Hinduism in Bengali and Hindi throughout the states of Bengal, Bihar, and Assam. This formal involvement with the traditions and texts of Hinduism, coupled with plentiful opportunity to observe and learn firsthand about Hindu customs and beliefs, leaves no doubt as to her knowledge of Indian religion. However, even at this time she was already developing her own Aryo-Nazi religion, sprinkling her lectures with references to *Mein Kampf,* and seeking correspondences between Hitlerism and Hinduism as supposed joint heirs of ancient Aryan wisdom.

She received encouragement in this project from a number of highly educated Hindus. During the 1930s, when India was chafing under British rule, the restrictions imposed on Indian nationalists led many to regard Soviet communism and the Third Reich with its Aryan racial doctrine and holy swastika sign as potent alternatives. Those who were religiously inclined even saw Stalin and Hitler as possible redeemer figures and made them the objects of *bhakti* devotion by displaying their photographs on the family shrine alongside the images of their personal deity, be this Vishnu, Shiva, or another god. It was with amazement and joy that Savitri Devi first observed pictures of the Führer on the household altar of Indian families. When she asked Srimat Swami Satyananda, the president of the Hindu Mission in Calcutta, if she might make reference to Hitler and *Mein Kampf* in her official lectures, he replied that Hitler was for them an incarnation of Vishnu, the god who keeps things from rushing to destruction, who keeps things back and goes against time. She was welcome to say what she liked in her lectures, provided that she said it from a Hindu point of view. Satyananda repeated this view of Hitler in 1942, adding that they needed National Socialism in India. She encountered similar pro-Hitler attitudes among many other educated Brahmins besides Asit Krishna Mukherji, and even among illiterate Sudras.[1]

Satyananda's references to Hitler as an "incarnation of God" and the "Saviour of the world" were in fact commonplace among high-caste Hindus. Writing of his impressions of university life in India during the 1950s, Agehananda Bharati declared that the active Hindu loves all dictators due to incurable hero worship. This he attributed to the avatar idea—that in every powerful man there is some cosmic power that manifested itself in the god-kings and heroes of the epics and mythology. But Hitler was especially popular, particularly with the aggressive nationalists, for he trounced the British in the early years of the war. Also, Hitler proclaimed the superiority of the Aryan, which is how the Hindu sees himself. Last, the memory of Max Müller's Aryan researches was still fresh: Hitler was the leader of the Sanskrit-knowing Germans.[2] Bharati was exceptionally well placed to observe this sympathy. Born Leopold Fischer in 1923, he spent his youth in Vienna and embarked early on the scholarly study of India. During the war he was a member of Bose's Indian Legion, serving mainly in France and Germany. Embracing Hinduism, he became a monk in the Dashanami Order, originally founded by Shankara in 800, and pursued an academic career at Benares Hindu University after the war. He has also written on Golwalkar's Rashtriya Swayamsevak Sangh (RSS) and Hindu fascism.[3]

Back in Europe during the early postwar years, Savitri Devi began to write the first major statement of her Aryo-Nazi philosophy, which drew together her own long-held convictions, her enthusiasm for National Socialism, and those elements of Hinduism that she regarded as the legacy of immemorial Aryan tradition. This work, entitled *The Lightning and the Sun*, was eventually published in Calcutta in 1958 after her return to India following thirteen years in Europe. She began writing the book in April 1948 in Edinburgh while employed as the wardrobe manager of a traveling dance company, continuing work on it during her propaganda missions and in prison at Werl in the summer of 1949. She returned to the manuscript while living at Lyons in 1951 and 1952, and then, after her pilgrimage to Germany, she completed it between 1954 and spring 1956 while staying as Katja U.'s guest at Emsdetten in Westphalia.

The most important inspiration from Hinduism in her Aryo-Nazi doctrine is the cyclic view of history, according to which the whole of creation commences at a point of perfection, but then declines through successive stages into final decay, until everything once more regains its pristine state and the cycle begins anew. Hindu thinkers had evolved a cyclic theory of time in the *Mahabharata* epic and similar ideas about the cycles also appear in the *Vishnu Purana*, a book of legends dating from the first few centuries A.D. These ancient Indian notions of cosmology and chronology offered a perspective upon the nature of time and its influence on the created universe. The latter work describes the Puranic divisions of time in the cycle of the ages in terms of the four Yugas, or ages. The Sanskrit names for the four ages refer to their relative duration: Krita or Satya (four units), Treta (three), Dvapara (two), and Kali (one). Thus, the Krita Yuga lasts some 1,728,000 years, the Treta Yuga 1,296,000 years, the Dvapara Yuga 864,000 years, and the Kali Yuga 432,000 years. Accordingly, their sum of ten units makes up a Mahayuga equivalent to 4,320,000 years.

The Hindu chronology of the *Vishnu Purana* made provision for even longer periods and cycles, including a thousand Mahayugas or a

Day of Brahman, also known as a Kalpa, equivalent to 4,320,000,000 years. A Year of Brahman was composed of 360 such Days and Nights (i.e., two Kalpas), and the life of Brahman was deemed to last for a hundred such years, yielding the astronomic total of 311,040,000,000,000 years. Such a figure was deemed to define the period of the universe through a complete cycle of creation, development, and collapse. But even this figure was itself just one cycle within a limitless and unending sequence of cycles. However, such large cycles all repeated the basic tenfold pattern of the four Yugas, corresponding to the Golden, Silver, Bronze, and Iron Ages, which determined the nature of life and society from prosperity to decay.[4]

In the *Mahabharata* these ages are described in some detail. The Krita Yuga is characterized as an age in which righteousness is eternal. In this most excellent of Yugas everything had been done and nothing remained to be done. Duties did not languish, nor did the people decline. There was no buying and selling, no efforts needed to be made by men, the fruits of the earth were abundant. No disease or decline of the organs of sense arose through age, there was no malice, weeping, pride, or deceit, no contention, lassitude, hatred, cruelty, fear, affliction, jealousy, or envy. All creatures were devoted to their duties, all the castes were alike in their functions, they were devoted to one deity and used one rule and one rite. During the Treta Yuga righteousness decreased by a fourth. Men now acted with an object in view, seeking rewards for their rites and gifts, while still being devoted to their duties and their ceremonies. The decline became more marked in the Dvapara Yuga, when righteousness was diminished by two quarters. The Veda became fourfold, and with this proliferation of rules, rites, and ceremonies people no longer knew unity. Once men had fallen away from goodness, many diseases, desires, and calamities assailed them and these in turn drove men to practice austerities.[5]

The Kali Yuga, or Iron Age, represented the cosmological and moral nadir in the Hindu cycle of ages. Only a quarter as much righteousness prevailed in comparison with the Krita Yuga. Sacred practices were neglected. Calamities, diseases, fatigue, and faults such as anger, distress, anxiety, hunger, and fear became commonplace. Political and social order collapsed, cities became violent, civilization receded. Evil was everywhere evident and triumphant. The *Vishnu Purana* describes many aspects of this moral and social decay in the Kali Yuga. The observance of caste and order is neglected with promiscuous intermarriage among all classes and peoples; women are unfaithful and consort with worthless men; the family and other blood ties lose their meaning; the acquisition of wealth, commerce, and money govern all men's actions and aspirations; liberalism and moral relativism prevail so that any idol or authority is revered on the basis of popularity and individual choice. The rulers oppress and plunder the masses, who then desert the intolerable cities and settle in remote places. There they live in scarcity and want, suffering exposure, and subject to decreasing vigor and longevity. In due course, the entire race is destroyed.[6]

Savitri Devi believed in the former existence of the Golden Age, the most recent Satya, or Krita, Yuga, which had passed away more than two million years ago. In terms reminiscent of the account in the *Mahabharata*, she described the social and political order on earth in that "Age of Truth" as a perfect replica of the eternal order of life:

> There was, then, nothing to be changed; nothing for which to shed one's own or other people's blood; nothing to do but to enjoy in peace the beauty and riches of the sunlit earth, and to praise the wise Gods—the "devas" or "shining Ones" as the ancient Aryans called them—Kings of the earth in the truest sense of the word. Every man and woman, every race, every species was, then, *in its place*, and the whole divine hierarchy of Creation was a work of art to which and from which there was nothing to add or to take away.

The end of the Golden Age began with the self-exaltation of a man-centered spirit at the expense of living nature and its naturally superior individuals and races. From then on, violence became unavoidable, "the very law of Life in a fallen world."[7]

The Hindu cycle of ages supplied an implacably deterministic philosophy of history, according to which each Golden Age was followed by successively less righteous ages until evil prevailed and no good could come of anything. Savitri Devi was profoundly impressed by these ancient cosmological notions, for they confirmed some of her earliest convictions. Even as a child in France, she had been contemptuous of the bold progressive idealism of the French Revolution. The ideas of 1789, those man-centered beliefs in liberty, equality, and fraternity, had early struck her at best as a wan secular reflection of Christianity, at worst as an expression of the superficial intellectual optimism of the modern age, which had lost all sense of tradition and man's rootedness in nature. Inspired by her vision of the former glories of the beautiful, strong, and warlike Aryan race at the dawn of the present cycle, she could not but regard recorded history as a slow process of Aryan corruption and decline. As a cultural pessimist and devotee of Leconte de Lisle, she had no doubts that the world had long been passing through the gloomy Kali Yuga.

In her view early postwar Europe with its grim austerities, ruin, and exhaustion, and, above all, the defeat of Nazi Germany, the focus of her hopes for regeneration and the start of a new Satya Yuga, only served to confirm that the world had yet further to go through the era of gloom. Writing in April 1948 in Scotland, she described the decadence and banality of the modern age as characteristics of the Kali Yuga, which included selfishness, conceit, hypocrisy, and false ideas of human equality and liberty. The Western belief in progress was her especial target and she roundly dismissed its advocates' celebration of literacy, individual freedom, equal opportunities, religious toleration, and humaneness. According to her view, universal education and literacy only rendered the masses more suggestible to the mass conditioning and control of the media and vested interests; the individual could revel in the exercise of trivial choices concerning consumer goods and services while remaining enslaved by the whole commercial system of exploitation and profit and ignorant of any traditional wisdom. Equal opportunities she regarded as no more than a mendacious myth that flew in the face of natural hierarchies, while tolerance and humaneness were for her mere liberal humbug.[8]

As she restlessly traveled around postwar Europe, confronted by Nazi atrocity exhibitions in London, daily reminded of the trial of her heroes at Nuremberg, or seeking escape from the overwhelming evidence of Nazi defeat in remote Iceland, she saw a world that was still rushing onward through the downsweep of the Kali Yuga:

> There is no hope of "putting things right," in such an age. It is, essentially, the age . . . described in the . . . Book of books—the *Bhagavad Gita*—as that in which "out of the corruption of women proceeds the confusion of castes; out of the confusion of castes, the loss of memory; out of loss of memory the lack of understanding; and out of this, all evils"; the age in which falsehood is termed "truth" and truth persecuted as falsehood or mocked as insanity; in which the exponents of truth, the divinely inspired leaders, the real friends of their race and of all the living,—the god-like men—are defeated, and their followers humbled

and their memory slandered, while the masters of lies are hailed as "saviours"; the age in which every man and woman is in the wrong place, and the world dominated by inferior individuals, bastardised races and vicious doctrines, all part and parcel of an order of inherent ugliness far worse than complete anarchy.[9]

Armed with the Hindu cyclic theory of time, Savitri Devi believed that "human history, far from being a steady ascension towards the better, is an increasingly hopeless process of bastardisation, emasculation and demoralisation of mankind; an inexorable 'fall.' "[10] Against the dismal cosmological background of the Kali Yuga, she developed her own doctrine of Men in Time, Men above Time, and Men against Time. These three types of historical actors represented three quite distinct responses to the bondage of time as understood in the cycle of the ages. Of the three types, Men in Time are the essential and most active agents of the Kali Yuga. Their conduct and aims typify the dark age and all its vicissitudes. Men above Time are properly at home in the perfection of the Satya Yuga, or Golden Age, and Men against Time act with ruthless violence in an attempt to restore the conditions of the Satya Yuga at the end of the Kali Yuga. By violent means, these martial heroes work to redeem the world from the thrall of the dark age and to initiate a new time cycle.

Men in Time, according to Savitri Devi, are those few strong individuals who wholeheartedly accept the iron law of history and act entirely in their own narrow self-interest. Whether in lust for personal enjoyment, in greed for gold, or in the search for honors, position, and power, this selfish drive is shameless and undisguised by such "noble" ends as the ideas of 1789 or the solidarity of the international proletariat. In seeking only their own personal ends with the utmost intelligence, unscrupulousness, and energy, these Men in Time are "the most thorough, the most mercilessly effective agents of the Death-forces on earth . . . working without hesitation and without remorse in the sense of the downward process of history and, for its logical conclusion: the annihilation of man and all life."[11]

Men in Time represent the most naked and powerful expression of egoism in the benighted era of the Kali Yuga, an age that is given over to the play of atomistic individual wills striving for their materialistic gratification with no understanding of the wisdom or higher collective goals of happier ages. By seeking their own individual advantage in a

constant war of wills, Men in Time drive history along that opposi-
tional path that is the hallmark of the dark age and its decline. Their
gains, profits, or victories are entirely personal; even if they bring wider
fortune and prosperity, this is quite incidental to their motive of self-
gratification. And all the while they are fighting and struggling and
winning, the world around them is violated, thereby growing older,
wearier, and less abundant until it is exhausted and reaches the end of
the time cycle.

Savitri Devi regarded Genghis Khan (1157–1227) as an outstanding
example of a Man in Time. The Mongol leader who rose from a fa-
therless outcast to the uncontested master of a vast Eurasian empire
stretching from the Danube to the Yellow Sea acted only to extend his
power. He followed no ideology, no other ends save survival and more
power. Although an agent of the dreary Kali Yuga, he also hastened
its consummation and end; Genghis Khan was thus a personification of
the divine destroyer Mahakala, or Shiva, possessing the awful splendor
of the great devastating forces of nature. Due to his powerful and destructive participation in the world, he represented the "lightning" in
the title of her book.[12] But because he espoused no higher cause than
his own personal gain and power, his empire scarcely survived him.
Indeed, Savitri Devi attributed the later rise of European colonialism
in Asia under the Portuguese, Dutch, French, and British and its commercial, money-worshiping spirit to the very failure of Genghis Khan
to found a more enduring state in this region. The self-seeking and
destructive force of the Mongol Empire was thus linked to the rise of
Jewish international finance, the great adversary of Aryan rule.[13]

Men above Time are those individuals who have attained the highest
enlightenment described in the *Upanishads*. In recognizing the fundamental unity of the divine Self (*Atman*) and the all-pervading God
(*Brahman*), they represent the spiritual authority in the Satya Yuga,
or Age of Truth, in which complete perfection and righteousness prevail. In ancient India the Brahmins were the counselors and mentors
of kings and warriors who were anxious to act in accordance with the
commands of timeless wisdom. However, as the world proceeds
through the time cycle with increasing disorder and decay, such Men
above Time enjoy less and less authority. During the Kali Yuga they
just seem to be unworldly mystics whose entire outlook and conduct
barely equips them to survive in a world of struggle and conflict, let
alone to act as guides and rulers of men. These lonely ascetics abstain

from all violence and cannot change the collective conditions of mankind. At best they can offer personal salvation in breaking the time bondage of individual souls; it is not within their power to re-create the Golden Age before its due time.[14]

Savitri Devi described Men above Time as "exiles of the Golden Age in our Age of Gloom," who live in their own inner world, while renouncing or simply forgetting the nature of the real world around them. In her view, both Buddha and Jesus Christ (whom she regarded as a genial mystic quite unlike St. Paul, the founder and organizer of Christianity) were Men above Time, too good for the fallen earth. Her chief example was Akhnaton, the Egyptian pharaoh of Aryan ancestry, whose ill-fated attempt to institute a golden-age state in the fourteenth century B.C. ended predictably in chaos and failure. Already in *A Son of God* (1946) she had described Akhnaton as a Man above Time "who had tried to impose his lofty ideals upon this Dark Age (both his *and* ours), *without taking into account the fact that violence is the law of any revolution within Time,* specially in the Dark Age (the Kali Yuga of the Hindus)."[15] He came already thousands of years too late for his solar theocracy to have succeeded. But like the sun, his symbol, he shed the last rays of the long-forgotten Satya Yuga while the downsweep of time continued in the ancient world.

In Hindu chronology the Kali Yuga suddenly and momentously gives way at its lowest point of degradation, suffering, and evil to the opening of a new Satya, or Krita, Yuga, which begins the cycle anew. According to Savitri Devi, Men against Time play a crucial role in the struggle to restore the Golden Age as the Kali Yuga nears the completion of its term. Although possessed of the sunlike qualities and mystical ideals of the Man above Time, the Man against Time employs the practical means, ruthlessness, and violence of the Man in Time for the achievement of collective salvation and the regeneration of the world. In her scheme of things, Men against Time combine the qualities of "Lightning" and "Sun" as the real heroes of history, the builders and defenders of all new churches who devote their whole life and energy to the reshaping of tangible reality on the model of their vision of truth. These divinely inspired militant mystics are rare individuals who suddenly intervene in the downsweep of time with the promise of redemption and the return of the Golden Age. The revolutionary implications of the Man against Time are obvious. Like a fiery comet from the heavens he bursts through the gloomy pall surrounding the earth in the Kali Yuga to herald the spreading sunshine of a new order of perfection, divine justice, and righteousness.

In Savitri Devi's opinion, the greatest Man against Time in all recorded history was Adolf Hitler, the Führer of the Germans, and the divinely appointed leader of the Aryan world in the West. His demand for German national unity in a strong new Reich in defiance of the humiliating Versailles Treaty clearly identified him as a champion of the old tribal principle against the degenerate capitalist and cosmopolitan world of the Allies. His adoption of racist ideas, his anti-Semitism, and the Nuremberg race laws forbidding intermarriage and sexual relations between Aryans and Jews convinced Savitri Devi that he intended the revival of the Aryan caste system on a global basis. An avid believer in Hitler's propaganda image, she saw his love of children and animals, his domestic modesty, vegetarianism, and abstention from alcohol as typical traits of the kindly ascetic. His ruthless use of military violence against his enemies in a resistant fallen world, no less his uncompromising plan to exterminate the Jews, the age-old adversary and counterimage of the heroic Aryans, identified him as the essential Man against Time.

Savitri Devi's notion of the Man against Time is derived from the Hindu idea of the periodic descent of the Deity, typically Vishnu, in a human, superhuman, or animal form. This mediator between God and men is known as the *avatara* (avatar), or divine incarnation, and represents a development from the extrahuman gods of the Vedic period.[16] The origin of the concept of avatar is obscure, and precursors have been traced to Aryan Iran in the *Bahram Yasht*, a Zoroastrian text, which may even show traces of Chinese influence and mythology. However, in none of these beliefs does the concept play such an important part as it does in the post-Vedic Hindu thought of the epics and the *Bhagavad Gita*. Both the *Ramayana* and the *Mahabharata* describe the descent of avatar in the form of Rama and Krishna, who both reappear as the favorite incarnations of Vishnu in the *Puranas*, ancient legends forming a further part of popular Hindu scripture.

In the *Mahabharata*, Vishnu incarnates ten times successively as a swan, fish, tortoise, boar, man-lion, dwarf, Rama (twice), Krishna, and Kalki. The *Bhagavad Gita* (a section of the *Mahabharata*) tells how Krishna, posing as a charioteer, manifested as an avatar to Arjuna on the battlefield of Kurukshetra during the war of the Koravas and Pandavas in 3102 B.C. Krishna's advice to the warrior prince concerning his martial duties and divine wisdom comprise the full text of the *Bhagavad Gita*. Puranic avatars also catalyze the cycle of ages as the Yuga avatars: in the Treta Yuga, Vishnu appears as Rama, and as Krishna at the end of the Dvapara Yuga and the beginning of the Kali Yuga. The Kalki avatar appears as the tenth and final incarnation of Vishnu: he arrives in the form of a sword-bearing rider on a white horse to end the dark age and initiate a new golden Satya Yuga.

Savitri Devi is unquestionably the first Western writer to identify Adolf Hitler as an avatar. In a manner suggestive of *bhakti* devotion, she frequently quotes Krishna's verses from the theistic *Bhagavad Gita* with reference to Hitler. One particular couplet appears as the motto of her book *Pilgrimage* and elsewhere in its pages: "When justice is crushed, when evil is triumphant, then I come back. For the protection of the good, for the destruction of evil-doers, for the establishment of the Reign of Righteousness, I am born again and again, age after age."[17] Her eulogy of Hitler's life and political career in *The Lightning and Sun* begins with the incarnation of the divine collective Self of Aryan mankind as "the late-born child of light" in Braunau am Inn in 1889. Her description of the youth and his dawning sense of mission is based on August Kubizek's account of their adolescent friendship in Linz and Vienna during the years 1904 to 1908. Whether enthusing over the magical power of Wagner's music or boldly outlining plans for new cities, buildings, and monuments, Hitler is for her the true friend of his people, ever inspired by the inner vision of a healthy, beautiful, and peaceful world, a real earthly paradise reflecting cosmic perfection.[18]

Savitri Devi was sure that Hitler had realized he was an avatar while still a youth. She found compelling proof of this in Kubizek's account of young Adolf's dramatic reaction to a performance of Wagner's *Rienzi* they had seen together during November 1906 in Linz. Both boys were caught up in the great epic of Rienzi's rise to become the tribune of the people of Rome and his subsequent downfall. When the performance ended, it was past midnight. Hitler, usually very talkative after an exciting opera, was silent and withdrawn. He led his friend through the cold, foggy streets up the Freinberg hill on the western side of the town. Kubizek recalled how Hitler strode on, looking pale and sinister, until they reached the summit. They were no longer engulfed by the fog and the stars shone brilliantly overhead. Then Hitler began to speak, his words bursting forth with hoarse passion. Kubizek was utterly amazed. Hitherto he had always understood that Hitler wanted to become an artist, a painter, or an architect. None of that mattered now. It was as if another Self spoke through him in a state of ecstasy or complete trance. "In sublime, irresistible images, he unfolded before me his own future and that of our people. . . . He now spoke of a mandate that he was one day to receive from our people, in order to lead them out of slavery, to the heights of freedom." With perfect recall of this starry hour in a conversation with Winifried Wagner and Kubizek at Bayreuth in 1939, Hitler solemnly added "In that hour it began."[19]

Savitri Devi believed that Adolf Hitler was the western Aryan counterpart of Rama and Krishna among the eastern Aryans of India. She visited Linz and Leonding on her pilgrimage of 1953 in the selfsame spirit that had drawn her in the 1930s to Ayodhya where Rama, the miraculous conqueror of South India, had lived and ruled, and to Brindaban, where Krishna, the immortal teacher of the doctrine of detached violence, had spent his early youth. Both these avatars personified to her the warlike wisdom and the territorial expansion of the hallowed race, and each of them inaugurated a new epoch in the history of the awakening of Aryan consciousness in antiquity.[20] Just as Rama and Krishna were Yuga avatars, she so could invoke Hitler, the race savior, as the perennial avatar of the *Bhagavad Gita*. Sitting in the garden of Hitler's former classmate's in Leonding, she visualized the beloved features of her Führer suddenly merging into the impersonal Essence of the many-featured One, who spoke Krishna's words to Arjuna. She was certain that she had sought him for centuries, in life after life, until she realized that the founder of the Third Reich was indeed he—the one who comes back, whenever he should "to establish the reign of Righteousness."[21]

Savitri Devi believed that it was impossible to understand National Socialism apart from the cyclic conception of history suggested by Hindu tradition. She considered that Hitler's vision ultimately transcended even Germany and the Aryan race. The Nazi philosophy set at nought man's intellectual conceit, his naive pride in "progress," and his futile attempts to enslave nature and instead made the mysterious and unfailing impersonal wisdom of forests, oceans, and outer space the basis of a global regeneration policy for an overcrowded, over-civilized, and technically overdeveloped world at the end of the Kali Yuga. She saw Hitler embodying that eternal nature wisdom against the false science, false religion, false morality, and false political ideas of a decadent age. He made Germany's struggle for freedom, healthy living conditions, and power part of a broader struggle for the liberation of mankind from the Kali Yuga. He made Germany, "the holy Land of the West, the Stronghold of regenerate Aryandom."[22]

Savitri Devi also found the faithful echo of ancient Sanskrit wisdom in the institutions and organizations of the Third Reich. Her enthusiastic description of social life in Nazi Germany dwelt on the high moral tone, new housing, and sports and leisure facilities in a sunlit world of energetic purpose. Hitler's measures for the physical and moral protection of his predestined people were intended to foster the natural leaders of the Aryan race. His new laws for the welfare of mother and child, for the creation of ideal living conditions for workmen's families, and for the education of a healthy, self-confident and self-reliant, proud and beautiful youth, and his Nuremberg race laws, all promoted the regeneration of the pure-blooded Germanic race and arrested the threatening tide of inferior humanity, whose rise is always the index of an advanced stage of the Kali Yuga.[23]

But Savitri Devi neither ignored nor denied the dark side of Nazism. For her the SS was the supreme Nazi organization, the physical and moral elite of awakening Aryandom, the living matrix in which a new race of gods on earth was to take shape and soul. She dwelt lovingly on the harsh rigors of its discipline and on its high standards of cleanliness, presentation, and drill. Purity of blood and flawless physical perfection were the conditions of admission to the SS: prospective members were obliged to submit a family tree of exclusive Aryan-Germanic descent back to 1750, and superiors took great care in vetting the future spouse of each SS man. Savitri Devi recalled that SS men always gave their religion as *gottgläubig* (believer in God) rather than any denomination. This had nothing to do with Judaeo-Christian notions of universalism but embraced the idea of a natural and biological hierarchy, in which the SS would form a blood aristocracy to rule over the rest of mankind. The SS knew nothing of meekness and humanity; its watchwords were strictness and pride. The black uniforms and ominous death's-head insignia symbolized the harsh forces "in Time" employed for the achievement of a golden age.[24]

Savitri Devi regarded the SS attitude toward war as the living expression of that ancient Aryan wisdom of detached violence necessary to overcome the dark age. Rigorous selection and training guaranteed the SS man's complete self-mastery and military skill. However, National Socialism was pitted against all the forces of darkness and decay in a fallen world, and this great cosmic battle required terrible deeds on the part of its elite military vanguard. The SS was involved in the liquidation of Jewish ghettoes and the administration of concentration camps; after the Wehrmacht attack on the Soviet Union, the SS Einsatzgruppen shot hundreds of thousands of Jews and communist officials in mass executions; millions of Jews were murdered in the extermination camps in occupied Poland. Savitri Devi saw the SS as the living enactment of the ancient Aryan warrior code described in the *Bhagavad Gita*: "Perform without attachment that action which is duty, desiring nothing but the welfare of Creation."[25] And again, "Taking as equal pleasure and pain, gain and loss, victory and defeat, gird thyself for battle." With frightful logic, she saw the embodiment of this Aryan *kshatriya* warrior spirit in Otto Ohlendorf, the commander of an SS Einsatzgruppe, condemned to death as a war criminal at Nuremberg.[26]

In her millenarian expectation of the end of the Kali Yuga, Savitri Devi combined the Hindu cyclic theory of time with more Manichaean and dualistic notions of Judaeo-Christian apocalyptic prophecy. Savitri Devi saw the Jews as the embodiment of the Kali Yuga. Her broad surveys of ancient history often touched on the rise of the Semites, initially in the overthrow of the Mitanni by the Assyrians and the migration of the Hebrews into Palestine during Akhnaton's reign. While the Aryans were refining the caste system in India and their western cousins were first settling as Teutons and Mycenaean Greeks in Europe, the Jews, she believed, were elaborating a cunning strategy for world dominion. Strictly adhering to their own tribal identity, the Jews encouraged racial mixing, cosmopolitanism, liberalism, and skepticism among all other peoples to promote their disintegration and downfall. Scattered by the Romans in the first century A.D., the Jews entered Europe in the early Middle Ages and became in due course the ferment of its nations. During the modern period the atomistic self-seeking individualism of money capitalism served their purposes as much as Marxism, another Jewish doctrine intended for Gentile consumption, which cynically preached international raceless brotherhood.[27]

Savitri Devi presents a metaphysical anti-Semitism, according to which the Jew is the expression of the downsweep of the time cycle, and whose purpose is the dissolution of all races, all nations, all communities, and ultimately all life upon the planet. From the fourth century B.C. onward until the time of Philo, she argued, hellenized Jews had begun blending their cabbalistic notions with Greek ideas to create that religion of man opposed to all other living creatures. This exaltation of man over nature led, either through capitalism or communism, to a general bastardization of the whole human species and its exponential proliferation as producers and consumers at the expense of all other creatures in "a reign of quantity" characterized by money, rational calculation, and the growth of human numbers. However, such philosophical falsehood was matched by its ecological folly. Mankind would simply create one vast international slum in which he completed the exhaustion and destruction of nature itself. In her account the Jews are thus the epitome of the death forces in the era of gloom.[28]

Certain passages in Hitler's *Mein Kampf* do indeed possess a strange cosmic quality. Especially when writing of the Jews or Marxism as the enemies of the Aryan race, Hitler often raises Nazi ideology to the level of a principle of order in the universe. Terms like the "planets," the "world ether," "destiny," "millions of years," and all "creation" lend a cosmological note to his accounts of nature, the struggle for life, and the survival of the fittest.[29] Hitler also identified the human conquest and transcendence of nature as a dangerous illusion of Jewish origin. Should the Jew, with the aid of Marxism, prevail over mankind and the laws of nature, Hitler prophesied that "the planet will go its way, void of human beings, through aetherial space, as it did millions of years ago. . . . [B]y defending myself against the Jew, I am fighting for the work of the Lord."[30] Savitri Devi seized upon such passages as striking evidence of Hitler's divine mission to eradicate the man-centered faiths in the Judaeo-Christian orbit of the modern Western world in favor of that doctrine "in the interest of the Universe."[31]

She regarded Hitler as an avatar like Rama and Krishna, the most widely remembered Aryan heroes of ancient India, who also knew that the end of the Kali Yuga can be achieved only by responding to the decay of the dark age with yet greater violence.[32] Savitri Devi glorified Hitler for his avataric intervention against the forces of death and disintegration in a battle for the future of the universe. At the mass meetings and rallies of the 1920s and 1930s "he spoke with the wild eloquence of emergency, knowing that the struggle he was about to start had to take place then or never."[33] He knew that his German people and the whole Aryan race "were threatened in their existence by the agents of the Death-powers; cornered; and that their definitive downfall and disappearance would mean the definitive downfall of higher organised Life upon this planet, with no hope of resurrection."[34] She extolled the mystical insight, elemental logic, and violence of Nazism as the collective expression of Hitler's own iron will, militant brutality, and fanatical faith.

The Yuga avatar was a harbinger of the apocalypse and the onset of the next age. The Hindu mythology of the *Puranas* foretold the advent of Kalki, the tenth and final avatar of Vishnu as the divine incarnation who will end the Kali Yuga and initiate a new Krita Yuga.

> When the close of the Kali age shall be nigh, a portion of that divine being who exists of his own spiritual nature in the character of Brahma, and who is the beginning and the end, and who comprehends all things, shall descend upon earth: he will be born in the family of Vishnuyasas, an eminent Brahman of Sambhala village as Kalki, endowed with the eight superhuman faculties. . . . [H]e will destroy all whose minds are devoted to iniquity. He will then reestablish righteousness upon earth; and the minds of those who live at the end of the Kali age shall be awakened, and shall be as pellucid as crystal. The men who are thus changed by virtue of that peculiar time shall be as the seeds of human beings, and shall give birth to a race who shall follow the laws of the Krita age, or age of purity.[35]

The critical and final nature of the Kalki avatar in the cycle of the ages has led to speculation that this is a borrowing from Christian apocalyptic prophecy concerning the Second Coming of Christ. This particular myth in the *Vishnu Purana* has been dated to the first couple of centuries A.D., and scholars have wondered whether this idea entered India with the Parthian invasions in the same period. Kalki is always portrayed in Hindu iconography as a sword-bearing warrior mounted on a white horse, which would again suggest a link to the redeemer figure or warrior Christ in the Book of Revelation. This close parallel between Christian and Hindu ideas of the savior, in the first case as one who ends all history, in the second as one who restores perfection for the period of a new cycle, go some way to explaining the peculiar attraction of Kalki to the Western millenarian mind. Savitri Devi devoted the final part of *The Lightning and the Sun* to the coming of Kalki and the end of the age of gloom.

Did Savitri Devi believe Adolf Hitler was Kalki? She almost certainly did during the heyday of the Third Reich and the first half of the Second World War. As Hitler's avataric battle escalated into a global conflict with the declaration of war against the Soviet Union followed by the United States, she shuddered at his colossal challenge to the combined dark age forces of Jewry, Marxism, and international capitalism. However, by late 1944 even she and her husband could no longer have expected an Axis victory; it was clear that Hitler had not ended the Kali Yuga. But her hopes for its ending remained undimmed, and she also clung to the belief that Hitler was still alive, awaiting the right moment to resume hostilities against the world. It was only certain that Kalki would come and Hitler might indeed reappear as Kalki at this final Armageddon. But even if Hitler himself did not return, Kalki would combine the qualities of the Krishna avatar on the Kurukshetra battlefield in the *Bhagavad Gita* with those of Adolf Hitler and of all Men against Time who come back to reestablish the reign of righteousness.

In the meantime, she believed that Hitler had offered not only himself but his beloved German people in sacrifice, for the fulfillment of the highest purpose of Creation: the survival of a superior mankind. Krishna's words appeared as the second motto of *Pilgrimage*: "I am the Oblation; I am the Sacrifice . . ." (*Bhagavad Gita* IX, 16). In early 1956 when Germany was divided and Nazism reviled, Savitri Devi fondly imagined that Hitler would survive in songs and symbols: "[T]he Lords of the new Time-cycle, men of his own blood and faith, will render him divine honours, through rites full of meaning and full of potency, in the cool shade of the endless re-grown forests, on the beaches, or upon the inviolate mountain-peaks, facing the rising sun."[36] For Savitri Devi the place of Adolf Hitler in the future Aryan pantheon was quite secure.

8

DEFIANCE

In May 1945 Europe lay in ruins. Because of the sustained Anglo-American bombing campaign since 1943, countless German cities were reduced to shells and rubble. Hitler's reckless policy of "no surrender," coupled with his wild hopes of miracle weapons, a falling-out among the Allies, or other freak reversal in the grinding defeat of the German armed forces had brought the war deep into the Reich. By the end, whole industries were destroyed; basic amenities and transport systems shattered; food and fuel scarce. The soldiers were demoralized, captured, or dead. The ragged civilian survivors searched for the missing amid a wasteland of defeat and enemy occupation. This burden of defeat, loss, and death was compounded with horror and disgrace. The Allied discoveries of the concentration camps, notably Belsen and Dachau, revealed the depravity of the Third Reich to the world at large. The emaciated victims and piles of corpses became the symbol of Nazi bestiality and German shame. Hitler and the Third Reich were reviled; Germany was an outcast among the nations.

Savitri Devi returned to this war-ravaged Europe in late 1945 to make her belated contribution to the Nazi cause. She knew she had left this mission too late; that while the Third Reich was martial, ebullient, and expansive, she had been far removed from action in India. Now, the defeat of Hitler and disgrace of Germany reduced her from a triumphant votary of the New Order to a quasi-gnostic sectary of Nazism in a world of Western ascendancy. Her sense of frustration at missing the "great days" of the Third Reich were overwhelming. Whenever she met Nazi loyalists, former SS men, and Wehrmacht veterans in occupied Germany, her admiration and compassion for these people was matched only by regret that she had failed to stand beside them during the heyday of Nazi rule. She was always repining that she had not shared with them the excitement and inflationary sense of power amid the thunderous applause of the Nazi crowds. Now she could only join them in their suffering, losses, and martyrdom. This desire to identify belatedly with the defeated Nazi cause and its devotees propelled her into a quixotic and hopeless mission on behalf of the Third Reich. Her subsequent detention as an Allied prisoner fulfilled her burning desire to share the fate of the Nazi faithful.

She approached her Nazi mission by degrees, not entering Allied-occupied Germany until the spring of 1948. But the total defeat of Germany cast its long shadow over her return to Europe. In November 1945 she had sailed on a passenger liner bound from Bombay to Southampton. During the several weeks on board there was no other conversation among her English fellow passengers but the defeat of Nazism. After a brief stay in London she traveled to France to visit her mother in Lyons, only to learn that she had been active throughout the war in the French Resistance against German occupation. Reunited for the first time since 1934, mother and daughter now found that a bitterly fought war as well as an ideological gulf divided them, and their relations were duly strained. However, Savitri Devi stayed on in Lyons, completing her classic misanthropic book *Impeachment of Man* there in March 1946.

Back in London, she arranged for the publication of *A Son of God* by the Theosophical Society at its press on Great Russell Street in London. This publication under the auspices of the society is understandable given its promotion of esoteric and Hindu ideas throughout Europe and America from the late nineteenth century onwards. But while Theosophists were interested in the subject of ancient Egypt and its mysteries, Savitri Devi had no time for their cosmopolitan and universal philosophy. The book led to some public lectures on the mystical pharaoh and his sun cult. She soon found new friends with similar interests in the capital. Muriel Gantry, a young theater costume designer, had long been interested in Minoan Crete and they spent many hours absorbed in the history of the ancient Mediterranean world. Muriel Gantry never shared Savitri Devi's Nazi interests but remained a loyal, lifelong friend. Through her own contacts in the theater world, she was able to obtain employment for Savitri Devi, who thus secured a livelihood during her time in London.

Wherever she went in London, Savitri Devi felt oppressed by the constant barrage of anti-German sentiment and propaganda, the suspicion and hatred of National Socialism. On Oxford Street she saw a photographic exhibition of Nazi atrocities and newsreels of the liberation of the concentration camps. She hurried on. But everywhere, in milk bars and cafes, in railway station waiting rooms and private houses, the radio ceaselessly recounted the horrors of Hitlerism and impugned all that Savitri Devi stood for. She stayed in cheap accommodations and suffered the conversation of fellow boarders. At the supper table in Mrs. Ponworth's boardinghouse at 37 Wood Lane, Highgate, she endured a Jewish woman's account of Nazi infamies and general support for the Nuremberg trials that were then nearing completion. The only dissenting voice came from a black Christian, whose plea for mercy enraged the Jewess and earned Savitri Devi's cynical approval.[1] These and many similar discussions about the terrible deeds of the Nazis and the overwhelming case for prosecuting the leading war criminals only hardened her extremist convictions.

The fearful prospect that her heroes would shortly be sentenced by the International Military Tribunal now filled all her waking hours. A few days later, while staying at a nurses' hostel at 104 Grosvenor Road in Pimlico, she dreamed one night that she entered the Nuremberg cell of Hermann Goering. He saw her and was rather astonished, but she reassured him that she was a friend. She declared that she wished she could save all the Nuremberg defendants from the ignominy of the trial, but the heavenly powers had granted her leave to save only one man. She had chosen Goering because of his kindness to animals. (She understood that Goering, as Reich Forestry Commissioner, had established extensive conservation areas in the Third Reich.) She then felt something small in her hand, and although she did not know what it was, she handed it to the former Reichsmarschall, saying, "Take this, and do not allow these people to kill you as a criminal." She bid the surprised prisoner a farewell "*Heil Hitler*" and then vanished. The next morning she overslept until ten o'clock, which was most unusual. It was the sixteenth of October and a rainy day in London. Outside the hostel at a newspaper kiosk she read with amazement the headlines "Goering found dead in his cell at 2.30 A.M. No one knows who gave him the poison. Potassium Cyanide." This experience of astral travel in her subtle body was her only contact with the top leadership of the Third Reich.[2]

Still she hesitated to travel to Germany and witness the defeat of the Third Reich. Wishing to escape the constant reminders of Germany's disgrace, she seized an opportunity to lecture on Akhnaton in Iceland. On 28 November 1946 she sailed from Hull to Iceland, arriving seven days later at Reykjavik with only five pounds in her pocket. Following her lecture engagement, she stayed on, found employment, and began learning Icelandic. In the hard winter of early 1947 she worked as a maid on a farm outside Reykjavik. Later she took a job as a French tutor to an Icelander's Austrian wife. Although she found the Icelandic people splendid specimens of the Aryan racial type, she was bitterly disappointed by their general hostility to Nazism. Even on this remote island in the Arctic Circle it proved impossible to escape the general abhorrence of the Nazi creed. She consoled herself by writing a play about Akhnaton and the persecution of his sun cult, which was a thinly veiled allegory of the defeat of Hitler.

The barren, austere landscape of Iceland mirrored the iron in her soul as she contemplated the defeat of her ideals. But this strange world of glaciers, geysers, and volcanoes also offered a rich pageant of nature, that amoral power that she worshiped in Shiva and his dance of creation and destruction. On the night of 5 April 1947, she rapturously watched the full eruption of Mount Hekla, Iceland's most famous volcano, which had already erupted eighteen times before 1845. At other times her mood was reflective. On 9 June she visited the Godafoss (Waterfall of the Gods), where a priest had once thrown the images of the old pagan gods as a demonstration of his conversion to Christianity about the year 1000. Deeply moved, she stood beside the waterfall, thinking of Odin, Thor, and Baldur, whom her Viking ancestors had once worshiped, lying for more than nine hundred years at the bottom of the icy waters of the Skjálfandafljót and still waiting for the "great Heathen Renaissance." In one of her ritual acts she recited the verse of Leconte de Lisle, which a Norse god addresses to the child Jesus:

Thou shalt die in thy turn!
Nine times, I swear it by the immortal Runes,
Thou shalt die like I, god of new souls!
For man will survive. Twenty centuries of suffering
Will make his flesh bleed and his tears flow,
Until the day when thy yoke, tolerated two thousand years,
Will weigh heavily upon the necks of the rebellious races;

When thy temples, standing in their midst
Will become an object of mockery to the people;
Then, thy time will be up . . . [3]

Invoking the Aryan gods, she implored their aid in her struggle to restore the Nazi cult of youth, health, and strength, before casting the paper into the roaring cataract.

She remained in Iceland until the end of 1947, when she returned to England. Once again she found theatrical employment as the wardrobe manager of the Randoopa Dancing Company, which traveled around England, Scotland, France, and Scandinavia giving performances of Indian dance. By early April 1948 she was in Edinburgh, beginning work on her final statement of Aryan doctrine and Nazi witness, *The Lightning and the Sun*. She next accompanied the group from Scotland across the North Sea to Sweden, arriving in May. In Stockholm she chanced to meet an old acquaintance from 1946 in London, a zealous English Nazi sympathizer, who introduced her to a number of Swedish Nazis, including the famous explorer Sven Hedin, then eighty-three years old.

By the first decade of the century Sven Hedin (1865–1952) was regarded as one of the world's leading Asiatic explorers. Immediately after leaving school he had traveled three thousand kilometers on horseback through Persia and Mesopotamia. In 1890 he was attached to King Oscar's embassy to the shah of Persia and then visited Khurasan and Turkestan. His later expeditions in the Pamir, China, and Tibet between 1893 and 1897, 1899 and 1902, and 1906 and 1908, recounted in his numerous books of adventure, brought him international recognition and honors. A lover of the desert and remote places, Hedin was a political reactionary. He detested the liberal government in Sweden and was a great admirer of Wilhelmian Germany. During the 1914–1918 war he had met the kaiser, Hindenburg, and leading commanders at the western front and was bitterly disappointed by the German defeat. After the rise of the Nazis, he became a loyal supporter of the Third Reich, frequenting the dining tables of Hitler, Goering, and other top Nazi brass throughout the war. His last major political work, *Amerika im Kampf der Kontinente* (1942), condemned Roosevelt's intervention in European affairs, recalled the 1918 "stab-in-the-back" legend beloved of German militarists, and generally followed the Nazi Foreign Office line. After

1945, Hedin's reputation was severely tarnished by these associations and writings.[4]

Hedin's aura of heroic adventure, his daring and hazardous travels across Asia, his triumphant homecomings to receive the tribute of monarchs and the adulation of crowds had been the stuff of legend. But now in 1949 all this was past. Expelled from various international societies, he bemoaned the modern world. His Nazi enthusiasm had rendered him a political pariah. A meeting at a Stockholm reception with the liberal Thomas Mann on 24 May remained at the level of small talk. On 4 June Hedin penned his thoughts on the defeat of communism and the unbreakable spirit of the Germanic race to Johannes Lehmann, editor of a Danish journal.[5] Two days later he received Savitri Devi, a fellow diehard in the Nazi cause. On 6 June they conversed for four hours about the fate of Germany and the chances of a Nazi revival. The old Swede evidently gave her fresh hope, alluding to Germany's immense resources of courage and strength despite defeat and hinting that Hitler might indeed still be alive. Thus encouraged, she decided to set forth on what was to be the first of three sorties into occupied Germany as an agent of the vanquished Nazi cause.[6]

She prepared for her mission by laboriously writing out her own German text on five hundred slips of paper—a task that took two entire nights.

> Men and women of Germany, in the midst of unspeakable rigours and suffering, hold fast to our glorious National Socialist faith, and resist! Defy the people, defy the powers, which work to denazify the German nation and the whole world. Nothing can destroy whatever is built on truth. We are the pure gold which can be tested in the furnace. The furnace may glow and crackle. Nothing can destroy us. One day we will rebel and triumph again. Hope and wait! Heil Hitler![7]

Thus armed, she boarded the Nord-Express in Stockholm bound for Germany on 15 June and distributed her leaflets in cigarette packets and other small gifts of sugar, coffee, sardines, cheese, and butter from the train as it passed through stations from the frontier at Flensburg via Hamburg, Bremen, Duisburg, Düsseldorf, and Cologne to Aachen. The railway journey across Germany lasted fifteen hours and it was a rite of initiation for Savitri Devi. The sight of the devastated cities, the twisted wreckage of industrial installations, the misery and hunger of the defeated Germans made a deep impression on her, confirming her

love for Germany and her hatred of the Allies. There was also opportunity for political exchange: in Duisburg two German railway policemen boarded the train and expressed their appreciation of her gesture;
three Jews in the theater company traveling with her were outraged.
This minor mission completed, she returned to London for a short stay.

Later in the year she repeated the operation on a larger scale. A
military permit to visit Germany for a longer period was obtained from
the Bureau des Affaires Allemandes in Paris through the good offices
of a former schoolfriend who had influence in Free French circles and
knew nothing of Savitri Devi's political convictions. Savitri Devi stated
that she intended to write a book about Germany as her reason for
visiting the occupied country. Returning through France and the Saarland to enter the French Occupation Zone of Germany at Saarhölzbach,
she spent some three months between 7 September and 6 December
1948 distributing a further six thousand leaflets in the three Western
zones and the Saarland. In the course of this extended visit, she had
many opportunities to acquaint herself with the Germans and their
conquerors. A long conversation with a French occupation official at
Baden-Baden only confirmed her contempt for the Allies' hypocrisy,
their policy of reeducation, and the sham of democracy. In Koblenz she
was introduced to a group of Nazi loyalists, including Fritz Horn, whose
health had been broken by mistreatment in Allied POW camps on
German soil after the war. In Bonn she met an unrepentant Nazi veteran whose fulminations against the Allies and fantasies of future revenge warmed her heart.[8] This more substantial operation behind her,
she returned to London to spend Christmas with friends before mounting her third and final propaganda mission to the defeated Reich.[9]

"Gold in the Furnace," the phrase used in her first propaganda leaflet
to typify the endurance of the Germans even in the hardest trials of
their defeat and subjection, became the leitmotif and title of her book
describing her travels and reflections during 1948 and early 1949 in
postwar Germany. She had begun writing *Gold in the Furnace* in early
October 1948 at Alfeld an der Leine in Lower Saxony, shortly after
entering occupied Germany on her second, longer propaganda mission,
and three chapters were already completed by the time of her arrest in
February 1949. A further three were finished while she was in inves-
tigative custody, and the final eight chapters were written secretly while
she was imprisoned at Werl. She completed the book in her prison cell

on 16 July 1949, a month before her release. She called the book "her favourite child" and it is evident that she poured out her soul in these descriptions of the staunch Nazi loyalists she had met in the course of her autumn 1948 mission. Her heroes were set against a bitter and crushing background of urban ruin and rubble, the pressures of denazification, and other Allied impositions, restrictions, and economic reparations involving the dismantlement of German industrial plant and deforestation.

The encounters are interspersed with lengthy avowals of National Socialism and denunciations of the futile and declining Western world of democracy and Christianity. These verbatim records of her contacts with Germans in the early postwar years are especially interesting for the light they throw on the attitudes and expectations of defeated people unable to make sense of the catastrophe of defeat following the collective excitement and national pride of the Third Reich. Conversations with these individuals followed a regular pattern. If Savitri Devi's credentials were already established by personal introductions or clandestine recommendations, the exchange would usually provide mutual comfort and encouragement concerning the temporary nature of defeat, the imminent prospect (two to three years) of a Nazi revival, and on occasion the assertion that Hitler was alive in hiding and simply waiting for the opportune moment. When striking up a casual acquaintance, Savitri Devi would often mention that she was writing a book about Germany. Whenever admonished by a Nazi sympathizer to write the truth and eschew prejudice, she would protest delightedly that she was herself a staunch Nazi.

A chance encounter at Koblenz railway station with an old shopkeeper, Fräulein E., led Savitri Devi to Herr M. He ridiculed the Allied policy of reeducation, declaring that the Führer gave them a sense of life that was eternal, not to be believed in but seen with one's own eyes. Everything that had occurred since 1945 only served to convince them that the Nazi doctrine was right in all respects, namely, on the Jewish question, the rule of the fittest, and the racial principle. Even more Germans believed this now than during the Third Reich.[10] Herr M. in turn introduced her to two more Nazi loyalists, with whom she stayed for several days. Friedrich Horn and his companion, Fräulein B., occupied a cramped garret room at the top of a house amid the ruins of Koblenz. Savitri Devi was particularly impressed by Horn, whom she revered as a model Nazi and a martyr to the cause in consequence of his ill-treatment by the Allies. She related his story with reverence and pathos.

Horn was an architect by profession and an ardent Nazi Party member, having held the office of *Ortsgruppenleiter* from 1932 onward during the Third Reich. Arrested as a prominent local Nazi by the Americans at the end of May 1945, Horn was first held at Diez before being transferred by rail to a concentration camp at Schwarzenborn near Treysa, together with nine or ten thousand other National Socialists. Detained in a former cavalry stables, Horn shared a stall with two other men. The conditions were appalling: no blankets, no running water, and only half a bowl of thin watery soup and three hard biscuits to eat each day. One in twenty of the internees died of starvation within a fortnight. By the end of December 1945 Horn, had lost sixty-five pounds, could hardly stand up, and was admitted to the camp hospital. In February 1946 he was transported by cattle truck to a concentration camp in Darmstadt, where the temperature in the unheated cells fell as low as -25° C during the harsh winter of 1946–1947. After several nights, Horn was hospitalized once more for three months and finally released in December 1947. His health was permanently ruined as a result of his ill-treatment in the camps, where he had spent nearly three years.[11]

The case of Friedrich Horn simply illustrates the chaotic postwar conditions in the American and French concentration camps, both in their zones of occupation in Germany and in France.[12] But in her hatred of the Allies, Savitri Devi latched onto any such instances of suffering, hunger, and torture among Nazi prisoners. In the little garret with Horn and his companion, she was in the presence of such a martyr. She lovingly described Horn's open face, his proud bearing, above all the calmness and cheerfulness of a warrior-sage whose quiet faith and confidence in the ultimate victory of the Nazi idea transcended his own suffering. Horn fetched his copy of *Mein Kampf*, while Fräulein B. showed Savitri Devi a glass etching of Hitler's portrait on a pendant and pressed her to accept it as a gift. Savitri Devi was greatly moved by this gesture. All three spent the rest of the evening reading and commenting on passages of *Mein Kampf*, exchanging their views on the necessity of a heathen outlook, and the incompatibility of Nazism and Christianity. Gathered under the steep attic roof somewhere in French-occupied Koblenz, the new friends celebrated their secret Nazi

gnosis in devotional exercises like members of a persecuted sect. At
their final parting in August 1949, Horn presented Savitri Devi with
his only copy of *Mein Kampf* with the words "Go wherever you might
be the most useful and wait. Hope and wait . . . if, being alone, you feel
powerless, you have your burning faith,—our common Nazi faith—
to sustain you. And you have this: our Führer's immortal words; a
remembrance from Germany." As if concluding a religious rite, they
exchanged the Hitler salute.[13]

Earlier in September 1948 on a fine early autumn day Savitri Devi
had walked in the forest adjoining the Harz mountains with another
Nazi stalwart, Herr A. She had never met him before and owed her
introduction to Nazis living abroad. Mindful of spies and thin walls at
home, Herr A. suggested that they wander in the forest in order to
talk freely. Amid the golden foliage and birdsong, Savitri Devi told
Herr A. something of her life, her visit to Palestine in 1929 and repugnance at the Jews, her search in India for a traditional Aryan culture, and her unending regret at not coming to Germany during the
Third Reich. After all, she would have seen the Führer. Herr A. understood her perfectly. Hitler was alive, Herr A. knew where he was,
although he could not tell her now. He assured her she should see
Hitler and hear him tell her how pleased he was that she was among
the Germans during their darkest days in 1948. However, he cautioned
her to be more guarded in her enthusiasm, for she could easily betray
her real feelings to the enemy in this land of fear and occupation. Herr
A. confided to her his plans to build a sun temple as a Nazi shrine, a
project that found her wholehearted support.[14]

Another encounter took place in a café in Bonn. Here Savitri Devi's
attention was caught by a pair of German men at a neighboring table.
One of these was unlike any of her earlier contacts: an elemental and
fearsome fellow, whose head and shoulders reminded her of a bison in
the ancient Germanic forests. Energy and will power were written all
over his broad forehead, red angular face, and powerful chin. He was
the tough beer-hall-fighter type, the representative of the Nazi crowd.
Savitri Devi thrilled at the sight of this "warrior of Hermann in a
shabby modern suit"—she saw in him a symbol of Germany's resurrection. The beer-hall fighter struck up a conversation with her and
was soon telling her the story of his war. As a Wehrmacht soldier in
France, he had marched through the Arc de Triomphe, and his troop
had proceeded as far as the Spanish border. *Jawohl*, they had had a

great time. They had eaten and drunk but always remained gentlemen. They had brought order to the countries they ruled, maintained a strict code of honor and been generous and merciful to the conquered. But when they lost the war, many Wehrmacht soldiers were unable to leave France in good time and were severely mistreated in concentration camps, some even deported for many years to the tropics and Indochina. He himself had been interned in France until 1948.

Continuing his narrative to postwar conditions in occupied Germany, the old fighter's face darkened. "Nice people to talk about freedom and justice, these damned democrats! They have tied us hand and foot, so that we cannot move, they have muzzled us, so that we can offer no resistance, while they plunder our country left and right, dismantle and carry off our factories piece by piece, cut down our forests, take our coal, our iron, our steel, all that we have, and into the bargain make people believe that we were to blame for the war—these confounded liars!" He lusted for revenge. He longed for the day when the last Allies ran for their lives to escape Germany, when Paris would lie in ruins at its next German occupation; next time he would show neither mercy nor good humor. Savitri Devi felt a sense of mounting excitement as his mood became ever uglier and he began to describe in a raised voice how he would kill his enemies: this was the spirit she sought, the rolling eyes of a wounded animal, a war god of the Stone Age thirsting for blood, barbaric magnificence. It was a perfect meeting of minds: the violent resentful German and the Aryan prophetess of revenge. The day of reckoning seemed already nearer.[15]

In preparation for her third propaganda sortie to enemy-occupied Germany she had printed in London a small German-language handbill, headed with a swastika, exhorting the Germans to remain true to their Führer, who was reputed to be still alive, and to rise up against the Allied forces now stationed throughout the country. Her sense of mission, her Nazi piety, and her self-proclaimed membership in a tiny gathered remnant of Hitler loyalists are evident from the text:

> German People
> What have the democracies brought you?
> In war time, phosphorous and fire.
> After the war, hunger, humiliation and oppression;
> the dismantling of the factories;
> the destruction of the forests;

and now,—the Ruhr Statute!
However, "Slavery is to last but a short time more."
Our Führer is alive
And will soon come back, with power unheard of.
Resist our persecutors!
Hope and wait.
                    Heil Hitler!
                                    S.D.

This fervent appeal, coupled with apocalyptic hopes surrounding the reappearance of Hitler, was followed by a stanza of the well-known Nazi marching song:

> Wir werden weiter marschieren
> wenn alles in Scherben fällt;
> denn heute gehört uns Deutschland
> und morgen, die ganze Welt.[16]

Given the utter defeat and demoralization of postwar Germany, its shattered industries, depleted work force, the hungry cities, and the growing dependence on the occupying forces, such an appeal was at best symbolic. It chiefly served Savitri Devi's burning need to demonstrate her solidarity with Nazism, her loyalty to Adolf Hitler, and her loathing of the West and its supposed superiority. She began distributing the handbill on the night of 13/14 February 1949 in Cologne and soon found a comrade to help her. His name was Gerhard Wassmer, a former SS man who in 1945 had been transported by the French as a POW to work in hard-regime camps in the Congo. The German prisoners had been subject to black overseers, and conditions had been intolerable. Of the 11,000 sent out to the Congo, only 4,800 survived to see Europe again. Wassmer was receptive to Savitri Devi's mission, and they agreed to meet again after a week.

By this time she had successfully distributed 11,500 leaflets and handbills in West German cities during five months' clandestine activity. However, Wassmer was caught by British military police, who were waiting for her when she inquired after him at his Catholic Mission address in Cologne on 20 February. She was remanded in custody, initially in Cologne before being transferred to Düsseldorf on 7 March, when the hearing was postponed for a week. On 14 March she was driven by car through Dortmund and Duisburg to Essen for an initial court hearing. Pleading a call of nature among the ruins of Essen, she briefly left the car and chalked *"Heil Hitler!"* on a wall in a further act of defiance. At the hearing her accomplice denied any interest in her propaganda mission. But this did not surprise nor disappoint her. She recognized that most Germans were now exhausted by the long war and the occupation that she had missed far away in India; she alone now had the energy for this ritual defiance of the Allies. This was her duty and her destiny.[17]

At the hearing it was decided that Savitri Devi had a case to answer under Article 7 of Law No. 8 of the Occupation Status, which forbade the promotion of militarist and National Socialist ideas on German territory subject to the Allied Control Commission. The maximum penalty for the breach of this law was the death sentence. She was to be detained at the British military prison for women at Werl until her formal trial, which was fixed for 5 April 1949. During the ensuing three weeks she was further questioned by British officers about her motives and inspiration, chiefly in order to establish if she was acting on behalf of a renegade Nazi organization or underground network in Germany. Regularly interrogated by military intelligence officer Hatch, she supplied details of her first visit to India in 1932 on account of her interest in eugenics, the caste system, and Hinduism as a living survival of the old Aryan cults of Europe. Hatch probed in vain for political links and was simply confronted by her unabashed Nazi piety: she attributed her National Socialist conviction to her philosophy, her essentially aesthetic attitude to religious and social problems, and her interpretation of world history.[18]

Throughout her interrogation by Hatch and other British officers and in discussions with prison wardresses, Savitri Devi displayed aloofness and political contempt for the values of the West. Despite the evident military and economic might of the occupying powers, she clung fast to her Nazi faith and its ultimate victory. Her response to any challenge concerning the inhumanity of Nazism was haughty disdain for the trivial, secular man-centered values of Western democracy, liberalism, and Christianity. Her truths were wholly impersonal and cosmic; her vision rested on the life-centered pageant of nature, the great wheel of creation and destruction, beside which man's concerns, comforts, and rights appeared trifling and insignificant. Utopian images of natural beauty, racial purity, and flawless perfection underlay her conception of Nazi spirituality; man himself and his notions of comfort and mutual benefit she regarded with icy scorn. Arrogance and hatred defined her attitude.

As the date of the trial approached, she indulged in fantasies of martyrdom for the Nazi cause. In a conversation with her lawyer, she expressed her wish that she could receive the death sentence, noticing in her own voice the unmistakable accent of sincerity, the yearning of years, the burning regret of wasted time in India, and the thirst for redeeming martyrdom:

> There would be, also, the joy of the last sunrise upon my face; the joy of the preparation for the greatest act of my life; the joy of the act itself. . . . Draped in my best sari—in scarlet and gold, as on my wedding day in glorious '40 (I hope they would not refuse me that favour)—I would walk to the place of execution singing the Horst Wessel Song. I, Savitri Devi, the ambassador of southernmost and easternmost Aryandom as well as a daughter of northern and southern Europe. And, stretching out my right arm, firm and white in the sunshine, I would die happy in a cry of love and joy, shouting for the last time, as defiance to all the anti-Nazi forces, the holy words that sum up my life-long faith "Heil Hitler!" I could not imagine for myself a more beautiful end.[19]

These absurd, romantic, and self-dramatizing effusions are entirely characteristic of Savitri Devi's passionate need to affirm her loyalty to Hitler and National Socialism following their demise. Confronted with the painful facts of Allied victory and the total defeat of the Third Reich, she sought relief in ritual acts of devotion, prayers to a universal deity, and whimsical ideas concerning her valiant but isolated witness to the Aryan ideal. A picture of Adolf Hitler, which hung like an icon on her cell wall, was frequently clasped to her breast as she whispered with devotion. She bitterly regretted the absence of a similar talisman, an Indian gold swastika lost in London in November 1947. Her breathless prayers reveal the extraordinary sense of election and mission she felt as an Allied prisoner:

> Lord of Life, Thou hast raised the everlasting Doctrine under its modern form; Thou hast appointed the Chosen Nation to champion it. Lord of Death, Thou hast allowed the forces of death to prevail for a while. Lord of Order and Harmony, Lord of the Dance of appearances, Lord of the Rhythm that brings back spring after winter; the day after the night; birth after death; and the new age of truth and perfection after each end of an age of gloom, Thou shalt give my beloved comrades and superiors

the lordship of the earth one day. If I survive this trial, I shall take it as a sign from Thee that this will be in my life-time, and that Thou hast appointed me to do something in our coming new struggle.[20]

This prayer to Shiva fuses Hindu fatalism with Nazi apocalyptic.

The day of the trial arrived. Following lunch at the Stahlhaus, the British Police Headquarters in Düsseldorf, she was taken to the court in the Mühlenstrasse. In her heightened state of Nazi enthusiasm she was particularly annoyed by her husband's attempts to intervene on her behalf. Just prior to her trial Asit Krishna Mukherji had written from Calcutta to the chairman of the Military Tribunal at Düsseldorf, but she was angry at his diplomacy and exculpations, his attempts to minimize the political significance and motivation of her fanatical conduct, his embarrassing claims about how she was causing him so much worry. She dismissed the letter proudly with the assertion that she had come to court to bear witness to the greatness of her Führer. Taking the oath on "the sacred Wheel of the Sun," she swiftly turned the courtroom into an auditorium for a long and impassioned speech about the eternal value of National Socialism. "It is not only the military spirit, but National Socialist consciousness in its entirety that I have struggled to strengthen, for, in my eyes, National Socialism exceeds Germany and exceeds our times."[21] Her outspoken advocacy of Adolf Hitler and his Aryan worldview confirmed her standing as an unregenerate die-hard Nazi loyalist to her Allied prosecutors. There was no question of her guilt, though her sentence hardly gave her the martyrdom she so craved. Three years' imprisonment or deportation to India. Predictably, she chose imprisonment in order to prolong her Nazi mission and remain among her fellow sufferers in Allied captivity.

In the event, Savitri Devi served barely six months of her sentence. She was released on 18 August 1949 but expelled from the British Occupation Zone of Germany for five years. However, her few months in the Allied women's prison at Werl near Soest in Westphalia offered her an initiation into the Nazi world. Although she was kept in accommodations separate from the "political" prisoners in D wing, she was allowed to receive visits from these hardened Nazi women who had been variously convicted as abettors of the euthanasia program and overseers and wardresses of concentration camps. Only through her imprisonment at Werl was Savitri Devi enabled to join the Nazi movement as a comrade, to match her enthusiasm for the Aryan doctrine with passionate attachments to individuals who had played their full part in the Third Reich. The intense atmosphere of the women's prison with its emotional dependencies and fierce loyalties, a hothouse of political rumor and speculation among the inmates, was the reward for her defiance of the Allies. Here she entered a world of Nazi comradeship that would remain her supporting network in Germany for many years to come. Savitri Devi truly discovered the Third Reich at Werl.

Once behind bars in Werl, she met practitioners of the Nazi regime. Earlier conversations with Germans in the Western zones during autumn 1948 had revolved around sentimental avowals of Nazi loyalty and hopes, the glowing achievements of the Third Reich, and the terrible adversities of the occupation. By comparison, her prison notes record exchanges with convicted Nazi criminals. The female political prisoners she befriended at Werl were among those found guilty in the notorious Belsen war crimes trial, which was held at Lüneburg in the British zone in October and November 1945. These conversations are particularly odious because they confronted Savitri Devi with the most gruesome and inhuman aspects of the Nazi regime that generally attracted worldwide opprobrium and disgust. Her reaction was quite the reverse. Nazi war criminals accused of atrocity and inhumanity were in her eyes the higher functionaries of a noble Nazi doctrine and now the hostages of the blinkered and hypocritical West.

Belsen was a concentration camp in the northern part of Germany that had been liberated by British armed forces advancing toward Lüneburg and Hamburg in mid-April 1945. When they arrived, the camp was in the grip of a full-blown typhus epidemic among the inmates. The SS camp commandant Josef Kramer, a former Auschwitz camp commander, and his forty or so staff held sway over some 40,000 prisoners in terrible conditions. Of these, 25,000 were women, 18,000 of them Jewish women who had been evacuated in great haste from Auschwitz and other camps before the advancing Soviet armies. The 15,000 men consisted of Jews, antisocial and political prisoners, some of them German, and a small number of British and American POWs. Belsen had originally been a Wehrmacht prisoner-of-war camp holding Soviet captives, and many thousands had already perished there. From 1943 the camp had also served as a "short-stay" camp for Jews with neutral passports awaiting repatriation, but at the end of 1944 Kramer arrived and a hard regime began. By April 1945 the British forces were confronted by scenes of human suffering and misery that defied description. This was the first major concentration camp to be discovered by the Western Allied forces. Although the Soviet armies had overrun German death camps in the East as early as late 1944, the British were the first to ensure the publicization of such Nazi atrocity to a world audience.

Although Belsen was a forced labor camp in the center of Germany far removed from the dreadful extermination camps situated in German-occupied Poland, a number of factors combined to make it one of the most bestial examples of the Nazi regime uncovered during the liberation of Germany. Because Belsen had become an emergency over-flow camp for the evacuated inmates of other forced labor and exter-mination camps in early 1945, its population was largely drawn from the worst camps of the East, people broken mostly in body and spirit; the chaotic conditions due to Allied bombing raids and the rapid encir-clement of Germany had prevented regular food supplies from reaching the camp for many weeks; and a short while before the liberation of the camp, typhus had broken out, accounting for seventeen thousand deaths. Ten thousand corpses were still unburied when the British ar-rived. The stench of decay from piles of bodies, the prisoners dying amid their own excrement, the pallor and terrible emaciation of the survivors, and the death rate of hundreds each day made Belsen an unforgettable horror for those officers and men who took charge of the camp. Pictures relayed worldwide established its name as synonymous with Nazi inhumanity and depravity.[22]

Savitri Devi did not believe a word of it. She regarded the horrors of Belsen as a masterly exercise in Nazi atrocity propaganda on the part of the Allies. Whatever hardship, suffering, and death had occurred at Belsen she attributed to the disruption of food and medical supplies due to Allied saturation bombing; the overcrowding, lack of sanitation, and typhus epidemic she deemed likewise the consequence of wartime chaos. She was utterly convinced that it was the Allies and enemies of Germany who were persecuting the Nazis. She found evidence for this in the vengeful treatment of the Germans once the tide had turned and Allied armies were sweeping through formerly Nazi-occupied territory. She cited the beating of wounded and exhausted Wehrmacht soldiers in retreat from France, the sadistic outbreaks against the German pop-ulation in Poland and Czechoslovakia, and above all the mockery of the show trials of purported "war criminals." She had nothing but con-tempt for the International Military Tribunal at Nuremberg and related the story of Julius Streicher's abuse and ill-treatment by his jailers (notably British Jews) with shock and revulsion.

She conceded the existence of the concentration camps. They were necessary, she said, for the detention of enemies of Nazism, for those who opposed the establishment of a new Aryan world order. However, she was certain that violence was used only against those who broke camp rules willfully; the majority was treated in a friendly fashion.[23] She was therefore delighted to meet concentration camp wardresses in Werl prison and thereby confirm her own opinions that it was the Allies and not the Nazis who were guilty of any atrocities. She established warm and friendly relations with three Belsen wardresses, who gave her graphic accounts of their alleged abuse and humiliation at the hands of the British forces that liberated Belsen. Frau Hertha Ehlert, who became her best friend and to whom she dedicated her book *Defiance*, had spent many years in the Nazi concentration camp system. Since 1935 she had served in four Nazi camps as a female overseer and in another as a supervisor. She had latterly worked at Auschwitz for three years and been assigned to Belsen on 13 February 1945, only some nine weeks before its liberation. As one of the major defendants in the Belsen trial, she was sentenced to fifteen years' imprisonment for ill-treating camp inmates. Other Werl confidantes of Savitri Devi included Frau Herta Bothe and Frau H. (either Anna Hempel or Irene Haschke), both Belsen wardresses, who each received ten-year sentences.[24]

Savitri Devi first saw Hertha Ehlert working in the infirmary, when she was there for an examination. Her reaction to this strong, blond woman was at once idealizing, dramatic, and almost erotic. "I could not take my eyes off that prisoner," she recalled. Wearing her shabby blue prison uniform, Ehlert still had "the classical beauty of a chieftain's wife in ancient Germany." Her full figure was made for the comfort of warriors and birth of heroes, while in her face Savitri Devi detected strength, pride, dreams, authority, and inspiration. She wondered at her glossy blond hair, shining in the light, and her large blue eyes that, she thrilled, could often be as hard as stone.[25] The Belsen trial picture of Ehlert shows a heavy, tough woman and one can only speculate on the mixture of sentiment, sexuality, and fascination with violence that attracted her admirer.

Unless she was lying at her trial, Hertha Ehlert may have exaggerated her Nazi credentials to Savitri Devi. When examined under oath by Major Munro at the Belsen trial on 13 October 1945, she stated that she was a Berlin bakery assistant who had been called up for the SS through the labor exchange in November 1939. She was first assigned to Ravensbrück camp, with responsibility for working parties outside the camp. She claimed that she was thought by her superiors to be too kind to the prisoners, who were generally treated very severely. After three years at Ravensbrück, she was sent by way of a punishment transfer to Lublin, where the prisoner regime was even harsher. In the spring of 1944 she went to Cracow and in November 1944 to Auschwitz, where she swore that she remained only two months in the gardening unit at Raisko, which had no connection with the death camp at Birkenau. At the beginning of February 1945 she had arrived at Belsen and found the conditions worse than in any camp she had seen. In her subsequent cross-examination Ehlert claimed she had made several attempts to improve the conditions of the prisoners, but her dismal record of punishments, brutal beatings, and arbitrary acts of violence toward the wretched camp inmates was undeniable. Since she admitted to being at Auschwitz for only a very short time, the Auschwitz charge was dropped by the prosecution, but she was duly convicted for her crimes at Belsen.[26] Several of her fellow defendants, including Irma Grese, the notorious "Bitch of Belsen," who had literally whipped her victims to death, received a capital sentence.

The women at Werl barely mentioned the terrible conditions at Belsen in their long conversations with Savitri Devi. Given Hertha Ehlert's long service in various camps, including the extermination camp Auschwitz, this omission is all the more striking. Instead of describing their time in the camps when in authority, their self-serving stories all began with the misery and humiliations they had suffered at the hands of the British following the relief of Belsen. Allegedly tricked into returning from another camp to Belsen to maintain order, the wardresses claimed they were encircled by a screaming crowd of men bearing fixed bayonets, who drawing ever nearer, inflicted puncture wounds upon them. After being completely undressed and submitted to the most humiliating searches amid coarse comments, they were again attacked with bayonets, flung around by the hair, or beaten with rifle butts. Robbed of all their belongings, they were next thrust into the camp mortuary, where they remained for four days and nights in complete darkness without food, water, and sanitation. On their release they were forced at bayonet point for several days to bury the thousands of bodies still lying around the camp. Dead prisoners en masse aroused no compassion in the wardresses, but their shock and outrage knew no bounds when they discovered the mutilated and disemboweled corpses of SS comrade warders, apparent evidence of British atrocities committed during their four-day captivity.[27]

The Nazi women prisoners' self-pitying accounts of their experiences conjured an orgy of violence meted out upon them by their persecutors. They claimed that lorries full of frenzied, shouting Jews were sent specially to Belsen after its liberation in order to inflict all manner of ill-treatment upon the camp staff. Frau Bothe and Frau F. (either Ida Forster or Gertrud Fiest) claimed they had seen SS men disemboweled alive by men wearing the uniform of British military police, whom they took to be émigré Jews serving in the British forces. Again they recalled the screams of fear and pain they had heard from the camp while they were held in the mortuary. In an extraordinary inversion of their experience, these women had no recall whatsoever of the provenance of the thousands of bodies they were ordered to bury, no memory of the treatment they had meted out to their charges during the long grim years of the Third Reich; they projected their own inhumanity and brutality upon their own hate figure, the Jew, and indulged fearful scenes of their own abuse, torture, and killing at his hands in an act of wholly unjustified revenge. It was all music, however, to Savitri Devi's ears. "They have thrown you to the Jews," she exclaimed with an image of Kali before her mind's eye, "revenge them, o unforgiving, irresistible power. Mother of destruction, revenge them!"[28]

Bonds of affection and respect linked Savitri Devi to the female war criminals in Werl. One woman, identified as L. M., had been the head of a small work camp holding five hundred to six hundred Jewish women; another, Frau S., had received the death sentence, commuted to life imprisonment, for killing unwanted non-German children. Condemned by the world at large following the defeat of Nazism, these prisoners and the Belsen convicts represented to Savitri Devi the fearless, unflinching loyalty of committed Nazi womanhood dedicated to the creation of a wonderful, beautiful Aryan world of the future in accordance with the vision of Adolf Hitler. Their disgrace, ill-treatment, and imprisonment only confirmed their status as martyrs to the Nazi cause in Savitri Devi's eyes. These allegedly maligned and imprisoned women were outstanding examples of "Gold in the Furnace," the expression Savitri Devi used to characterize the loyal Nazis in the hell of Allied-occupied Germany. She was proud to be associated with them and to share their hardships at Werl.

In Savitri Devi's view, British military officialdom, Allied restrictions, the disabilities of former Nazis, the moral pressures of reeducation, democratic brainwashing, and denazification procedures had turned the whole of Germany into one enormous jail. Allied victory and occupation had overturned the former Nazi order to the extent that the diehard loyalists were transformed from a proud elite into martyrs or furtive sectaries keeping the flame of their Nazi faith alive in secret groups. This was Savitri Devi's mental world in trizonal occupied Germany in 1948 and 1949. However, her own martyrdom at Werl came to an end sooner than expected. Her husband had sent a petition for her release and deportation to India. When summoned by the prison governor, Colonel Vickers, she agreed that this was what she wanted. Cursing her own apostasy and weakness, she begged that the manuscript for her book be returned to her.[29] In possession of her papers, she was discharged from Werl on Thursday, 18 August 1949, after tearful farewells among her dearest friends, Hertha Ehlert and Herta Bothe. Expelled from the British zone for five years, she was driven to Andernach behind the French zonal border. The French authorities knew nothing of her case and she simply boarded a train to Koblenz to see her friends, eventually leaving Germany for Luxembourg.[30] Her defiance on behalf of Nazism had run its course, she had fulfilled her quixotic crusade.

9

PILGRIMAGE

In August 1949 Savitri Devi returned to France satisfied she had at last borne witness to her Nazi faith. She spent the next three years, besides visits to England and Greece, in her old hometown Lyons, engaged in the writing of new pro-Nazi books. Within two years she had published under her husband's imprint in Calcutta two books devoted to her experiences in occupied Germany. *Defiance* (1950) was largely an autobiographical account of her last ill-fated propaganda mission, and her ensuing arrest, trial, and conviction for "maintaining the military and Nazi spirit in Germany." The greater part of this book recorded her period at Werl prison with admiring descriptions of her new friends among the female Nazi war criminals and their life in the Third Reich. *Gold in the Furnace* (1952) was a more general essay about the condition of postwar Germany, in which she extolled the defeated Germans for their enduring loyalty to the ideals of National Socialism. Again, this book was interspersed with her firsthand experiences and encounters during her undercover missions in 1948 and 1949. She also continued work on her major statement of Aryo-Nazi doctrine, *The Lightning and the Sun*. During these years in France, she was eager to revisit her newfound Nazi loyalist friends. In late 1952 she decided to travel back to Germany in defiance of the five-year ban imposed on her at the time of her release.

An early return to Germany necessitated new personal documents. With this in mind, she returned to Greece in January 1953. In Athens she managed to secure a Greek passport in her maiden name of Maximiani Portas on the basis that her marriage in India had not taken place according to Christian rites and was not recognized in Greece.

She trusted this would be sufficient cover for her illegal reentry to Germany. In late April her journey then continued by air from Phaleron to Campini, culminating in her arrival in Rome. Here there were fond memories of fascism, and she paid a call on Camillo Giuriati, one of Mussolini's former state ministers, whom she and her husband had first met when he was Italian consul in Calcutta. From Italy she traveled by railway northward toward the Brenner Pass and into Austria. The train rolled on amid the splendid forested and Alpine scenery of the Tyrol through Innsbruck and Salzburg. In her view, of course, Austria was an inseparable part of Germany—as it had been following its *Anschluß* into the Greater German Reich in March 1938—but she was traveling to Linz for a very special reason.

In 1953 Savitri Devi visited Germany not as a missionary but in the spirit of a pilgrim. Her desperate desire to identify belatedly with the Nazi cause was relieved to some small degree by the penance of her brief imprisonment at Werl several years before. Although she was never to lose those dreadful pangs of remorse that she had failed to experience Germany during the Third Reich, she had through her propaganda missions exorcized the wretched sense of being a mere onlooker at German defeat and suffering. By 1953 Germany was recovering, its cities and industries were being rebuilt and beginning to flourish. Although Allied occupation in the western zones would continue until 1955, some three years of political normalization had elapsed since the founding of the Federal Republic of Germany in May 1949 when Savitri Devi was sitting behind bars in Werl prison. Her earlier sense of anguish at the horrors of devastation and oppression was no longer acute. This time she could return to Germany as a member of the silent, invisible and intransigent resistance to Allied suzerainty. Now she intended to make a personal pilgrimage to those places in the "Aryan Holy Land most hallowed by association with Adolf Hitler and the National Socialist movement."

Her pilgrimage began with the towns and villages where Adolf Hitler had spent his childhood and youth—Leonding and Linz in Upper Austria—followed by a highly charged visit to his birthplace at Braunau am Inn on 20 April 1953, the sixty-fourth anniversary of his birth. From here she traveled to Berchtesgaden, where she wandered among the ruins of Hitler's Alpine retreat on the Obersalzberg. Her route then took her to Munich, the birthplace of the Nazi movement, where she was able to pay her respects at such shrines as the Feldherrnhalle and

Königsplatz. She sought the spiritual proximity of Nazi war criminals through a visit to Landsberg am Lech. Here she paced around the prison where Hitler was jailed following the abortive putsch of November 1923 but which now served as the principal penitentiary for convicted Nazis in the former American zone. Her next station of remembrance was Nuremberg, the scene of the zenith and nadir of Nazi fortunes. At the Luitpoldarena and Zeppelinwiese she recalled and imagined the exultant Nazi Party September rallies of the 1930s; in a more somber mood she visited the Palace of Justice, where the surviving members of the Third Reich's leadership were tried from late 1945 until October 1946. Through all these stations she felt as if she had recapitulated the "great days" she had missed and drawn nearer in spirit to the Third Reich.

In its concluding stages her pilgrimage embraced a wider mythical and pagan conception of the "Aryan Holy Land" with visits to the Hermannsdenkmal in the Teutoburger Wald and the prehistoric solar temple and rock cliffs of the Externsteine, traditionally identified as an ancient Germanic sacred site. At all places of pilgrimage there was rich opportunity for reflection on the meaning of the Nazis' mission and their Aryan racial utopia, besides the comfort of pious exchanges with sympathetic Germans encountered along the way. Germany and the Germans were no longer an overwhelming novelty to her, nor was she constantly provoked into outbursts by the omnipresent signs of defeat, dismantlement, and occupation, as in 1948 and 1949. Through her visits to the shrines of Nazism and ancient Germany she evoked her love of Nazi Germany and her hopes for a future Aryan world order. By comparison with her first two postwar books about Germany, *Pilgrimage* (1958) is a more reflective and more revealing memoir of pious Nazi gnosis in a hostile world.

On the evening of 18 April 1953 Savitri Devi arrived at Linz railway station. Lying on the southern bank of the River Danube, the city just fell within the American zone of occupation in Austria, facing the Russian zone on the northern bank. The capital of Upper Austria, the city had long possessed a certain provincial grandeur with its Gothic cathedral, opera house, museum, and other impressive public buildings, surmounted by the Kürnberg Castle, where the famous medieval *Nibelungenlied* was said to have been composed. As she left the station and walked across a square and then a public park before joining the broad, well-lit Landstraße—the city's main promenade—Savitri Devi felt a constant sense of excitement that she had arrived at a place so closely associated with her idol and savior. " 'Can it be true that I am in Linz, the town in which our Führer has lived?' It had all seemed to me—and it still seemed to me—like a dream."[1]

Adolf Hitler had first come here as a nine-year-old, when his father, a newly retired customs official, had bought a house next to the church-yard in the outlying village of Leonding some three miles west of Linz in January 1899. After a carefree year in the village Volksschule, where he assumed the role of a natural leader among the peasant boys in their endless games of cowboys and Indians, the young Hitler began attending the Linz Realschule in September 1900. Until he finally left to seek his fortune as an artist in Vienna in February 1908, Linz was the focus of Hitler's youth. Following his father's death in January 1903, Adolf lodged in Linz during the week to save the long walk to school. He was confirmed in Linz Cathedral in May 1904, and in late June 1905 his mother sold the house in Leonding and moved to a flat at Humboldtstraße 31 in Linz. Having completed his final year of secondary school at lodgings in Steyr, Hitler returned to live with his mother the following month. For the next two and a half years he led a life of leisure in Linz, indulging his dreams of becoming an artist and attending performances of Wagner operas that fired his imagination with notions of Germanic myth and national redemption.[2]

A sympathetic hotel maid called Luise K., the widow of an SS man, was greatly moved by Savitri Devi's journey all the way from Athens to Linz to see the place where Adolf Hitler had lived. The next morning Savitri Devi took a local bus out to Leonding and alighted beside the village church, where she knew Hitler's parents were buried. Inside the empty church, sunlight poured through the narrow plain-glass windows upon the polished wooden pews and altar rail. Early afternoon, restful silence, an atmosphere of peace. She imagined how Hitler's mother had come to pray here after her household chores, her eyes lit with a longing for perfection and infinity within the frame of her Catholic faith. At Klara Hitler's side, she visualized a thoughtful, blue-eyed child, "a child in whose face the light of boundless love and the flame of genius already radiated: her son, Adolf Hitler, the Chosen One of the Invisible Powers." Overcome with emotion, the inveterate pagan Savitri Devi even crossed herself in memory of the mother of her leader and wept for a long time.[3]

Outside in the bright spring sunshine she walked around the graveyard until she found the grave of Alois and Klara Hitler. A few fresh flowers in a tin can were the only recent adornment to a grave decked with a withered wreath of fir twigs and overgrown with creeper. On a slab of black marble set in a rough block of stone, she read the simple memorial to the couple, while reflecting on the enormous significance of these simple Austrian country folk: "our Führer's parents; the last link in that endless chain of privileged generations destined to give Germany the greatest of all her sons, and the Western world, the one Saviour of its own blood."[4] Going in search of flowers to lay on the grave, she met Frau J., who could offer only forget-me-nots from her garden. Savitri Devi expressed her disappointment, saying that she wanted dark red roses for a very special grave. Frau J. guessed her purpose and warned her that it was forbidden to adorn Hitler's parents' grave. Once Savitri Devi had given vent to her anger against the oc-cupation authorities, Frau J. declared her own Nazi loyalty, mentioning that her husband was an SS man, and invited her into her home. Frau J. indulged her own hopes that many Austrians who had earlier rejected Nazism, were coming round to the Hitler doctrine now that they had a taste of the occupiers' democracy.

Frau J. then offered to introduce Savitri Devi to Hitler's old tutor and a former classmate a little further on in the village. Savitri Devi found the tutor, a friendly old gentleman of more than eighty years, sitting at his doorstep facing an open space where a beautiful old tree was growing. In reply to her request that he tell her something about Hitler, the old man declared that he was a healthy, clean-minded, lov-ing, and lovable child, the most lovable he had ever met. "All I have to say is contained within these few words. The grown man retained the child's goodness, honesty, love of truth. The world hates him only because it does not know him." Savitri Devi could not be other than most gratified by this witness of Hitler's youth, still more by the bib-lical allusion to the national savior. She then asked whether the young Hitler loved animals, to be told that he loved every living creature that God had made and that he never did harm to any. The old man became absorbed in his reverie, describing how the child Hitler used to come and go from this very house, greeting them with his frank face and his bright loving eyes. "We all loved him. The wide world that has brought ruin on us would have loved him too, if only it had known him as he really was." This pious and sentimental memory evidently owed more to the adulation Hitler received from Austrians at the time of the *An-*

schluß rather than as the boisterous ringleader of war games at Leonding that other witnesses have recalled.[5]

Under the fruit trees in the garden of Herr H., Hitler's former classmate, Savitri Devi was shown photographs of the Führer laying a wreath upon his parents' grave and another of him shaking hands with Herr H. from a car. These pictures had been taken on the morning of Sunday, 13 March 1938, when Hitler visited Leonding after staying the night at Linz on his triumphal progress from Munich to Vienna over the weekend when German armed forces invaded Austria and he was welcomed everywhere by enthusiastic and cheering crowds. Savitri Devi confessed to Herr H. that she envied him these memories of the "great days." She spent a further hour talking with him and his wife, happy in the thought that she was among those who had known Hitler and been among his friends. Leonding in the late afternoon sun with its innocent memories of the young Hitler seemed a safe refuge from the postwar world that so oppressed her. These friendly elderly people with their happy stories of the child Führer amid this soft, hilly landscape gave Savitri Devi solace. In this idyll it seemed possible to forget the Second World War and all the atrocities, ruin, and wreckage it had brought in its wake.

The sun was setting when she returned to the village churchyard with her forget-me-nots. She planted the humble flowers carefully, happy in the knowledge that they would still be alive in months to come. Kneeling before the grave, she saw Hitler's face in her mind's eye. Once again her thoughts turned to his present whereabouts and she asked, "Will you ever know how much I have loved you?" The face of her vision spoke back: "Live for my Germany! And you shall never part from Me, wherever I be."[6] It was a religious experience, a fitting climax to the day spent in Hitler's childhood home. Outside the churchyard she saw the little house where he and his parents had lived between 1899 and 1905. A light was lit behind the closed windows and she thought of the boy who had sat, played, and read in the garden. Later that evening, having returned to Linz, she visited the Realschule and walked up to the third floor at Humboldtstraße 31, where Hitler and his mother had lived from July 1905 to May 1907. Leaning against the windowsill on the staircase between the second and third floors she gazed out on the garden full of fruit trees in blossom, other houses, and in the distance a church spire dark against the evening sky. She was happy in the thought that his eyes had also rested on this view just less than fifty years before.[7]

Early the next day, 20 April 1953, she took a train to Braunau am Inn, Adolf Hitler's birthplace. From 1871 onward Alois Hitler had served as an Austrian customs official in this town on the river frontier between the Habsburg Empire of Austria-Hungary and the new German Reich. It is indeed symbolic that Hitler whose nationalist policy set so much store by the incorporation of German Austria into Germany should have been born at a border town between Germany and Austria. He himself described the place of his birth as a lucky sign of destiny on the first page of his political testament *Mein Kampf*. Alighting at the railway station, Savitri Devi walked along a sunny street to reach the town square surrounded by high, picturesque old houses. Through the archway of a town gate she entered the *Vorstadt* and the street in which the Pommer Inn stood along a terrace of early nineteenth-century facades. Here in lodgings on the second floor of the inn Adolf Hitler had been born to the third wife of Alois Hitler on 20 April 1889 at 6:18 in the afternoon.

Taking a seat in a *Café-Konditorei* on the opposite side of the street, Savitri Devi observed with pleasure the unhurried, placid life of the market town in the spring sunshine. Around her, mothers and children drank coffee and ate cakes. Elderly matrons conversed at a nearby table. Through the window she surveyed the neat and homely shops, the freshly whitewashed house fronts, the great blossoming chestnut tree just beyond the former inn and reflected that the scene had probably not been so different on that spring day, sixty-four years before, when Hitler came into the world. The small town idyll contrasted strangely with a feeling of awe as she let her mind wander back to that "Day of Destiny," imagining a cosmic nativity in which the savior of the Aryan race came down to earth.

> Alois Hitler, a custom-officer well over fifty, and twice a widower, lived in that house . . . with his third wife, Clara, who was then twenty-nine. The child to which the latter was about to give birth was neither her first one nor her last one. Just another baby in the family. . . . But the unseen Powers, Whose inscrutable Play lies behind the mystery of heredity, had ordained that all the intelligence and intuition, and all the will-power and heroism of generations and generations,—all the virtues and genius of the privileged Race, fated to rule—should find in that Child their highest

expression; that the Babe should be a god-like one: whose consciousness was, one day, to be none other than the deeper consciousness of his people and of the race at large, for all times to come, and whose dream was to inspire a new civilisation. And far beyond the clear blue sky of the little town and the thin atmosphere of this little planet, in the cold, dark realm of fathomless Void, the unseen stars had very definite positions; significant positions, such as they take only once within hundreds of years. . . . And at the appointed time—six o'clock 18 in the afternoon—the Child came into the world, unnoticed masterpiece of a two-fold cosmic Play: of the mysterious artistry of Aryan blood in infinite time; of the mysterious influence of distant worlds in infinite space. Apparently, just another baby in the family. In reality,—after centuries,—a new divine Child on this planet; the first one in the West after the legendary Baldur-the-Fair and, like He, a Child of the Sun; a predestined Fighter against the forces of death and a Saviour of men, marked out for leadership, for victory, for agony and for immortality.[8]

She wandered back through the arch into the large square and out onto the long bridge over the wide, swift, bluish-green River Inn, tributary of the Danube. This was the site of Alois Hitler's office in the Imperial Austrian customs service. Throughout the nineteenth century this river had formed the frontier between Austria and Germany until Hitler's *Anschluß* in 1938 had swept away this division of the nation. But now eight years after the fall of the Third Reich, when Savitri Devi came on her pilgrimage, Austria and Germany were again separate states, and a customs house and striped barrier stood once again on the bridge over the Inn as if in mockery of Hitler's achievement of German unity. Railing at the inconvenience, futility, and national outrage of the reimposed border to long-suffering customs officials, she was surprised to find that they too regarded their office with irony and resented the border themselves. When they lamented their powerlessness, Savitri Devi urged them to think of revenge day and night and to wait as she did. She was amazed at their outspoken agreement and exulted in this confirmation of Hitler's dictum: "Gleiches Blut gehört in ein gemeinsames Reich."[9]

She spent the afternoon wandering around the small town, pausing to buy buns in a baker's shop, posting a card showing Hitler's birthplace to Luise K. at Linz, sitting on a bench in a public garden and watching the children play, as she thought of the infant Adolf in this very place, and then entering a church where she supposed that his baptism might have taken place. At length she retraced her steps to the *Vorstadt* until she came to the three-storied house near the chestnut tree where Hitler had been born. It was now a library and a school. She passed through the entrance into the rear court and walked up the stairs to the first and second floors, then along the passage flanked by massive, white-washed stone arches with a view onto the court, trees, and other houses beyond. The arches shone, dazzling white, against the deep-blue spring sky. A woman looked out from one of the doors along the passage and cut off her inquiry with a curt and dismissive "There is nothing to see here." Bitterly disappointed and bewildered, Savitri Devi gazed out at the pure blue sky and thought of Hitler, the constant companion of her heart. It mattered only that she was here in the Pommer Inn on his birthday. Out on the street again, with one last backward glance, she returned to the railway station.[10]

Leaving these gilded scenes of Hitler's early years in Austria, Savitri Devi traveled on by rail to Germany. Crossing the border at Salzburg, she changed trains at Freilassing and took a local service bound for Berchtesgaden in the southeasternmost corner of Bavaria. A few kilometers east of the town lay the Obersalzberg, which had become world famous as Hitler's country residence. He had first come here for a spring break in 1923 and found the outstanding Alpine scenery with views of the Watzmann and Untersberg mountains a source of inspiration and recreation after the hectic politics of Munich. Following his imprisonment after the putsch, he returned to complete the first volume of *Mein Kampf* in spring 1925 and established his auxiliary head-quarters, first at the Pension Moritz on the Obersalzberg, then in Berchtesgaden. He also completed the second volume here in July 1926. In 1927 he was able to rent the Haus Wachenfeld on the Obersalzberg from a Nazi Party supporter and installed his half sister, Angela Raubal, as his housekeeper.[11] During the 1920s the Obersalzberg still retained the atmosphere of a traditional Alpine settlement with the Haus Wach-enfeld and some two dozen or so similar farmhouses scattered over the hillside and meadows in the midst of the most beautiful Bavarian coun-tryside, which also included the Königssee and the lakeside monastery of St. Bartholomä.

After Hitler became chancellor in 1933, the Obersalzberg witnessed dramatic changes. As Hitler's popularity grew, thousands of Germans would travel to Berchtesgaden to glimpse him and pay their respects to the restorer of the nation's fortunes. Hitler had always enjoyed long mountain walks around the Obersalzberg and mixed freely with the local population, but the enormous numbers of admirers eventually posed problems of organization and security. The development of the Obersalzberg from rural idyll into government enclave now began. Hitler bought Haus Wachenfeld and began to enlarge it through several stages into the Berghof. Other party leaders, including Martin Bormann, Hermann Goering, Josef Goebbels, Rudolf Hess, and Albert Speer, were drawn to the area and rented or bought properties that were converted and expanded into large country houses. First Hess, then Bormann, was entrusted with the overall planning of the Obersalzberg, which involved compulsory purchase and the creation of a "Führer territory" of some ten square kilometers and a circumference of twenty-seven kilometers. Most of the old farmhouses were cleared and the new pompous residences of the Nazi top brass arose, as well as extensive barracks for the SS guard and accommodations for the hundreds of employees and building workers. The former Pension Moritz, renamed the Platterhof, was also enlarged as a hotel for visiting Nazi bigwigs. An extensive system of underground tunnels and air raid shelters honeycombed the entire site. By the early war years Bormann had established himself as uncontested master of an enormous development project.[12]

The Berghof was transformed from the rustic farmhouse Haus Wachenfeld through three major conversions into the spacious mountain residence of the Führer arranged on three extensive floors. An open flight of steps led to a gothic hall decorated with old-master paintings and pieces of sculpture, which led into the famous conference room with the huge picture window framing views of the Untersberg. This large room's walls were hung with beautiful Gobelins and its floor was laid with a thick red carpet. There were three further reception rooms on this floor besides a large kitchen and dayrooms for staff and the adjutants' offices. Upstairs were Hitler's private living quarters as well as guest rooms. Here at the Berghof Hitler received prominent visitors from abroad, including the Duke and Duchess of Windsor, Neville Chamberlain, David Lloyd George, Mussolini, Edouard Daladier, Kurt von Schuschnigg, and Admiral Miklós Horthy. The coming and going of high officials and summit meetings contrasted with the cosy routine of the Führer's inner circle at mealtimes and the regular showing of a film in the evening. Obersalzberg was also a link between the public life of the Führer and his provincial Austrian origins: on a clear day

Hitler could look from the gigantic window of the conference room over the mountains as far as Braunau am Inn.

On 21 April 1953, Savitri Devi awoke in her hotel room in Berchtesgaden and threw open the window to gaze with rapture at the beautiful Alpine scenery all around: the steep fir-clad hills, then more distant hills, blue green in color, and beyond these the snowy peaks shining like silver against the radiant blue sky. The fragrance of the pine woods and the keen mountain air invigorated her as she set off on the road leading to the Obersalzberg. All was quiet save the call of birds, the lowing of cattle on the meadows, and the rushing sound of the river beside the road. She knew that little remained of the numerous Nazi houses on the Obersalzberg. On 25 April 1945, 318 Lancaster bombers of the Royal Air Force had led an air raid over the Obersalzberg, dropping 1,232 tons of bombs in an action aimed at preventing the use of the complex as an alternative government center for the last-ditch defense of Germany (the so-called Alpine Redoubt). The Berghof received three direct hits, the Bormann and Goering houses were destroyed, the SS barracks were leveled, and the Platterhof was badly damaged. The rubble and ruins had remained amid the greenery of the hillsides for several years until the Bavarian government finally blew up the surviving ruins in the spring of 1952. The shell of the Berghof was dynamited at 5:05 P.M. on 30 April 1952.

The peaceful surroundings served as a poignant reminder to Savitri Devi that the "great days" of the Third Reich were long past. At length, on the right side of the road, she came upon an enormous heap of sand, gravel, and pulverized blocks of mortar from which the cornerstone of a ruined wall projected. Tears welled into her eyes and her mouth quivered with emotion at the sight of this devastation. "Here the Berghof had once stood in all its loveliness, in the midst of lawns and flower beds and trees; *this* was what 'they' had reduced it to, so that no trace of it should be left; so that men should forget!" She shuddered at the hatred that urged men to work this systematic destruction seven years after the end of the war and asked herself how long the world would execrate the Führer and all he had stood for and created. Recalling the destruction of Akhnaton's new solar city in ancient Egypt, she reflected that the "money power" would forever persecute those it could neither buy nor frighten. However, she took comfort in the thought that the "Shining Ones," the Aryan powers of light and truth, would nevertheless prevail in the cosmic struggle of Manichaean opposites. "The sight of the desolation of this place, glaring sign of the victory of the evil forces for the time being, filled me with resentment, with hatred, with grief; once more, with the awful awareness of defeat."[13] She lay down and sobbed desperately at her sense of loss.

A soft warm breeze calmed her and she began to imagine Hitler at the Berghof in these magnificent natural surroundings as the hero of the new aeon:

> I pictured him on a spring day like this, letting his star-like eyes, athirst of infinity, rest on those meadows and woods, those dark-green and violet hills, those shining white ranges. . . . I pictured him alone, in tune with the Soul of this land that he so loved, breathing its power and its beauty, communing with it and through it, with the Essence of himself and of all things—immanent Godhead. . . . I pictured him . . . all-loving, all-knowing, above happiness and sorrow, detached in the midst of world-wide action, looking over this dream-like scenery on the border of that extended Germany, which he had reconquered, into the realm of eternity that was—and is—his impregnable realm; into that intangible world in which success and failure fade into nothingness before the one thing that counts: timeless Truth; sure that he was right whatever men might say, whichever events might occur, sure that Germany's mission was . . . (in the words of the most ancient Aryan Book of wisdom) "the interest of the universe." Sure, and therefore serene. Sure, and therefore sinless,—perfect.[14]

In her opinion this was the real Adolf Hitler, the Aryan savior, the one of whom no newspaper had ever spoken, and whom no man had ever understood. This was her adored leader, the only one she had loved, life after life, for millions of years.

Her reverie was broken by the arrival of three men come to explore the site. Joining the group, she was told they were standing just above the conference room whose huge window once overlooked the Untersberg with views beyond Salzburg. The men soon betrayed their Nazi loyalties and there was general denunciation of the Bavarian SPD government's desecration of this Nazi monument. When the men dejectedly referred to the defeat of Germany, she compared the Nazi doctrine to the rise of Christianity. She reminded them that their era had begun twenty years ago when Hitler became the master of Germany. Hitler himself had been born sixty-four years ago. How did the Roman world appear in the year A.D. 20 or 64? Christ was dead and his followers a small persecuted sect in the vast Roman Empire. Who would have then believed that Christianity was to become the dominant religion of the West for the next two thousand years? She had given them fresh hope. Together they all gave the Hitler salute. Alone again in the sunset, she sang a Nazi battle song after writing one of its lines upon the ruined wall of the Berghof: "Einst kommt der Tag der Rache." She then viewed the ruins of other Obersalzberg properties and took coffee in the restored Hotel Türken beyond the Berghof site that had served as quarters for the SD intelligence during the Third Reich. Late in the evening, under a bright moon, she walked back to Berchtesgaden.[15]

A highly introverted communion with the absent and the dead was the leitmotif of her solitary pilgrimage in these early stages. Arriving on 23 April in Munich, "the birthplace of National Socialism," she hastened to the Feldherrnhalle, an open loggia built in the early 1840s at the southern end of the Ludwigstraße and containing bronze statues of two great Bavarian commanders, Tilly and Wrede. It was here that the police had opened fire on the Nazi marchers in the putsch of 9 November 1923. Savitri Devi repeated the names of the sixteen martyrs who had fallen in the hail of bullets in an act of remembrance of their heroism and sacrifice for the resurrection of their country. Her next stop was the famous Hofbräuhaus, a roomy beer hall rebuilt after 1890 in neo-Renaissance style, where Hitler had begun holding the first mass meetings of the early Nazi Party in autumn 1919. It was here also that Hitler presented the twenty-five points of the new party program to a packed audience of some two thousand on 24 February 1920. These were the amazing days of growth, when Hitler's oratory transformed a tiny backroom club into a powerful political movement. Savitri Devi visited the great vaulted hall where the historic meeting had taken place. She saw her savior speak, young and confident, with the burning eloquence of love, hate, and despair; she saw the crowd, grateful and enthusiastic, listening to his message of German salvation.[16]

Returning to the present with a jolt, she saw workmen in the hall busily putting up decorations, colored streamers and a clown's face, for the Americans' May Day party. She angrily imagined the frivolous, mindless crowd of people who would shortly be amusing themselves, wearing paper hats and dancing to a jazz band, in this historic place. The grinning clown's face over the platform where Hitler had spoken seemed to her an eloquent symbol of the postwar West with its fatuous concerns for the individual and democracy, for peace and security.[17]

Elsewhere in the city she found the Nazi heritage had been covered and erased by the victorious Americans. She sought out the Bürgerbräukeller. In this fourteenth-century beer cellar Hitler had launched and masterminded the putsch; it also had witnessed his return to public life following imprisonment with a frenzied speech before the tumultuous applause of a four-thousand-strong audience in February 1925; here, on 8 November 1939, a communist assassin planted a bomb that exploded shortly after Hitler had left following his speech. Her disappointment was great when she was informed that the great hall had been destroyed by bombing in 1943 and rebuilt by the Americans as a recreational facility. The prospect of GIs playing table tennis in such a heroic setting was but another galling reminder of defeat. She was not surprised to find that the Brown House, the former national headquarters of the Nazi Party, was razed to the ground. The Königsplatz, the major center of Nazi ceremonial in the Bavarian capital, with its mighty neoclassical Glyptothek and Propylaea by Leopold von Klenze, recalled her memories of Athens and the common Aryan ancestry of Greek and German art. The twin colonnaded shrines of the sixteen Nazi martyrs on the stone-paved square had been blown up in 1947 but she touched their foundation-stones as a Christian pilgrim might revere the tomb of a saint.[18]

The next day she traveled fifty-five kilometers west to Landsberg am Lech to view the Allied prison for convicted Nazi war criminals. Throughout the early postwar years the Landsberg fortress had received substantial numbers of war criminals. Those detained or sentenced to death in the secondary Nuremberg trials held between 1947 and 1949 and the U.S. Army's Dachau trials of late 1946 had been brought here. Every week, from mid-October 1948 until the beginning of February 1949, executions took place at Landsberg, sometimes fifteen on a single day, bringing the total to more than one hundred in this period. The fate of the Nazis still awaiting execution had become the subject of international concern in early 1951. The newly established German government began putting pressure on the Americans to commute such sentences as a condition for supporting Western defense planning and the raising of a new German army. At that time there were twenty-eight remaining "red-jackets" on death row in Landsberg. Fourteen of these had been condemned in the Einsatzgruppen and SS Main Office trials at Nuremberg; the remainder had been sentenced at the Dachau trials, having been found variously guilty for their part in the massacre of U.S. soldiers at Malmédy, the murder of Allied airmen, and involvement in thousands of murders at Dachau, Buchenwald, and Mauthausen concentration camps.

In January 1951 the growing East-West conflict had just erupted in the Korean War, and the creation of a German military force in Europe was a crucial factor in the defense policy of the United States. Meanwhile numerous German lobby groups bombarded John McCloy, the U.S. high commissioner in Germany, and President Truman with appeals for clemency in the case of the "red-jackets" and the many others serving long sentences in Landsberg. Following a drastic reduction of prison sentences and numerous commutations for those facing execution, there was a huge campaign to save the final seven, whose death sentences still stood. The German lobbies rushed more than 600,000 signatures by airmail to the White House. Savitri Devi had herself written from Lyons to McCloy and sent a telegram to Truman. After five months of delaying tactics in the American courts, the last seven "red-jackets" were hanged at Landsberg on 7 June 1951. The seven were Otto Ohlendorf, the commander of Einsatzgruppe D, who admitted murdering at least 90,000 civilians in the Soviet Union, as well as Erich Naumann, Werner Braune, and Paul Blobel from the Einsatzgruppen trial; Oswald Pohl, who had directed the Final Solution from Berlin; and two Dachau SS guards. Their deaths brought the total number of Nazi war criminals executed in this prison to 257.[19]

At the time of Savitri Devi's visit to Landsberg, some 160 prisoners still remained in custody. These included Sepp Dietrich, the former Waffen-SS general, reputedly Hitler's favorite, and Jochen Peiper, who had ordered the Malmédy massacres. Besides the top brass there were the numerous concentration camp sadists, such as Andreas Schilling, an SS corporal at Mauthausen who had injected inmates in the camp hospital with motor oil, and Horst Dittrich, who had dispatched Soviet POWs with a bullet in the neck as they stood against the wall during a fake medical examination. As Savitri Devi walked around the outer enclosure of the prison, a long white wall surmounted by several rows of barbed wire, she centered her thoughts on her brothers in faith behind the barred windows. The sound of the prison siren punctuating the inmates' interminable day reminded her of the dreary routine and rations at Werl. "Avenge my Führer's faithful people," she prayed. She completed her vigil for those languishing inside the prison with a Nazi marching song and the Hitler salute. "My loved ones, my superiors, from behind the barred windows of your work-rooms and cells, did you hear my voice? Or did you at least, on that afternoon,—24th April, 1953—feel . . . the certitude of our coming dawn?"[20] Unbeknown to her, at this very time Chancellor Konrad Adenauer was in Washington discussing with President Eisenhower the Landsberg inmates. Releases began in May 1954, and all were out by Christmas 1956.

The following two days spent in Nuremberg represented the climax of her tour of Nazi remembrance. After sadly inspecting the ruined streets and gutted houses of the historic old town, once famed for their gabled roofs, and elaborate gilded facades and doorways, she made her way out to the party-rally grounds to the south. Alone on the vast stone-flagged parade grounds, now sprouting rank weeds, and before the gigantic terraced tribunes of the Luitpoldarena and the Zeppelinwiese, she imagined all the glories of the huge Nazi pageants she had missed while far away in India during the 1930s. Before her mind's eye arose the enormous crowds gathered to witness the annual September rally. She saw the endless ranks of party formations, the SA, the SS, and the youth organizations, bearing their flags and standards into the arena. Above the tribune hung the great red, white, and black swastika banners. At the Zeppelinwiese the sun shone down upon the brilliant white monumental walls of the colonnaded tribune that stretched over the 400 meters between two huge pylons bearing great bronze eagles. Day after day the crowds came to give ritual expression to their shared belief in Hitler, Germany, and its world mission. She recalled the martial music and heard the cadences and rhythms of the Führer's speeches before 200,000 party faithful, the speaking choruses and the exhilarating climaxes when the frenzied swaying crowd joined in the chant of *"Sieg Heil!"*

She imagined the scene by night when Hitler addressed the crowds on the Zeppelinwiese illuminated by special lighting effects. All around the huge enclosure, at 40-foot intervals, 130 powerful antiaircraft searchlights with a range of 25,000 feet threw up great pencil beams of light into the dark night sky, conjuring the spectacle of the "cathedral of light." Above the tribune flames flickered in three great bronze vessels, casting a glow upon the pylon walls, the deep-red swastika flags and the upturned faces of the crowd. There was tumultuous applause as Hitler's speech ended and then, after a momentary hush across the great darkened space, the periodical thunderclap of the repeated *"Sieg*

Heil!" resounded again and again. She remembered that this was where the thousands had heard the proclamation of the Nuremberg race laws in defense of mankind's Aryan elite in 1935 and saw herself listening to it all on the radio in faraway Lucknow. Again she felt the bitter sense of regret and self-reproach: Why, why had she missed all the glory of the "great days," why had she missed her real duty and spoiled her life? The moonlight gleamed on the white tiers and walls of the deserted monuments. Where the thousands and tens of thousands had gathered, she was now alone.[21]

At the Palace of Justice she viewed the courtroom where the International Military Tribunal had opened on 18 October 1945 and continued in session for just less than a year. At the trial seven defendants had drawn prison sentences: Deputy Führer Rudolf Hess, Grand Admiral Erich Raeder and Reich bank President and Minister of Economics Walther Funk for life; Minister of War Production Albert Speer and Hitler Youth Leader Baldur von Schirach for twenty years; Foreign Minister and "Protector of Bohemia and Moravia" Baron Konstantin von Neurath for fifteen; Grand Admiral Karl Doenitz, Hitler's successor as head of the Third Reich in its last days, for ten. Eleven of the top leadership received the death sentence. In the early morning of 16 October 1946, Foreign Minister Joachim von Ribbentrop mounted the gallows in the execution chamber of the adjoining prison, followed at short intervals by Field Marshal Wilhelm Keitel; SS-Lieutenant General and Chief of the Reich Security Main Office Ernst Kaltenbrunner; Ministers Alfred Rosenberg, Hans Frank, Wilhelm Frick; the former Nuremberg Gauleiter, a fanatical antisemite, and editor of the Jew-baiting *Stürmer* magazine, Julius Streicher; Reich kommisar for the occupied Netherlands Arthur Seyss-Inquart; Gauleiter Fritz Sauckel, in charge of all forced labor programs; and General Alfred Jodl. Hermann Goering cheated the hangman by swallowing a smuggled cyanide cartridge hours before his turn. The same day their ashes were cast into a small stream in a Munich suburb by American soldiers. Not a trace of their power nor a place of remembrance was to remain.

Savitri Devi now surveyed the benches where her idols had once sat and touched the polished wood where their hands had rested. Asking her guide where each individual had sat, she angrily imagined the endless stream of lies poured out against them and her own Nazi faith in this place. Her thoughts were with the eleven martyrs: "March in spirit within our ranks, and live in us for ever, great Ones, whom I have never seen, alas, but whom I love; close collaborators of our immortal Führer, live in *me* as long as I live!"[22]

Her pilgrimage of remembrance ended in Nuremberg. After her communion with the absent and dead at shrines of the past, she sought out her new Nazi friends. Traveling north to Homburg vor der Höhe she visited the husband of Hertha Ehlert, her best friend still imprisoned at Werl as a convicted overseer at Belsen, and learned that she was shortly to be released. In early May she was reunited at Koblenz with her old friend Fräulein B. Together they stood before the grave of Fritz Horn, who had given her his copy of *Mein Kampf* with words of encouragement for her mission. His health broken by his treatment in Allied concentration camps, he had finally succumbed in December 1949. At Hoheneggelsen she walked along a country lane beside the widow of Otto Ohlendorf to visit his grave. One of the last seven "redjackets" executed at Landsberg, Ohlendorf aroused her special admiration as a modern Aryan hero. With fearless detachment before the Allied judges at Nuremberg he had explained his role as commander of a dreaded Einsatzgruppe responsible for the summary execution of some ninety thousand Jewish and Soviet prisoners in the wake of the Wehrmacht invasion of the Soviet Union: "[I]n war as in peace individual life does not count. Duty alone matters." This ruthless spirit reminded her of the warlike wisdom of the ancient Aryans she attributed to the *Bhagavad Gita*.[23]

A highpoint among reunions took place at the Fischerhof convalescent home near Uelzen. Here Hertha Ehlert had been sent on her release from Werl prison on 8 May. Savitri Devi was introduced to her fellow residents Leo B., a SS-Oberscharführer just out from Werl; Heinz G., another SS man from Werl; and Erich X., who had recently returned from captivity in the Soviet Union. An air of jollity animated the group as they met at the station and drove off in a cramped car. There were many stories to exchange in a café. Ninety-seven men and five women remained in the cells at Werl, but several hundreds still sat in Landsberg according to Hans F., a SS-Sturmführer released from there just two months before. Back at the Fischerhof, she met Lydia V., condemned to death by the French but recently released from Fresnes; listened approvingly to Hans F. justify the extermination camps of Auschwitz and Treblinka as the dispassionate defense of Aryandom; and talked with a young SS man from the Oradour reprisals trial. On

30 May she went with her friends to a dancing party at Uelzen organized by the Heimkehrerverband (Homecomers' League) to celebrate the
homecoming of German POWs from the Soviet Union and Nazi war
criminals released from Landsberg, Werl, and other Allied prisons.
These were happy and hopeful days for Savitri Devi. Surrounded by
those she loved and admired, she enjoyed the fleeting experience of the
world in which she had so much wanted to live, where she felt she
belonged.[24]

Through her stay at the Fischerhof, Savitri Devi also found a new
home in Germany. One of the residents was Leokardia ("Katja") U., a
twenty-six-year-old German woman born in the Soviet Union, who
overheard her pro-Nazi views and was duly impressed as a former
member of the Bund Deutscher Mädel. She invited Savitri Devi to stay
and write at her home at Emsdetten in Westphalia, where she lived
with her husband and two children. This proved a most satisfactory
arrangement and Savitri Devi stayed for at least two years in Emsdetten, where she completed *Pilgrimage* and wrote most of *The Lightning
and the Sun,* her final statement of Nazi faith. Westphalia with its open
heaths and mountainous forests became Savitri Devi's elective German
homeland. Above all, she was impressed by the Teutoburger Wald's
historic role in the defense of ancient Germanic independence, once in
antiquity, when Hermann the Cherusker (Arminius) defeated the le-
gions of Varus in A.D. 9, and again in early medieval times, when
Charlemagne destroyed the pagan shrines of the Saxons and converted
them on pain of death to Christianity in his campaign between 772 and
787. A visit to the Teutoburger Wald in late October 1953 represented
the final station of her pilgrimage.

On a fine early autumn day she took the tram from Detmold to
Hiddesen, marveling at the magnificent brown, orange, yellow, and red
colors of the forest. Her first destination was the Hermannsdenkmal,
the gigantic copper statue of the liberator mounted on a gothic base,
which stands more than 160 feet high and towers above the trees on
the Grotenburg hill. Built over thirty-seven years with funds raised by
subscription, the monument represented the lifework of the indefati-
gable architect Ernst von Bandel (1800–1876) and was finally completed
in 1875. The inspiration and symbolic importance of the statue are
attributable to the development of German national feeling and the
movement toward unification in the nineteenth century. Savitri Devi
gazed upon the copper colossus with his winged helmet and upheld

sword with feelings of awe and admiration. Hermann personified to her "the spirit of joyous defiance, the aggressive pride of a young, strong, healthy, beautiful Nation, jealous of her freedom and conscious of her invincibility."[25] In Savitri Devi's view, Hermann's victory had forestalled Roman colonization. Germany had thereby retained its ancient language, avoided the racial mixing prevalent throughout the cosmopolitan Roman world, and avoided early Christianization. Thus Germany remained the "kernel of militant Aryan mankind in the West," implacably opposed to all forms of artificial internationalism, until the Third Reich emerged as the leader of a pan-Aryan world order.

She reached the Externsteine near Horn before sunset on the same day. These bizarre great sandstone rocks, four in number, have long been identified as an important religious site. A flight of steps leads up the third rock to a small bridge giving access to the upper chapel perched high upon the second rock. Through a circular aperture in its wall the rising sun may be observed at the summer solstice. The first rock, standing beside a dark lake, is hollowed by caves and decorated with various Christian reliefs believed to represent the site's reconsecration to the new faith. One relief shows the pagan Germanic Irminsul or world pillar bent beneath figures supporting Christ; such an Irminsul belonging to the pagan Saxons was destroyed nearby at Altenbeken by Charlemagne in the late eighth century. At the edge of the lake stands the so-called Tomb Rock containing a hollowed-out cavity not unlike a stone coffin for a recumbent human body. Anyone lying in the coffin experiences complete silence and isolation, and some think that this "tomb" was used by pagan priests or shamans for initiations into mysteries and a new life. During the years of the Third Reich the *völkisch* archaeologist Wilhelm Teudt had published several books devoted to the pagan solar cults of the Externsteine that had been read by Savitri Devi.[26]

She had seen other sun temples, Delphi and Delos in Greece, Karnak and the pyramids in Egypt, and the Black Pagoda near Puri in India, but this was the first time she had visited a putative prehistoric solar temple in Germany. She climbed up the steps to the "chamber of the sun" upon the second rock and there imagined old Aryan sages celebrating the solstice rites at a time when the Twelfth Dynasty pharaohs were building their temples in Egypt, the Minoan sealords ruled the Aegean, and the eastern Aryans were invading the Middle East and

India. She pictured the destruction of the old shrine by Charlemagne and his Frankish Christians, and the imposition of their alien creed opposed to natural and racial hierarchy upon the healthy and fearless Aryan warriors. It seemed to her that this assault upon the Saxons in 772 had been worse than the defeat of 1945, for it had taken Germany more than a thousand years to recover its natural heathendom in the Third Reich. Charlemagne and Eisenhower were both apostate Germans who, forgetting their racial origins, had persecuted the old faith and their kinsmen.[27]

At all stations of her pilgrimage Savitri Devi had experienced a thrill at being in a place closely linked with the growth or conquest of the Aryan spirit. But a feeling of sadness was also ever-present. Hitler's birthplace, the Feldherrnhalle in Munich, the Nuremberg party-rally grounds all evoked memories of the promise of Nazism to restore the Aryan world and a bitter sense of its recent defeat. Time after time, in place after place, she nevertheless took fresh hope from her surroundings to imagine the coming Reich, Hitler's return in even greater glory, the establishment of a worldwide Aryan order. Her thoughts and feelings at the Externsteine rehearse this passage from reminiscence through despair to new hope. Alone in the sun chamber on the evening of 23 October she saw the circular aperture lit by the moon. Struck by its deathly symbolism, she was reminded how Nazism had been obliterated and was seemingly dead since 1945. But through her solitary rituals she was certain that she could help speed its resurrection.

Returning a week later before daybreak on 30 October to the rocks, she performed further rituals for the resurrection of Nazism. Descending to the Tomb Rock beside the lake, she climbed into the stone coffin beneath its semicircular arch and saw a small violet spark flash from the rock vault above her head. The uncanny silence associated with the interior of the coffin made a deep impression on her. She was removed from the world like some ancient shaman undergoing an initiatory ordeal for personal transformation. While her limbs grew cold and heavy, she fervently prayed for spiritual rebirth and a Nazi revival. "How long did I remain in the attitude of death, at the bottom of that stone coffin? I could not tell. It was no longer dark when I stepped out." High up in the Chamber of the Sun she shouted the ancient Sanskrit words in invocation of the Vedic deities: "Aum Shivayam! Aum Rudrayam!" followed by "Heil Hitler!" It was still cloudy and raining at the Externsteine, but she knew the sun had risen. Her spirits soared, she could already see the swastika flag flying once again above the rocks of the sun. The celebration of her lonely Nazi gnosis made her certain of Aryan victory.[28]

10

THE ODESSA CONNECTION

The complete and utter defeat of the Third Reich, the exposure of its crimes and atrocities, and the accompanying programs of denazification and reeducation of the German people combined to vilify Adolf Hitler and National Socialism throughout the Western world. After 1945, Savitri Devi had exchanged her former isolation in India for the marginal role of a die-hard Nazi agent in occupied Germany and elsewhere in Europe. In the late 1940s and early 1950s she was an obscure figure inhabiting a twilight world of bewildered Nazis filled with bitterness, revanchist ideas, and wild hopes of Hitler's return. We have seen her distributing leaflets amid the ruined cities of the fallen Reich, meeting secretly with small conventicles of unrepentant Nazis, and offering comfort to fellow prisoners at Werl, war criminals' widows, and other devotees of the defeated idol. The quixotic and sectarian nature of her postwar activity is highlighted further by her pilgrimage to Austria and Germany in 1953. Throughout this tour she regularly invoked the gods and performed solitary rituals at such places as the Nuremberg rally grounds and the Externsteine in a passionate if desperate attempt to reverse the Allied defeat and urge the resurrection of an Aryan Germany.

This situation of isolation and helplessness was soon to change. Through her reckless and outspoken advocacy of Hitler's cause, she was becoming known in clandestine Nazi circles. She had undertaken her one-woman propaganda crusade in the British zone of occupied Germany without the involvement or knowledge of any Nazi support organization, much to the frustration of several interrogators following her arrest. But the story of her mission and imprisonment soon spread among the inmates of Werl prison and she became a trusted comrade of these and other detainees following their release from Allied prisons. Many of these new friendships offered her an introduction into the political organizations dedicated to a nurturing and revival of Nazism. Above all, this network of Nazi organizations was itself growing and becoming more securely established at the time of her release from Werl.

Once denazification had been sacrificed to the Allies' fresh interest in wooing the Germans for the Cold War against the Soviet Union, new political parties began to spring up in Germany that owed much of their inspiration to National Socialism. One of the earliest was the Sozialistische Reichspartei (SRP) founded in October 1949 and led by Otto Ernst Remer, who had been promoted to general following his role in foiling the bomb plot of disaffected high military and aristocrats against Hitler on 20 July 1944. In the May 1951 Land elections the SRP polled 11 percent of the vote and won sixteen seats in the Lower Saxony diet. The Nazi affiliation of the SRP was manifest in Remer's trenchant attacks on the Americans, whom he accused of constructing fake gas chambers at Dachau to discredit the Germans, and on the Adenauer government together with the "criminals of the 20 July." Such overt Nazi political activity was deemed illegal under the Basic Law of the newly founded German Federal Republic and Remer was sentenced to three months' imprisonment. The Karlsruhe supreme court declared the SRP unconstitutional in July 1952 and the party was banned. Meanwhile Adenauer's Christian Democratic Union (CDU) and other parties scrambled to pick up the 367,000 votes of the outlawed SRP, and the CDU succeeded in boosting its share of the vote in Lower Saxony from 17 to 33 percent. However, considerable numbers of SRP voters and supporters were not long in expressing their nostalgic Nazism through a successor party, whose activities were in the ascendant by the time Savitri Devi returned to Germany in April 1953.

The Deutsche Reichspartei (DRP) traced its origins to a merger of two small far-right parties first launched in the aftermath of defeat in November 1945. After 1952 the DRP was the most influential electoral force on the extreme right with some sixteen thousand paid-up members, a few seats in the Land diets, and about half a million votes across the country in federal elections. Led by Adolf von Thadden, the DRP boasted such former celebrities of the Third Reich as Werner Naumann, a former Nazi secretary of state and Hitler's choice to succeed Goebbels;

SS General Wilhelm Meinberg; a number of Wehrmacht generals; and the Luftwaffe ace Hans-Ulrich Rudel. However, the DRP was only the most prominent of the neo-Nazi organizations that flourished in Germany during the 1950s. According to the Ministry of Interior's annual report on neo-Nazism, there were at least a hundred parties, leagues, movements, and associations, each claiming a Nazi succession, and whose total membership amounted to about eighty thousand persons in 1954. While the great majority of former Nazi supporters, careerists, and businessmen made their way in the new Germany under the auspices of the CDU—Adenauer had several former Nazi ministers in his own government—it was a hard core of Hitler faithful and inveterate Nazis who joined the political fringe of the far right. After her return to Germany in 1953, Savitri Devi made numerous contacts in this revanchist and nostalgic milieu of Nazi diehards.

Foremost among these was Colonel Hans-Ulrich Rudel (1916–1982), whom she frequently visited at Hanover and came to know well. The son of a village pastor in Silesia, Rudel had been fascinated by airplanes and flying from an early age, and joined the expanding Luftwaffe in 1936 during Hitler's buildup of the armed forces. By the spring of 1938, the newly developed Stuka dive bombers were rolling off the production lines in readiness for Germany's blitzkrieg campaigns, and Rudel volunteered to train as a Stuka pilot. At the time it was an unfashionable choice, for most of the young Luftwaffe bloods wanted to be fighter pilots, but it was the foundation of the Rudel legend. From the outbreak of war onward he was almost constantly engaged on bombing missions in Poland, in the Balkans, and above all in the campaign against the Soviet Union. He was the first pilot ever to sink a battleship, the Soviets' *Marat*, and also dispatched 2 cruisers, one destroyer, 70 landing craft, and more than 500 Russian tanks. By January 1945 he had 2,530 wartime operational flights to his credit and was regarded as Germany's greatest war pilot ever, and possibly the foremost air ace of all time. He was the first and only recipient of Germany's highest military decoration—specially created for him by Hitler in December 1944—the Iron Cross with Golden Oakleaves, Swords, and Diamonds.

Rudel believed that "an officer has a vocation in which he does not belong to himself but to his fatherland and to the subordinates committed to his charge. . . . [H]e must therefore . . . show an example to his men without regard for his own person or his life." He was not known to have taken any leave and when in April 1945 he lost his right leg below the knee, he returned to his unit and continued flying immediately after surgery. Rudel's military achievements and his reputation for courage and patriotic self-sacrifice were a living legend among the German public during the war. This legend enjoyed an even wider appeal because Rudel was not a member of the Nazi Party nor identified with any other political organization of the Third Reich. He was, quite simply, a hero of the fatherland for whom loyalty, duty, and obedience were the ultimate virtues. His bravery was also recognized by the enemy. After the German surrender, he met top pilots of the Royal Air Force in June 1945 at Tangmere to discuss operational tactics and technical matters. One of them, Group Captain Douglas Bader, wrote in his foreword to the English-language edition of Rudel's war memoir *Stuka Pilot* (1951) that he was a gallant chap and wished him luck.

When Rudel received his unique Iron Cross from Hitler in person, the Führer had praised him as the greatest and bravest soldier the German people had ever produced. Nor was this mere rhetoric. Hitler had boundless admiration for Rudel. He regarded him as the paragon of German soldierly virtue whose courage and devotion to Germany were unaffected by the political jockeying, placemanship, and hunger for power that permeated the party and the political organizations. According to Hitler's architect, Hermann Giesler, Hitler wanted Rudel to succeed him as Führer when the time came. His youth, his qualities of leadership, his powers of communication, his ability to remain calm and logical under stress, his unquestioned character, crowned by his wartime record, all combined to make him a worthier successor in Hitler's view than anyone else in the party.[1] Rudel knew nothing of Hitler's musings, but he did know that after the surrender of Germany, things could never be the same again. He could not forget that it was the Third Reich and Hitler's war that had made his reputation. A hostage to the aura of his own heroism, the selfless patriot became a Nazi die-hard.

After the war Rudel had fled to Argentina, where he became a popular and prominent member of the country's large Nazi community, which enjoyed the protection of the Perón government. Rudel formed a close link with Juan Perón (1895–1974), whose own successful political career owed much to his study of Italian fascism. The wartime hero now turned his mind to devising plans for assisting Nazi fugitives and war criminals to escape from Europe and became the head of such a rescue organization called the Kameradenwerk. He also founded the Rudel Klub as a mutual aid society in Argentina to help former Nazis establish themselves with new livelihoods. Throughout his stay abroad Rudel acted as a leading contact man between Nazis in exile and those still in Germany. On his return to Germany in 1951, he became the patron of the ultranationalistic Freikorps Deutschland, a right-wing extremist group founded that year whose name and aims recalled the private armies and revanchist squads set up by disgruntled soldiers after the First World War. Newspaper reports in January 1952 fueled suspicion that Rudel and former SS Colonels Otto Skorzeny and Eugen Dollmann were leading members of a Madrid-based Nazi center that cultivated close links with another Nazi center in Cairo directly involved in Nasser's anti-British plot that ended with the ousting of King Farouk.[2]

As soon as he had returned to Germany, Rudel publicly declared his undying admiration for Adolf Hitler and his vision of a resurrected, strong Germany. This outspoken loyalty to the Third Reich backed by the wartime legend of his Luftwaffe exploits firmly established him as the idol of the reviving neo-Nazi movement. His nationalist views found a regular outlet in the *Deutsche Soldaten-Zeitung* (est. 1951), which was edited by former officials of Goebbels's propaganda ministry and SS officers. Besides his support of the Freikorps Deutschland, he became a committee member of the Deutsche Reichspartei (DRP). When Savitri Devi first met Hans-Ulrich Rudel, he was already perhaps the most popular and visible figure of the neo-Nazi scene in the young German republic. His contacts among old Nazis in South America were extensive and he was a key player in the Nazi clandestine groups in Spain and Egypt. Although an activist by nature, Rudel could not help but be impressed by Savitri Devi's praise of Nazism as an international racist movement, a notion well suited to the clandestine and dispersed nature of postwar Nazi conspiracy. She met him several times at Hanover, completing her manuscript of *The Lightning and the Sun* on the occasion of a visit in March 1956.

Later that year Rudel returned to South America, living in Brazil and Paraguay, where he befriended President Alfredo Stroessner (b. 1912), the vintage dictator of German origin. By the early 1970s he had returned to Europe and settled in the Austrian Tyrol, but he remained in close touch with many wanted Nazis in South America, including Klaus Barbie, the Gestapo chief of Lyons; Josef Mengele, the

Auschwitz doctor; and Walter Rauff, who had planned the early extermination facilities for East European Jewry. All these men, and hundreds of others, including Martin Bormann according to Rudel, owed their new lives abroad to the postwar Nazi escape organizations in which the Luftwaffe ace had earlier played a key role. He later befriended President Augusto Pinochet (b. 1915) in Chile, where Rauff died at liberty in 1984. Hans-Ulrich Rudel's immense network of old Nazi survivors, South American politicians, and businessmen was as great a legend as his Luftwaffe record. Through her encounter with Rudel and his warm response to the propagandist value of her pro-Nazi books, Savitri Devi was properly launched into the international network of escape organizations, mutual aid groups, and new Nazi parties. Thanks to introductions provided by Rudel, she was subsequently able to meet leading Nazi émigrés in the Middle East and Spain.

The emergence of the Middle East as a haven for old Nazis during the 1950s had its roots in the anti-British and pro-Axis attitudes of Vichy Syria, Rashid Ali in Iraq, Mohammed Amin al Husseini, the Grand Mufti of Jerusalem, and even King Farouk of Egypt during the war. United by a common hatred of Jewry, the Third Reich had taken the Palestinian mufti under its protection following the Allied invasion of Iraq and he had lived throughout the war in a luxurious suite at the Hotel Adlon in Berlin. Hitler had enjoyed quite a following among the nationalist youth of Egypt during the war, after Nassiri Nasser, the later president's brother, had published an Arab edition of *Mein Kampf* in 1939, describing its author as the "strongest man of Europe." Even after the defeat of the Third Reich, Arab feelings remained very warm toward the Germans, who were still regarded as potential allies against British colonial power in the region.

Egypt became a favored destination for old Nazis in search of responsible jobs and high office. King Farouk had been impressed by his palace garage mechanics recruited from Afrika Korps POWs and wondered what he might achieve with officers from the elite units of the Gestapo and SS who had fought so hard against the hated British. A number of Nazi experts who had escaped the Allied dragnet were hired by the king as military, financial, and technical advisers. This Nazi influence in Egypt was to survive its royal patron, for the young Egyptian officers who planned the military coup d'état that ousted King Farouk in January 1952 were themselves great admirers of the Germans and availed themselves of further large-scale imports of ex-Nazi expertise. Thus it came about that the former Gestapo chief of Düsseldorf, Joachim Däumling, later actively engaged in SS operations in Croatia, was employed to set up the Egyptian secret service along the lines of the SS Reichssicherheitshauptamt (Himmler's Reich Security Main Office), while the former Gestapo chief of Warsaw organized the security police.[3]

Hans-Ulrich Rudel and his fellow conspirators Otto Skorzeny and Eugen Dollmann played an important role in recruiting large numbers of former Nazi fugitives from Argentina for key posts in the new republican regime. As early as January 1952 they were in contact with influential Egyptian army officers and the former Grand Mufti of Jerusalem, who had lived in Egypt since the fall of the Third Reich. According to Israeli and French intelligence reports, the Egyptian secret service and political police were staffed by such men as SS General Oskar Dirlewanger, chief of the infamous SS penal brigade; SS Major Eugen Eichberger, battalion-commander in the Dirlewanger brigade; SS Colonel Leopold Gleim, chief of the Gestapo department for Jewish affairs in Poland; SS Lieutenant Colonel Bernhard Bender, Gestapo official in Poland and the Soviet Union whose knowledge of Yiddish enabled him to penetrate Jewish underground organizations; SS General Heinrich Selimann, chief of the Gestapo in Ulm; SS Major Schmalstich, Gestapo liaison officer to French collaborationists and organizer of Jewish transports from Paris to Auschwitz; SS Major Seipel, Gestapo official in Paris; and SS General Alois Moser, a war criminal who was involved in the extermination of Ukrainian Jewry.[4]

Wehrmacht General Wilhelm Fahrmbacher took over the central planning staff in Cairo, while a number of former Nazi officials and sixty military experts, mostly former Waffen-SS men, assisted in the organization and training of the Egyptian army. Several of these were reported in 1958 as closely associated with the then Algerian exile government. These included SS Colonel Baumann, a participant officer in the destruction of the Warsaw ghetto; Willi Berner, an SS officer at Mauthausen concentration camp; and Erich Alter, implicated in the murder of Professor Theodor Lessing at Marienbad and later commissioner for Jewish affairs in Galicia. Economic and ideological advisers followed fast on the heels of their military colleagues. Financial specialists from Goering's Four Year Plan and the German Labor Front were soon employed in Egyptian ministries.

President Gamal Abdel Nasser's anti-Jewish and anti-Zionist propaganda apparatus discovered an ideological treasure trove among Nazi émigrés. Supervisory among these was Johannes von Leers, who had been responsible for anti-Semitic campaigns at Goebbels' Propaganda Ministry, together with Franz Bünsch and Alois Brunner, who had held top jobs in Adolf Eichmann's "Jewish department" of the SS Reich Security Main Office. The Egyptian propaganda ministry also employed Walter Bollmann, Nazi espionage chief in Britain before the war and later, as SS major, active in antiguerrilla and anti-Jewish operations in the Ukraine; Louis Heiden, an SS official transferred to the Egyptian press office during the war; Franz Bartel, an "old fighter" of the early Nazi Party and Gestapo officer; Werner Birgel, an SS officer from Leipzig; Erich Bunz, SA major and expert in the Jewish question; Albert Thielemann, a regional SS chief in Bohemia; and SS Captain Wilhelm Böckler, another participant in the liquidation of the Warsaw ghetto.[5]

Nasser himself was well disposed toward the Germans, but all the more because these asylum seekers wished to join him in the destruction of Israel. Around 1958 Egypt began to arm itself with new supersonic planes and rockets. At least two hundred German and Austrian scientists and other personnel were deployed in the new aircraft and missile center at Helwan, where rockets were aimed at Israel. The two production units were under the supervision of Austrian experts, Hans Schönbaumsfeld and Ferdinand Brandner. The latter, a former SA colonel and notorious Nazi, appointed Dr. Hanns Eisele, SS captain and medical torturer in Buchenwald, as staff physician at Helwan. By October 1962 the presence of German scientists at Helwan had been exposed in the world press. In April 1963 these matters precipitated a government crisis in Israel (whose secret service had made attempts on the lives of several Germans). There was also consternation in Bonn over this German contribution to Egypt's military potential against Israel.[6]

Savitri Devi left Europe to return to India in the spring of 1957. Under cover of her maiden name she had illegally spent four years in West Germany, completing her books *Pilgrimage* and *The Lightning and the Sun* while staying with her friend Katja U. at Emsdetten and otherwise traveling around the country to make contact with old Nazis. The supply of Indian gold and jewelry that she had brought with her to cover her costs of subsistence was now all but gone. She decided to return home by the overland route through the Middle East. In May 1957 she sailed across the Mediterranean to Egypt with a warm personal recommendation from Hans-Ulrich Rudel to leading Nazi personalities in Egypt. Her first stop was in Cairo, where she made contact with Johannes von Leers. He was a well-known senior Nazi placement in Nasser's new administration, having arrived with his family from Argentina in 1954 through Rudel and Skorzeny's recruitment consultancy. At the time of his meeting with Savitri Devi, Leers was a specialist in Zionist affairs with top responsibility for Cairo's anti-Israeli radio broadcasting.

Although the door of his ministry office bore an assumed Arab name, Professor Dr. Omar Amin von Leers could only have been taken for a German. The pink-cheeked, white-haired man with bright-blue marblelike eyes rose to greet Savitri Devi with old courtly Prussian charm. Of course, he had heard of her and her splendid books on behalf on the international Nazi cause. Colonel Rudel had spoken warmly of her. Would she accept his invitation to stay for a while and see what the Germans were now doing in Egypt? He lived a short distance to the south of Cairo in the town of Méadi (El-Maâdi) on the east bank of the River Nile. However, the Leers house was full at present, and he would arrange for her accommodation at the house of a neighbor, a Palestinian Arab called Mahmoud Sali with a great admiration for the Führer. This gentleman would be greatly honored if Savitri Devi accepted his hospitality. She was delighted. Leers suggested that she come and dine with them that evening.

Johannes von Leers (1902–1963) had very high qualifications for his Egyptian assignment. A Nazi university professor and an SS officer, Leers had also held a senior appointment in Goebbels's Ministry of Propaganda, where he specialized in vicious anti-Semitic campaigns targeted at both domestic and overseas audiences. His long publication list of anti-Semitic diatribes included *14 Jahre Judenrepublik* (14 years Jewish republic) (1933), the sinister photo album *Juden sehen Dich an* (Jews look at you) (1933), *Blut und Rasse in der Gesetzgebung* (Blood and race in legislation) (1936), and twenty-four other books. Leers's entire literary output revolved around the concepts of race, blood, and soil. During the Third Reich his two titles *Geschichte auf rassischer Grundlage* (History on a racial basis) (1934) and *Der Weg des deutschen Bauern* (The way of the German peasant) had both been published in large popular editions by Reclam. In the first work he described Hitler as "absorbing the powerful forces of this Germanic granite landscape into his blood through his father." From 1933 onward he and wife jointly edited *Nordische Welt*, a monthly periodical published by Herman Wirth's Gesellschaft für germanische Ur- und Vorgeschichte (Society for Germanic Prehistory), and after 1935 he wrote regular articles for the *SS-Leithefte* published by the SS Race and Settlement Office under the auspices of Richard Walther Darré. Leers's racial ideas were saturated with ideas of the Aryan polar homeland, sun worship, and the power of the native soil. During his Argentian exile Leers published a vicious attack on the anti-Nazi resistance as *Traitors of the Reich* (parts 1 and 2).

Over the next few days Savitri Devi spent many hours in the company of Johannes von Leers. The professor could trace his learned interests in *völkisch* and racial anti-Semitism back to the late 1920s and recalled the people he first met while living in Munich at that time. These included Darré, the pioneer of Nazi "blood-and-soil" doctrine and, after 1933, Reichsbauernführer (national peasant leader) and minister of food and agriculture in the Third Reich. Before her marriage, Gesine von Leers had been the personal secretary of Herman Wirth, the renowned if controversial Dutch-German scholar of Nordic traditions and ancient Germanic institutions. She believed herself the reincarnation of a Bronze Age priestess and affected barbarous gold jewelry. Another member of their Munich circle was Karl Weisthor, an Austrian racial occultist who claimed ancestral-clairvoyant memories of the distant Germanic past. Savitri Devi was thrilled to hear Leers's account of the fashionable parties he and his wife had given for Nazi top brass in Berlin in the early 1930s. Here he had introduced Herman Wirth to Heinrich Himmler, who had henceforth become his patron and created the SS Ahnenerbe (Ancestral Heritage Office) under Wirth's direction. The elderly Weisthor also found favor with Himmler and became a valued member of his personal staff, advising his chief on ancient Germanic religion, runes, and the mysteries of race.[7]

Thrilled as Savitri Devi was at these reminiscences of the Third Reich, she was even more excited by Leers's account of the new international Nazi mission against Jewry and communism. He told her of his successive escapes from Soviet and Western detention camps in Germany; of how the secret escape organizations had sent him and his family to safety in Argentina by 1946; and of the web of international Nazi conspiracy that in turn had brought him and many other highly qualified Germans to Egypt to participate in Nasser's new assertion of Arab power against Britain, France, and Israel, culminating in the recent Suez crisis of 1956. The Third Reich may have gone down in flames in Berlin more than a decade ago, but here in the Middle East, in Latin America, and Spain the old Nazis had new schemes for global racketeering and political resurgence. He impressed upon her that Germany had not lost its friends among those who resented the old colonial powers. Germany was rearming itself economically at home, diplomatically and ideologically abroad. In proof of his assertions, Leers offered her further introductions to senior SS officers now ensconced in Damascus and Baghdad, whom she might like to meet as she continued her journey to India.

She walked with Leers from his home in Méadi along the palm-tree-bordered esplanade beside the wide stream of the Nile, across which stood the ancient pyramids of Giza in the parched desert landscape. In Egypt she was daily reminded of the immemorial sun cults and the young idealistic pharaoh Akhnaton's ill-fated utopia so many centuries before, about which she had written in Calcutta in the early 1940s. But meeting Johannes von Leers and hearing about his numerous Nazi and SS comrades in Egypt also reminded her of her own self-imposed exile from the Third Reich in India. She had always regretted those years spent so far removed from her idol and the "great events" in Europe. Here she found herself again in a foreign setting, outside Europe, only this time she was accompanied by Nazi loyalists who were emerging across the world to prepare for Germany's resurrection. The din and squalor of downtown Cairo recalled her memories of wartime Calcutta, and once again she felt that her years of lonely witness, her passionate prophecies of Aryan revival, and the end of the Kali Yuga had a universal significance. The Third Reich had passed, but the Fourth Reich was surely coming. Now there were devotees of the Aryan faith throughout the world in such places as this.

After visiting Tell-el-Amarna, the site of Akhnaton's solar city some 190 miles south of Cairo, she returned to Méadi to bid farewell to Leers and his family and took a Greek ship from Alexandria to Beirut. She traveled on to Damascus by car but found to her disappointment that her Nazi contacts there had decamped for the hot summer months. She then continued her journey across the desert by bus, first to Baghdad, and thence to Teheran, where she spent three weeks. From the Iranian capital she traveled out to Pahlevi to see the Caspian Sea and then continued by road from Teheran through Mashhad to Zahedan on the Iranian-Pakistan frontier. Here she waited for a week at a small Greek hotel that recalled the campaigns of Alexander the Great in this ancient Persian border country until she could board the train that would take her to Lahore. As the steam locomotive puffed across the burning desert of Baluchistan—one of the hottest places on earth—she suddenly felt a great sense of relief to be away from Europe and at long last back in Asia where she could once again flaunt her Nazi convictions without fear of incrimination or sanctions. She had left India at the end of that dark year of defeat in 1945 and since that time she had spent long years in occupied Germany as an undercover agent for Nazism, as an Allied prisoner, and again as a Nazi propagandist and sympathizer in the German neo-Nazi underground. But now India and Pakistan were independent, the British no longer ruled, and she was free to sing the Horst Wessel Song at the top of her voice out of the carriage window.

She arrived in Delhi on 30 July 1957 and within two days was back in Calcutta with her husband at the old apartment in Wellesley Street. The postwar years had not been easy for Asit Krishna Mukherji in view of his pro-German and pro-Japanese wartime activities, and he had found it difficult to find other sponsors for his editorial and journalistic work. However, during the 1950s he had been making a living as a Hindu astrologer and had raised sufficient money to pay for the printing of his wife's books and send her regular financial support. Savitri Devi now wanted to fund the printing of her latest books and for this she herself needed well-paid employment. In the late summer she found a job as field interpreter for three East German engineers who were building a funicular railway at the iron ore mines of Jordania-Barajonda in the Orisa province. When this project was completed, she returned to Calcutta to take up a post as a teacher at the French School in September 1958. The proceeds of her interpreting job covered the production costs of *Pilgrimage* and *The Lightning and the Sun*, which were both published in 1958.

Although she was free to publish Nazi books in Calcutta, she suffered once again from a sense of standing on the sidelines. Now independent, India was eager to emphasize territorial nationality to avert racial strife, and with the British gone, there was little interest in their former German enemy. By 1960 Europe beckoned to Savitri Devi once again as a more promising stage for neo-Nazi activity. Her mother had died at Lyons in March 1960 and there were affairs to be settled. In any case, she wanted to join forces again with her German die-hard friends in preparing for a Nazi revival. For the second time she bid farewell to her husband, in September 1960, and sailed via South India and Ceylon to Marseilles. After docking at the great French port, through which she had so often passed en route to Greece, India, and Egypt, she traveled directly into Spain. Once again Hans-Ulrich Rudel had secured her a top-level introduction into the neo-Nazi network by sending her books *Gold in the Furnace* and *The Lightning and the Sun* to his colleague Otto Skorzeny in Madrid.

SS Colonel Otto Skorzeny (1908–1975) was another archconspirator in Nazi escape organizations, and in political, and business intrigues, whose postwar adventures are as astonishing as his daring wartime exploits. He had been one of the first members of the Austrian Nazi Party in 1935 and had joined Das Reich Division of the Waffen-SS at the outbreak of war. Thanks to his close links with the Austrian SS police leader and later SS General Ernst Kaltenbrunner, Skorzeny took command of a new SS commando unit in 1943. Commando raids of breathtaking audacity and risk were the trademarks of Skorzeny's warfare. On 12 September 1943 he entered the history books when his special glider forces liberated the deposed Mussolini from a mountaintop hotel in the Gran Sasso, where he was being held prisoner by the new Italian government. In July 1944 he received a special secret authorization from Hitler and was effective commander in chief of all German home forces in the confusion following the bomb plot and played a crucial role in foiling its success. In November 1944 he was appointed head of the sabotage section of the SS Reich Security Main Office and led commando raids in U.S. uniform (thereby contravening the Geneva Convention) in the Ardennes during the Battle of the Bulge. Later he was involved in Operation Werewolf, a code name for the resistance fighters, guerrillas, and foreign agents who were to continue the war behind Allied lines.[8]

At the end of the war Skorzeny was apparently charged with creating a special corps to defend the Alpine Redoubt, supposed to provide a major bloc of military resistance and a refuge for Hitler and the Nazi leadership in a large mountainous area centered on the Austrian Tyrol, southern Bavaria, and the Alto Aldige in northern Italy. From early 1945 Goebbels had mounted a journalistic campaign to produce stories about impregnable positions, underground supply dumps, elite troops, and mountainside factories. The entire operation was a myth, intended to create confusion among the invading Allies and distract them from the assault on Berlin. Skorzeny's actual task was to coordinate the es-

cape and evasion networks of leading Nazis. Skorzeny is usually credited with the creation of the most famous network of all, the ODESSA
(Organisation der ehemaligen SS-Angehörigen) and its Bremen-Bari
(B-B) line, which provided a secure chain of some 250 friendly agents
with safe houses, money, and documents across Europe. The B-B line
was the preferred route for Nazi fugitives making their way southward
through Germany, over the Alps, and into Italy to reach Mediterranean
ports, where they embarked for Latin America. Thousands of war criminals had benefited from Skorzeny's highly reliable escape line between
1949 and 1952.

But Otto Skorzeny's ambitions and love of adventure extended far
beyond the domestic operations of Nazi rescue organizations. He was
an early recruit into Reinhard Gehlen's new West German intelligence
organization (Bundesnachrichtendienst), itself a creation of the American CIA under Allen Dulles with its overriding concern to use the
indispensable knowledge of the former German intelligence corps
against the new Soviet enemy. Basing himself in Madrid from 1950,
Skorzeny built up an international intelligence-gathering and merce-
nary-recruitment agency under cover of an engineering and import-
export business. He was appointed security adviser to several
right-wing dictatorships in Latin America and was a trusted consultant
to Spain's Ministry of the Interior. Skorzeny was further credited with
being the treasurer of enormous Nazi funds and gold reserves that had
been salted away on behalf of major German industrial concerns (the
so-called Circle of Friends) in neutral countries during the last year of
the war. He also dealt in arms and sold the supplies of weapons cached
by the SS at the end of the war in France, Austria, and Italy. Through
his father-in-law, Hjalmar Schacht, Hitler's former finance minister,
Skorzeny was invited by Dulles in 1953 to help reorganize the security
forces of the new Egyptian Republic. In the course of his clandestine
intelligence and commercial dealings, Skorzeny regularly traveled from
Madrid to Cairo, Tangier, Buenos Aires, and Rome besides many towns
in Germany and Austria.

Although principally a man of action and affairs, Skorzeny was well
placed to take an interest in the political and ideological side of international neo-Nazism. Following the first postwar gathering of various
neofascist and neo-Nazi parties and movements in Rome in March
1950, about a hundred delegates from these parties in Germany, Italy,
Austria, France, Spain, and Sweden assembled in May 1951 at Malmö

in southern Sweden. Among these were Sir Oswald Mosley, leader of the prewar British Union of Fascists and the Union Movement since 1948; Maurice Bardèche, brother-in-law of the French fascist Robert Brasillach and representative of the Comité National Français; Fritz Rössler of the Sozialistische Reichspartei; and Karl-Heinz Priester, a former leader of the Hitler Youth who had a close connection with Skorzeny and the SS international. The Malmö International was a milestone in the history of postwar fascism, for it created the first confederation of parties in the "European Social Movement," which advocated a third force in Europe against the superpower blocs of the United States and the Soviet Union. Its right wing subsequently founded the Nouvel Ordre Européen (NOE), an extreme anti-Semitic confederation, in Zurich in September 1951. These internationals joined about fifty national movements and numbered perhaps several thousand members worldwide. In his undercover operations Skorzeny was always able to access these extensive Nazi networks.

Skorzeny regarded Savitri Devi as an exceptional ideologist on behalf of a revived Nazi International and invited her to visit him in Madrid on her return to Europe. They evidently found plenty to discuss for she remained his guest for six weeks. Skorzeny was convinced that conditions were growing more favorable for a fresh wave of neofascist sympathy in Europe. The loss of the Congo had unleashed revanchist sentiments in Belgium, and now, in late 1960, French extremists were seeking to delay any settlement of the conflict in Algeria. There was a widespread hope among neofascists that the Algerian issue would repeat the ideological conflict of the Spanish Civil War on a European stage. The fascist organization Jeune Europe supported the Organisation Armée Secrète (OAS) in Algeria and later found safe hideouts for its leaders. The increased levels of colored immigration in Great Britain were leading to a racial backlash and further support for far-right groups. New German neo-Nazi groups and youth movements were being established, including the Bund Vaterländischer Jugend and the Notgemeinschaft reichstreuer Verbände, sponsored by Skorzeny's friend Karl-Heinz Priester. Skorzeny had read Savitri Devi's books and was impressed by their praise of German virtues in the general context of a revival of the white Aryan world. He felt she was someone to be encouraged, someone who should write more for the Nazi International.

Here in Madrid Skorzeny could show her something of the prestige and protection that notorious wanted Nazis enjoyed in their Spanish refuge. For instance, there was Ante Pavelić (1899–1959), the leader of the Nazi puppet state of Croatia between 1941 and 1944. Inspired by a tribal desire for an independent Croat nation, Pavelić's fascist Ustaše movement had waged a savage war of vengeance, which claimed more than 800,000 victims among the Serbs and Jews of Croatia. At the end of the war, the Croat dictator had been sent along the ODESSA escape lines to Spain. From here he had gone to live in Argentina, until he was shot by a Yugoslav enemy in Buenos Aires. He returned to Madrid, dying there in 1959, a short while before Savitri Devi's visit to Skorzeny. The list of foreign fascists in Spain also included Horia Sima (1906–1993), commander of the Romanian Iron Guard, and senior Nazi officers of the Condor Legion, who had earlier fought for Franco and destroyed Guernica in the Civil War. Besides Skorzeny himself, the most notable Nazi exile in Madrid at the time of her visit was Léon Degrelle (1906–1994), the former Belgian Rexist leader and commander of the Wallonie Waffen-SS division on the eastern front. During her stay Skorzeny introduced her to Degrelle, who greatly impressed her with rousing stories of his anti-Bolshevik crusade in Hitler's pan-European army. She would later quote from his book *Hitler für ein tausend Jahre* with warm approval in her own memoirs.[9]

Degrelle had begun his political career in 1930 with the foundation of a publishing house and an authoritarian Catholic and anticommunist political movement called Christus Rex. After the Rexists had obtained 275,000 votes in the 1936 general election, which gave them twenty-seven seats in the lower house and seven in the Senate, Degrelle became a force to be reckoned with in Belgian politics but was interned by the government for his pro-German position at the outbreak of the war. After the German occupation of the Low Countries in 1940, Degrelle was freed and resumed his political activity. When Germany attacked the Soviet Union in June 1941, Degrelle volunteered to form a French-speaking Wallonian unit to fight alongside the Germans against Bolshevism. Thousands of young Belgians flocked to join his new unit from which the Wallonie and Langemarck Waffen-SS divisions were swiftly formed. Degrelle was involved in seventy-five direct combat actions on the eastern front and was wounded thirty-four times. By the end of the war he had risen to the rank of SS-Standartenführer as commander of the 28th SS Wallonie division. Refusing the unconditional surrender demanded by the Allies, Degrelle escaped from Oslo in Albert Speer's light plane, which crashed into the sea off the Spanish coast near San Sebastian.

Franco was greatly impressed by Degrelle and his Catholic anticommunist credentials. After the Belgian courts had sentenced Degrelle to death in absentia as a traitor on two occasions, Franco refused all demands from Belgium for his extradition from Spain. By way of further protection, the Spanish authorities also provided him with an armed guard in case of a kidnap attempt or assassination. Once he had recovered from his crash injuries, Degrelle established himself as a businessman in Madrid. Rumor linked Degrelle and his Falangist friends in Spain with the safehousing of Martin Bormann in Madrid en route to Argentina during 1947. However, Degrelle's chief contribution to the postwar Nazi cause was the ceaseless glorification of the Third Reich and the encouragement of a younger neo-Nazi generation. He published a dozen major books on Nazism, including *Die verlorene Legion* (The lost legion), *Hitler — geboren in Versailles* (Hitler—born at Versailles), *Denn der Hass stirbt . . .* (Because hate dies . . .), and *Hitler für ein tausend Jahre* (Hitler for a thousand years), and regularly wrote for the far-right European press. As a prewar Belgian fascist and a highly decorated Waffen-SS commander, Degrelle was a powerful symbol of the self-styled pan-European, anti-Bolshevik crusade of Nazi Germany. When the statute of limitations on his Belgian convictions lapsed, Degrelle became a considerable public figure in the neo-Nazi movement, receiving many visitors from abroad and addressing large international right-wing youth rallies from the 1960s onward until he was well into his eighties.[10]

In the course of her six weeks' stay with Otto Skorzeny, Savitri Devi was able to gather a great deal about the work of ODESSA and the other Nazi escape organizations, which had brought so many wanted Nazis and SS to safety abroad. She was excited to learn something of the far-flung intelligence networks that Skorzeny had expertly woven through the espionage and security needs of Germany, Egypt, Spain, and Latin America, often with financial support from the United States. She was greatly impressed by the clever interplay of his financial, commercial, and political activities on behalf of the "Circle of Friends" that had safeguarded German industrial and financial interests through surrender and defeat. But Skorzeny was not just a man with a Nazi past. His interests and influence reached far into the governments and councils of contemporary states. He played the part of a Spanish grandee to perfection, meeting his contacts at a restaurant where most of Franco's cabinet took their lunch. He lectured in Spanish universities on new military strategies and guerrilla warfare, and in 1960 he was a leading figure in the West German government's negotiations for Bundeswehr bases in Spain. Savitri Devi's admiration for Skorzeny was practically boundless; many years later in Delhi she would recall him as "one of the finest people I have ever met."

The bravado and mystique of Otto Skorzeny were notorious. Time and time again during the 1950s and 1960s his name was linked in the world's newspapers with Nazi plots and foreign intelligence services, above all with the ODESSA and its power to put former SS men in high places. So great was his aura of competence and intrigue that he was even tenuously linked to the planning of the Great Train Robbery in 1963. It seemed that Skorzeny's resources of daring and imagination could never be underestimated in view of his successes in the liberation of Mussolini, his bold guerrilla tactics, and the plans for Operation Werewolf in an enemy-occupied Germany.

And yet the myth always, perhaps necessarily, exceeded the man and his works. The Skorzeny myth was in turn part of the wider myth of the Fourth Reich. Adolf Hitler and the top Nazi leadership were long dead or imprisoned at Spandau; the Third Reich, the Nazi Party, and the SS had vanished in the inferno of a defeated nation; West Germany practiced parliamentary democracy under the watchful eye and tutelage of its victors. And yet, on the fringes of that safe, liberal Western world, in Spain, the Middle East, and Latin America, such figures as Otto Skorzeny, Hans-Ulrich Rudel, Léon Degrelle, and their countless confederates were powerful symbols of Nazi survival. Through her meetings with the men from ODESSA, Savitri Devi joined that world of regenerate Nazism.

11

INSIDE THE NEO-NAZI INTERNATIONAL

On leaving Spain, Savitri Devi returned to France and in January 1961 found a job as a supply teacher at Montbrison near Lyons. From here she followed Skorzeny's advice and continued to keep abreast of the growth of international fascism. During that year the larger neofascist parties in Europe were moving toward a new International, and the National European Party was founded by a convention of Mosley's Union Movement, the Deutsche Reichspartei, Jeune Europe, and the Movimento Sociale Italiano in Venice in March 1962. The National European Party clearly echoed Mosley's new postwar "Euro-Fascism." Its manifesto proposed the creation of a federal European state extending from Brest to Bucharest, the withdrawal of all American and Soviet forces from the old continent, and a scheme for white rule in parts of Africa. Its economic policies upheld the familiar fascist "third way" between capitalism and communism.[1]

This Venice International, like the preceding ones in Rome, Malmö, and Zurich, was eager to promote new ideas for old causes in the postwar world. However, these Internationals were usually careful to avoid any embarrassing references to Hitler, the SS, Nazism, and the Holocaust. Such caution was completely cast aside in the spring of 1962 by Colin Jordan, the British neo-Nazi leader, who admired Hitler and revived all the Nazi props of brown shirts, breeches and jackboots, and swastika armbands, together with the slogans of *"Sieg Heil!"* and *"Juden 'raus!"* and the Horst Wessel Song. When Jordan founded the World Union of National Socialists (WUNS) as a self-proclaimed Nazi International in August 1962, Savitri Devi became a founding member and was closely involved throughout the 1960s.

John Colin Campbell Jordan (b. 1923) had begun his preparation for the role of "world Führer" soon after the war. Demobilized from the Army Education Corps, he went up to Sidney Sussex College, Cambridge, in 1946 with an exhibition in history awarded before his war service. He contacted a number of British nationalist and neofascist groups with a view to promoting the cause at Cambridge. Foremost among these leads was Arnold Leese (1878–1956), an inveterate anti-Semite who had founded the Imperial Fascist League in 1929, a small (two hundred members) party that was the most pro-German and openly anti-Semitic group in England during the 1930s. It had always remained independent of Oswald Mosley's British Union of Fascists. Leese had published the pro-Nazi magazine *The Fascist* (1929–1939) and been detained during the war under the 18B regulation against suspected German "fifth columnists." Upon his release he resumed anti-Semitic publishing with his scurrillous periodical *Gothic Ripples* (1945–1956) and was briefly imprisoned in 1947 for giving aid to two fugitive Dutch members of the Waffen-SS. Jordan regarded Leese as a mentor figure, and the two men remained close friends until the latter's death. Leese's widow was a staunch supporter of Jordan in his subsequent struggles on the far-right scene and gave him the personal right to use a house in Notting Hill as a political headquarters.

But anti-Semitism and Nazism were limited in their appeal to a few racist sectarians like Leese and Jordan. It was colored immigration to Britain that provided a new impetus to their racism and held out the prospect of a mass movement on the extreme right. The postwar shortage of labor in the economies of Western Europe had been met by importing workers from other countries, and in Britain's case these people typically came from colonies or former colonies, especially the West Indies, India, and Pakistan. The first group from the West Indies arrived in 1948 and from that year to 1954 some 8,000–10,000 immigrants came into Britain each year. In 1954 and 1955, immigration from the West Indies rose to more than 20,000 each year, while that from India and Pakistan rose to about 10,000. A total of 132,000 colored immigrants from the Commonwealth arrived in Britain between 1955 and 1957, of whom 80,000 came from the West Indies. The newcomers were widely perceived with apprehension, especially by those working-class communities in which they were expected to settle. Because all the major political parties wished to avoid making immigration a political issue, it was foreseeable that new groups would arise to demand immigration control.

The immigration issue was squarely confronted by the National Labour Party (NLP) and the White Defence League (WDL), which were founded, respectively, by John Edward Bean (b. 1927) and Colin Jordan in 1957 when they left the League of Empire Loyalists (LEL), a right-wing society begun in 1954 to reverse British policies of decolonization. In August 1958 there were race riots in Nottingham, and in September similar riots in Notting Hill in West London. Jordan ran the White Defence League from Arnold Leese House at 74 Princedale Road in Notting Hill, and organized nightly rallies in the streets of this immigrant neighborhood throughout the tense summer of 1958. He also published a local newspaper, *Black and White News*, and a flood of racist pamphlets to provoke strong feelings of resentment against the newcomers. In Jordan's view, the great importance of the immigration issue was that it forced people to think in terms of race and thus become more receptive for his primarily anti-Semitic convictions. In 1959 he was advocating the cause of Nordic racial unity through the publication of a small periodical *The Nationalist*. By February 1960 the WDL and NLP had merged as the new British National Party (BNP) under the motto "For Race and Nation," with Andrew Fountaine, a Norfolk landowner, as president; Mrs. Leese as vice president; Jordan as national organizer; and John Tyndall (b. 1934), also formerly in the LEL, as a founder member.[2]

The potential for the extreme right in Britain seemed very great in the years 1960 to 1962. In 1960 some 60,000 immigrants from the West Indies, India, and Pakistan were added to the population, three times as many as in 1959, and in 1961 the net increase exceeded 100,000 for the first time. It was BNP policy to send all colored immigrants back to their homelands and to impeach the Tory cabinet and the 1945–1950 Labour cabinet for "complicity in the black invasion." Despite its limited funds and small membership (about 350), the party's activities were highly sensational and headline-grabbing, including demonstrations at London railway termini to confront immigrants arriving from the ports, two public meetings in Trafalgar Square, and demonstrations against the parade of a Jewish lord mayor of London and the Anti-Apartheid Movement. To expand into the provinces and to attract younger members, an organization called Spearhead was started within the party.

It was early in the spring of 1961 that Savitri Devi made her first contact with the British neo-Nazis. She was spending her Easter holidays in England with Muriel Gantry, her old friend first met in 1946 through a common interest in the pharaoh Akhnaton. Once in Britain, Savitri Devi quickly noted the widespread publicity that the BNP was attracting as a result of its confrontational stunts and demonstrations over the ever-increasing levels of colored immigration into the country. The growth of this fringe movement committed to racism, virulent anti-Semitism, and folkish nationalism fired her enthusiasm.

She lost no time in contacting Andrew Fountaine, the president of the BNP. A spring camp, attended by twenty delegates from European nationalist groups, was held on Fountaine's estate at Narford, Norfolk, in May 1961. Those present included Robert Lyons, a young leader in the American National States' Rights Party, which violently opposed desegregation in the South; representatives from German neo-Nazi groups; and Savitri Devi. Another key figure was ex-SS Lieutenant Friedrich Borth. Born in 1928, this blue-eyed, blond Austrian Nazi had served in the Luftwaffe and the Waffen-SS. As a teenage officer, he had commanded an assault group and won the Iron Cross. After serving a three-year jail sentence in postwar Vienna, he published an SS veteran magazine, *Das Kamerad*, which was swiftly suppressed by the Soviet authorities. Thereafter he was connected with numerous extreme right-wing groups and attended most international fascist gatherings. He led the Bund Heimattreuer Jugend until its banning in 1959 and then ran the Legion Europa, the Austrian section of Thiriart's Jeune Europe, another international grouping inspired by the French OAS in Algeria and Belgian rancor over the loss of the Congo.[3] After a busy schedule of lectures at Narford, the participants celebrated their Nordic racial identity with folkish songs and tankards of traditional ale around the campfire.

Savitri Devi was soon on friendly terms with John Tyndall and Colin Jordan, with whom she had first corresponded while staying with Skorzeny in Spain, and she kept in touch following her return to France. It was through this early contact that she was able to follow the subsequent wranglings in the BNP between Fountaine and Bean on the one hand and the brazen neo-Nazi tendency of Jordan and Tyndall. The latter commanded her instinctive allegiance and in due course she was their devoted supporter in the schismatic National Socialist Movement.

Despite the runaway success of the immigration issue for racial nationalism, ideological divisions were becoming apparent in the BNP leadership. In February 1962 Bean presented a resolution to its national council that "Jordan's wrongful direction of tactics is placing increasing emphasis on directly associating ourselves with the pre-war era of National Socialist Germany to the neglect of Britain, Europe and the White World struggle of today and the future." Bean and Fountaine clearly saw that Jordan's chief motive was admiration for Nazi Germany, whose example he wanted to translate, together with all the paraphernalia of swastikas, uniforms, and Hitler cult into contemporary Britain. What they wanted was a modern British nationalist movement addressing the issues of the 1960s. Jordan was defeated by a vote of seven to five, but he refused to stand down and reminded everyone that he held exclusive right to the use of Arnold Leese House. The BNP thereupon split, with Bean and Fountaine taking the party name, the magazine *Combat*, and more than 80 percent of the membership. Jordan retained the headquarters, John Tyndall and most of the Spearhead group, and the Birmingham and West Essex branches of the BNP.

The real issue behind the split was whether or not to make the BNP a self-proclaimed Nazi party. Colin Jordan wanted just this. Since 1960 he had edited a magazine called *Northern European* (1960–1962), which was flagged as the "voice of Nordic racial nationalism." He now called his rump faction the National Socialist Movement (NSM) and, together with John Tyndall and Denis Pirie, began to develop a British neo-Nazi party with all the forbidden trappings of Hitlerism. He launched the NSM with an inaugural party on 20 April, Hitler's birthday, with a swastika-decorated cake. Great excitement attended a transatlantic telephone call to Lincoln Rockwell, the leader of the American Nazi Party, to exchange congratulations, "*Heil Hitlers,*" and "*Sieg Heils.*" Jordan then made a speech about Britain's "loss and shame" for its role in the Second World War and the defeat of Hitler. However, he ended on an exultant note about the prospects of the NSM: "In Britain—in Britain of all places—the light which Hitler lit is burning, burning brighter, shining out across the waters, across the mountains, across the frontiers. National Socialism is coming back." In May he began editing a new magazine, *The National Socialist* (1962–1966), and published the NSM manifesto: ". . . the greatest treasure of the British people—the basis of their greatness in the past, and the only basis for it in the future—is their Aryan, predominantly Nordic blood; and that it is the first duty of the state to protect and improve this Island."[4]

Racial nationalism and the glorification of German National Socialism were distinctive features of Jordan's NSM which repeatedly seized
the tabloid headlines in 1962. This year also witnessed a climax in the
public concern over immigration, with some 212,000 colored immigrants having entered Britain over the eighteen months before the new
Immigration Act was finally passed in July. On 1 July 1962 the NSM
held a rally before a crowd of 4,000 in Trafalgar Square, at which Jordan
declared: "More and more people every day are opening their eyes and
coming to see that Hitler was right. They are coming to see that our
real enemies, the people we should have fought, were not Hitler and
National Socialists of Germany but world Jewry and its associates in
this country." John Tyndall fulminated in a similar anti-Semitic dia-
tribe that "in our democratic society, the Jew is like a poisonous maggot
feeding off a body in an advanced state of decay." This open avowal of
Nazi sentiments and vicious anti-Semitism quite overshadowed the
precipitating factor of colored immigration. The NSM was true to the
spirit of Arnold Leese and the interwar Imperial Fascist League. The
rally ended in a riot with a mob of Jewish people, Communist Party
members, and CND (Campaign for Nuclear Disarmament) supporters
storming the platform. The NSM would claim that the rally unleashed
the racialist strife that summer. Oswald Mosley's Union Movement
held rallies during July in protest at colored immigration in Trafalgar
Square, Manchester, and the East End, which were all met with uproar
and disorder. In early August race riots lasted for three nights in Dud-
ley near Birmingham, and again many arrests were made.

Secret military training had been a penchant of John Tyndall's ever
since he began leading his Spearhead group in the provinces on week-
ends. The Special Branch had already started to take an interest in its
activities in July 1961, when policemen found such slogans as "Race
War Now" and "Free Eichmann Now" (Eichmann had recently been
abducted by Israeli agents from Argentina to face trial in Jerusalem for
his part in the Final Solution) on the wall of an old stable at Culver-
stone Green in Kent. Tyndall and his lieutenant Roland Kerr-Ritchie
were subsequently observed drilling a squad of eighteen men, dressed
in the Spearhead uniform of gray shirts, sunwheel armbands, boots,
and belts. After the BNP split, Tyndall and Jordan continued to foster
the paramilitary stormtrooper spirit in the NSM. During April and
May 1962 Jordan was regularly watched by detectives as he led the
Spearhead squad on military maneuvers involving mock attacks on an

old tower on Leith Hill near Dorking in Surrey. Such paramilitary training was an integral part of the NSM ideology based on the rise of the Nazis in Germany during the 1920s, while Jordan and Tyndall especially were attracted to the swashbuckling romance of armed struggle in the event of a national crisis. But the Spearhead maneuvers were also intended to rehearse the prowess, drill, and discipline of the British contingent at the Nazi International camp that Jordan planned to host in England for August 1962.

Jordan had already announced before the ill-starred Trafalgar Square rally that the NSM would hold a summer camp, incorporating an international Nazi conference. Against a background of the Union Movement rallies, Mosley's inflammatory speeches, and the NSM's sensational incident, Parliament was seeking action on public disorders and there was demand for a debate on Mosley by the end of July. Labour and Jewish MPs and members of the Jewish community had meanwhile put pressure on the Home Office to refuse the Nazi delegates visas to attend the NSM conference. Once Jordan revealed that Lincoln Rockwell might be attending the camp, the authorities swung into action. On 1 August the home secretary announced that the foreign delegates would not be permitted to land in Britain, and all the airports and seaports were put on a special alert to watch for Rockwell and other known supporters of international Nazi intrigue. Unbeknown to the authorities, Jordan was already confident of Rockwell's attendance by the time he announced its possibility. On 29 July, several days before the Home Office ban was imposed, Rockwell had arrived at Shannon airport and been met by Jordan and Tyndall in Eire. There were no further immigration checks between Ireland and the British mainland, and they had traveled by ferry from Dublin to Liverpool. Rockwell was therefore already staying at a secret accommodation in London by the time that the ports were on the lookout for him. The belated official interest in Rockwell's entry to Britain also enabled most of the other delegates to arrive undetected.

By the time the Home Office ban was announced, Savitri Devi was also among those already in England. She had come to visit Muriel Gantry at her Drury Lane flat in London on 26 July, proudly bearing a large red, white, and black swastika flag for the camp. Miss Gantry did not share her friend's enthusiasm for Hitler and was very troubled when her unpredictable guest unfurled the Nazi flag with excitement at a large window overlooking the busy street. On Tuesday, 31 July the two friends made a long-planned visit to Stonehenge, where Savitri Devi surreptitiously consecrated her flag on the sarsens to the old Aryan gods of Europe. Aware of her friend's plans to attend the NSM international camp and now mindful of the recent reports of Home Office interest in the newspapers, Miss Gantry warned her of the risk that she might be banned from future visits to England. But Savitri Devi was already far too enthused by the prospect of the conference to consider withdrawal. She was determined to plant her Nazi colors on British soil.

On Friday, 3 August, she went to the NSM headquarters at 74 Princedale Road in order to receive instructions on how delegates were to reach the secret camp location. She was admitted to the shop-fronted premises and found a large number of people already present. The atmosphere of Arnold Leese House impressed her greatly. Here right in the midst of Notting Hill, an area of growing colored immigration, the NSM had raised its flag. Young men in uniform shirts with sunwheel armbands, leather belts, and jackboots bustled from room to room with messages and commissions. Meanwhile documents, leaflets, and literature were being stacked in readiness for the conference. Looking around the headquarters, Savitri Devi felt that she was witnessing the emergence of a new Nazi Party, a faithful copy of its original at Munich in the early 1920s. Pictures of Hitler and Rudolf Hess hung on the walls, back numbers of Jordan's various racist and anti-Semitic newspapers and magazines lay around with their shouting headlines and provocative pictures of blacks, while uniforms and jackboots lay stacked in the basement ready for action. All that she saw conjured the image of the Brown House in the early years of the Nazi Party. She shivered with excitement when she recalled that the scene of this new activity was London in the 1960s.

Colin Jordan had two main purposes for holding this international Nazi conference. In the first place, it was important to him to boost the profile and membership of the NSM. At the time of the split with the BNP, he had been left with as few as twenty activists, including John Tyndall, Denis Pirie, and Roland Kerr-Ritchie. While the Trafalgar Square rally had kept the NSM in the spotlight, Jordan was aware that he had to attract more members, not least to compete with the BNP, which was now claiming a membership of one thousand active supporters. The BNP was again holding its annual summer camp over the weekend of 4–5 August on Andrew Fountaine's land at Narford, and

Jordan felt that the NSM had to go one better. By convening and sponsoring an international Nazi conference under NSM auspices, Jordan was essentially outflanking the BNP's claims to be the major neo-Nazi party in Britain and placing himself and his party at the head of a new initiative to coordinate and liaise with other groups worldwide devoted to racial nationalism, anti-Semitism, white supremacism, and the glorification of German National Socialism. His chief motive for the NSM summer camp was to place himself at the head of an international Nazi movement.

Colin Jordan explained to her and other delegates that the camp was being held at a secret site in Gloucestershire and that strict security measures were being taken to ensure that as few people found out about it as possible. They would therefore leave NSM headquarters in small groups to attract minimal attention. Each group would make its way to Paddington railway station and take a train to Cheltenham, where a second rendezvous would be held. From there cars would take them to the camp in the Cotswold Hills. Savitri Devi's excitement mounted at these clandestine arrangements. Taxis set off in different directions to confuse any pursuers and she and several companions were soon steaming down the main line through Swindon to Cheltenham.

It was already evening when she entered the secret camp at Pinnock Cliffs on the edge of Guiting Wood, about a mile from the village of Guiting Power. The camp was sited in a secluded woodland glade beside the headwaters of the River Windrush amid the rolling scenery of the Cotswolds some ten miles east of Cheltenham. John Tyndall was already there with the Spearhead Landrover and about half a dozen large, brown bell tents had already been pitched. Savitri Devi's swastika flag was hoisted on a flagstaff, and several fires were soon alight for an evening meal. After supper the Nazis enjoyed singing German marching songs amid campfire camaraderie. Savitri Devi shared a tent with a Belgian woman, whose son was also attending. After nightfall the camp fell quiet as everyone got a good night's sleep in anticipation of next day's activities.

Soon after dawn on Saturday, 4 August, Savitri Devi awoke to hear John Tyndall's voice booming from one of the other tents. Determined to set a military example, he was calling out that only soft democrats lay abed in the morning. Feeling challenged, she arose and went for a cold bath in the nearby river. Over breakfast she began to make the acquaintance of some of the other foreign delegates, the majority of whom were Germans and Austrians, including former SS Lieutenant Friedrich ("Fred") Borth. There were also a number of Swedes, some Spaniards, one or two Frenchmen, one or two Italians, some Belgians and Dutchmen, and some Americans.

The first morning of the camp passed agreeably while the early arrivals settled in, describing to one another neo-Nazi activities in their various home countries, exchanging and reading their magazines and books. More delegates arrived from Cheltenham in the course of the morning. Meanwhile there were logs to be cut and lunch to be cooked. It was noted that both Jordan and Tyndall had vanished that afternoon and a mood of expectation spread through the camp. Savitri Devi described the general amazement and delight when Lincoln Rockwell was suddenly seen, accompanied by Jordan and Tyndall, as they approached through the woods from the direction of the river. The Horst Wessel Song struck up on a portable gramophone and there was loud applause for the arrival of the leader of the American Nazi Party. As she recalled, the newspapers and the British government had said that Rockwell would be banned, but here he was in defiance of all. It was a special moment of triumph for Jordan and his fellow activists in the NSM that they had secured his presence at the international camp.

Rockwell began by giving a speech about the conspiracy of Jewish interests that dominated world politics and had mobilized all its agents to exclude him from participating in the camp. But National Socialism was getting stronger every day throughout the world, indeed this international camp was proof of this fact. Just as he had got through to the camp, so the future of National Socialism was assured. Savitri Devi was thrilled to see Rockwell and thought him a great personality. He was already well known in Nazi circles from pictures showing a tall, athletic figure, with a dashing lock of hair falling over his forehead, who wore sporting blazers and smoked a pipe whenever not marching in the gray-shirt uniform of his movement. That Saturday evening, at the lamp-lit camp in the depths of rural Gloucestershire, Rockwell spoke about his life, the American Nazi Party, and the future of international Nazism. The ensuing questions and discussions went on deep into the night.

George Lincoln Rockwell had been born on 9 March 1918 in Bloomington, Illinois, the son of theatrical performers.[5] His childhood years had been spent in Maine, New Jersey, and Rhode Island. In 1938 he began to study philosophy and sociology at Brown University, where he became politicized against the liberal, egalitarian tenor of social science and his teachers. He became convinced that liberalism was the "pimping little sister" of communism. Nevertheless, he was heavily influenced by the contemporary buildup of anti-German opinion and enlisted in the United States Navy in March 1941. He served as a naval aviator throughout World War II, commanded the naval air support for the invasion of Guam in August 1944, and was demobilized with the rank of lieutenant commander and several decorations in October 1945. Meanwhile he had married a girl he had known as a student at Brown. Rockwell spent the first five years after leaving the navy studying art and then taking a variety of jobs as a commercial photographer, a painter, an advertising executive, and a publisher, in Maine and New York. In 1950 with the outbreak of the Korean War, Rockwell returned to active duty, training fighter pilots in southern California.

It was here that Rockwell first became politically engaged. The anticommunist revelations of Senator Joseph McCarthy dominated this period, and Rockwell was suspicious of the motives of those wished to smear and discredit him. Through further reading in the San Diego public library, he became convinced of the existence of a Jewish-communist world conspiracy. Rockwell was staggered by the seeming magnitude of the conspiracy as well as the official and media silence concerning its existence. Down in the dark bookstacks of the library one autumn day in 1950, Rockwell experienced his political illumination and awakening. He had always felt that the world was out of joint, that mischief was afoot, but now he had the key to the past and the present. How could he fight against this monstrous and universal plot? The example of Adolf Hitler and his crusade against world Jewry and communism quickly came to mind. Early in 1951 Rockwell found a copy of *Mein Kampf* in a local bookshop, read it, and saw the world anew:

> [Here] I found abundant "mental sunshine," which bathed all the gray world suddenly in the clear light of reason and understanding. Word after word, sentence after sentence stabbed into the darkness like thunderclaps and lightningbolts of revelation, tearing and ripping away the cobwebs of more than thirty years of darkness, brilliantly illuminating the mysteries of the heretofore impenetrable murk in a world gone mad. I was

transfixed, hypnotized. . . . I wondered at the utter, indescribable genius of it. . . . I realized that National Socialism, the iconoclastic world view of Adolf Hitler, was the doctrine of scientific racial idealism—actually a new religion. . . . [6]

Thus was Lincoln Rockwell converted to the religion of National Socialism.

Some eight years were yet to elapse before he became an outspoken Hitlerite at the head of an American Nazi Party. Meanwhile, in November 1952, the navy had assigned him to a base at Keflavik in Iceland, where he spent two years, marrying for a second time and achieving the rank of commander. On returning to civilian life, he decided to enter magazine publishing, hoping to find both a livelihood and a forum for his political ideas. He was also active among conservative groups, planned some sort of confederation, and tried to advance by concealing his Nazi hard-core ideology behind a respectable front. But eventually he despaired of this strategy because it failed to attract dedicated racists and anti-Semites. Prompted by a series of recurrent dreams in the winter of 1957–1958 that always ended with his meeting Hitler, he decided to go public against Jewish power in the United States with the financial patronage of Harold N. Arrowsmith, a wealthy anti-Semite. They formed the National Committee to Free America from Jewish Domination in Arlington, Virginia.

Rockwell's first opportunity for confrontation was provided by the U.S. government's military aid in May 1958 for the Chamoun regime in Lebanon, which was unpopular with Lebanese Arabs but enjoyed the support of the Israelis. On 29 July 1958 Rockwell led a picket of the White House, protesting against Jewish influence on the government, and organized simultaneous demonstrations in Atlanta, Georgia, and Louisville, Kentucky. When a synagogue was blown up in Atlanta on 12 October, the police seized Rockwell's supporters there and newspapers around the world carried stories implicating Rockwell. Now he and his family were harassed and his home was attacked; Arrowsmith retreated from the glare of the publicity and withdrew his support.[7]

Rockwell's wife and children soon found the strain too great and returned to Iceland. Deserted by his family and former supporters, Rockwell faced a bleak and solitary future in the early months of 1959. One cold March morning in his house in Arlington, he found himself alone communing with a huge swastika banner and a plaque of Hitler. Following a "religious experience" involving a brief state of universal awareness, he felt he had attained "wisdom." Now he was utterly convinced he had to fulfill Hitler's mission in a total, global victory over the forces of tyranny and oppression. He would henceforth become an overt National Socialist and self-proclaimed devotee of Hitler, abandoning all thought of liaison with conservative groups and respectability.[8] He proudly displayed his Nazi banner, recruited a handful of storm troopers, to whom he issued gray-shirt uniforms and swastika armbands, mounted an illuminated swastika on the roof of his house, and founded the American Party, later called the American Nazi Party. Besides the party headquarters at his house at 2507 North Franklin Road in Arlington, Rockwell also maintained a barracks in a nearby farmhouse for his growing detachment of storm troopers.

Once Rockwell had decided on a flagrant, open avowal of Nazism, his activity was wholly directed toward the provocation of the Jewish enemy and society at large, which he regarded as its passive victim. Besides the flaunting of Nazi uniforms and insignia, he and his storm troopers missed no opportunity to shock and outrage domestic opinion. From 1960 onward his brash and sensational exploits were designed to achieve maximum press coverage for an otherwise crackpot fringe group. Before curious crowds and eager reporters and surrounded by American and Nazi flags, Rockwell gave speeches advocating a national and then global program of eugenics to purify the Aryan race. He ceaselessly denounced the Jews as representatives of Marxism, unbridled capitalism, racial degeneration, and cultural bolshevism, and demanded their extermination by gassing. Rockwell effectively forced the media to give him publicity by concentrating on the distribution of inflammatory leaflets, creating public incidents, and haranguing crowds to provoke violent opposition. The American Nazi Party also pursued a racist policy toward blacks. In 1961 Rockwell and his storm troopers drove a "Hate Bus" through the southern states. Rejecting all race mixing and desegregation as Jewish wiles to mongrelize the American racial stock, Rockwell proposed to resettle all American blacks in a new African state, to be funded by the U.S. government.

By the time Lincoln Rockwell attended the NSM summer camp in August 1962, he was probably the most notorious neo-Nazi on the contemporary world scene. His intentional clowning tactics had won him international news coverage, in which he could regularly invoke the name of Adolf Hitler, quote *Mein Kampf*, and pay tribute to the Nazi racial crusade against the Jews and all non-Aryan races. It is possible that Colin Jordan noted his exploits in the United States from 1960 and decided to follow his example after the split with the BNP in April 1962. In any case he was in touch with Rockwell as soon as he had launched the NSM. Having convened this international Nazi conference, Jordan was eager to impress his guest of honor with his own credentials for Nazi world leadership. On Sunday morning Jordan demonstrated the military prowess and efficiency of the British Nazis to his guests by putting the Spearhead unit through its paces. Led by John Tyndall, uniformed NSM members were deployed down the valley and attacked sham strong points, rushed imaginary enemy concentrations, and fought off make-believe counterattacks, while Jordan, Rockwell, and Borth watched the maneuvers through field glasses from high ground.

The climax and real business of the camp took place that afternoon and involved all delegates, including Savitri Devi. A new neo-Nazi International called the World Union of National Socialist (WUNS) was set up under the terms of the Cotswold Agreement, whereby Jordan, Rockwell, and the leaders of the foreign National Socialist parties formed a confederation. The major objectives of the WUNS were defined as follows:

1. To form a monolithic, combat-efficient, international political apparatus to combat and utterly destroy the international Jew-Communist and Zionist apparatus of treason and subversion.
2. To protect and promote the Aryan race and its Western Civilization wherever its members may be on the globe, and whatever their nationality may be.
3. To protect private property and free enterprise from Communist class warfare.

Long-term objectives included the "unity of all white people in a National Socialist world order with complete racial apartheid." While much of this would have been quite acceptable to other right-wing and nationalist groups, paragraph 7 of the twenty-five-paragraph codicil formally established the Nazi credentials of the WUNS: "No organization or individual failing to acknowledge the spiritual leadership of Adolf Hitler and the fact that we are National Socialists shall be admitted to membership." Likewise, the long-term objective, "To find and accomplish a just and final settlement of the Jewish problem," identified the WUNS as a direct heir of Hitler's plans for a Final Solution. Jordan was elected world Führer and Rockwell his deputy and heir by the twenty-seven delegates, who with their respective parties became founding members of the WUNS.

But this rural Nazi idyll could not elude the press and public curiosity for long. The comings and goings at the camp, the military maneuvers of the Spearhead group, the constant shouts of "*Sieg Heil!*" and the strains of the Horst Wessel Song deep into the night inevitably drew the attention of local inhabitants and members of the press were informed. On Sunday evening Rockwell was quietly smuggled away from the camp and went to stay at Jordan's Coventry home. Meanwhile some reporters had arrived and a *Daily Mail* photographer, Ann Ward, was struck by an air-gun pellet. She later received an apology from John Tyndall. The press interest became more intense, and on Monday Jordan addressed journalists over a gate at the edge of Guiting Wood. He held up a film showing Rockwell at the camp on Sunday evening and offered it to the highest bidder. He also confirmed that the police had visited the camp that morning but had soon left. However, in the course of the afternoon a Bristol newspaper photographer, Eric Hanson, entered the camp and was set upon by a group of men and his camera was damaged. John Tyndall also held an impromptu meeting by the gateway leading to the camp and fielded questions from a crowd of youths about the uniforms, the flying of the swastika flag, and the liquidation of the Jews in Nazi Germany. Newspaper stories with such enticing headings as "Secret 'Nazi' Camp" and "Jackboots in an English Glade" appeared in *The Daily Telegraph.*[9]

Although the Cotswold Agreement had now been signed and Rockwell had left, it was intended that the camp should continue through the week. Another couple of delegates were still expected from America, and on the morning of Tuesday, 7 August, Savitri Devi volunteered to travel to London in order to collect them. However, on the same day the camp was plunged into crisis. Angry at the unwelcome publicity, a crowd of some twenty villagers from Guiting Power decided to storm the camp on Tuesday evening. After jeers and catcalls, a shot was fired at the swastika flag flying above the tents. This was quickly hauled down by the Nazis, but the villagers managed to grab it. The fighting lasted for about twenty minutes until police reinforcements arrived and the villagers were persuaded to leave the site. Later on, Superintendent Dennis Blick of Cirencester advised Jordan to close the camp in order to avoid further trouble. Meanwhile, the authorities were concerned about the emerging evidence of the American Nazi leader's presence in Britain. On Tuesday evening the home secretary signed a deportation order on Rockwell and asked the police to find him.[10]

Savitri Devi met the American couple at London airport on 8 August. They were concerned to read in that morning's newspapers that the camp had broken up after trouble with the local population and the police were involved. While the Americans decided to stay away, Savitri Devi felt she had no option but to return to collect her suitcase. With mounting anxiety she traveled back by railway to Cheltenham and then by car out to the campsite. Arriving in the early afternoon, she found the camp in turmoil but was able to recover her luggage from a pile of stowed equipment. However, Special Branch officers were present and demanded to see the identification papers of all aliens in the camp. Her Greek passport was examined and a stamp was inserted that she only later discovered barred her from reentry to Britain for a number of years. After returning to London to stay with Muriel Gantry, Savitri Devi was able to keep in touch with the events following the much-publicized Nazi International.

Rockwell and Jordan had talked by telephone with the police from their hideout in Coventry, and Rockwell had decided to give himself up once he had sold his story to the *Daily Mail*. However, the news-paper informed detectives of Rockwell's intentions and he was arrested near its offices in Holborn on Wednesday evening. Meanwhile, a NSM official, Roland Kerr-Ritchie, announced that a letter from Rockwell requesting an audience with the Queen had been delivered to Bucking-ham Palace. After being held overnight at Cannon Row police station, Rockwell was deported by a DC-8 airliner on a scheduled flight to Boston on Thursday morning. Halfway up the steps to the aircraft, Rockwell turned and raised his hand in a Hitler salute. Jordan was evidently kept in ignorance of these rapid developments, for he was still seeking legal advice on how to thwart the deportation order on Thursday afternoon.[11] Worse was to follow for the British Nazis. Just before 8:00 P.M. on Friday, 10 August, a truck covered with a green tarpaulin drew up outside the NSM headquarters in Princedale Road, whereupon a dozen Special Branch officers raided and searched the building for two hours. No arrests were made, but large quantities of documents, flags, uniforms, and weapons, together with portraits of

Hitler and Hess, were seized. Jordan and ten other men were questioned by the police, and three women were also found in the building.[12]

The authorities' clampdown on the NSM effectively removed Colin Jordan from the center of WUNS activities at an early stage following its birth. On 16 August, Jordan, Tyndall, Kerr-Ritchie, and Pirie were charged under the Public Order Act with organizing and equipping a paramilitary force. On 20 August, Savitri Devi attended the magistrates' court at Bow Street, where the NSM leaders were sent to prison for a fortnight for petty offenses. When the main Spearhead trial was held at the Old Bailey in October, the prosecution rested on the more serious charge of the group's self-conscious emulation of the Nazi storm troopers, not least its possession of firearms and materials for making explosives. Jordan was sentenced to nine months' imprisonment, Tyndall to six, and their lieutenants to three each. Leadership of the WUNS now passed to Lincoln Rockwell and the American Nazi Party. With its radical Nazi and anti-Semitic program, the WUNS soon succeeded in attracting many members of the Nouvel Ordre Européen (NOE), founded in 1951 at Zurich, into its own ranks. By the beginning of 1964, the WUNS announced that it maintained national sections in France, Germany, Great Britain, Belgium, Denmark, Switzerland, the United States, Argentina, Chile, and Australia. It was also under Rockwell's leadership of the WUNS that Savitri Devi ultimately became a more widely known figure in international neo-Nazi circles.

The initial contact with Colin Jordan's NSM and early involvement in the WUNS greatly extended Savitri Devi's range of contacts and ideological influence. Typical of these was her friendship with Françoise Dior, a wealthy French heiress and neo-Nazi whose sensational and subversive antics during the 1960s regularly guaranteed her newspaper coverage. Born on 7 April 1932, Françoise Dior was the niece of Christian Dior, the famous Parisian couturier. Growing up in France under the German occupation, she became an avid admirer of Hitler's new racial order; one of her sweetest memories was the compliment of an SS-man, "What a beautiful little Aryan girl." Her other abiding interest was pre-Revolutionary France and she believed, like Savitri Devi, that the ideas of 1789—equality, liberty, and fraternity—were nothing more than a cover for the activities of sinister international elites whose aim was national degeneracy. She was initially a fervent Royalist and married Count Robert-Henri de Caumont-la-Force, a scion of one of

France's oldest noble families. However, their union was unhappy. Disappointed by traditional aristocracy, Françoise Dior reverted to her juvenile enthusiasm for a racial elite. As a result of the sensational reports of Colin Jordan's Trafalgar Square rally, she traveled to London and became a frequent visitor to the headquarters of the NSM in the summer months of 1962.

Jordan began courting Françoise Dior and introduced her to Savitri Devi, whereupon the two women became close friends in France. When the NSM began to revive after the release of John Tyndall, Denis Pirie, and Roland Kerr-Ritchie in the spring of 1963, Dior again became a fanatical supporter of the British neo-Nazis. Romance also blossomed, and she was successively engaged to Tyndall and then Jordan, following their respective releases from prison. She and Colin Jordan were married on 6 October 1963 in a bizarre ceremony complete with Nazi regalia at 74 Princedale Road. Standing at a candlelit table draped with a swastika flag, the couple swore over a dagger that they were of Aryan descent and exchanged their vows. Each then made a small incision in the ring finger, their two fingers were joined to symbolize the union of the blood, and a drop of their mixed blood was then allowed to fall onto an open page of *Mein Kampf*. The couple held hands, and Jordan declared the marriage enacted.[13] The guests gave the Hitler salute and the Horst Wessel Song was played. Savitri Devi was bitterly disappointed that she was unable to be present at the wedding. She had been turned away by the immigration authorities at Dover on one of the several occasions that she tried to reenter Britain following her ban after the Cotswold camp.

Within three months the couple had separated, but they were reconciled once Dior was satisfied that Jordan had demonstrated his powers of leadership in the NSM, which had fallen prey to factionalism. This new split on the far right reflected the causes of the earlier division between the BNP and the NSM. John Tyndall wanted to develop a British form of National Socialism with due emphasis on patriotism, racial pride, and contemporary circumstances. He thought the overt Hitler worship and meticulous imitation of German Nazism so beloved of Jordan attracted ridicule and was a political liability. It is also likely that his humiliation over losing his fiancée to Jordan played a part in the break. In August 1964 Tyndall launched the Greater Britain Movement (GBM) with its own magazine *Spearhead* and some 130 members. Following their acrimonious rupture, Jordan and Tyndall each courted

Rockwell for his party to be recognized as the British section of the WUNS. But Rockwell instinctively sided with Jordan because Rockwell himself had long advocated brazen Nazism and was suspicious of Tyndall's plan to drop the swastika as a political symbol. After his failure to convince Rockwell, Tyndall cultivated contacts with rival U.S. white supremacist groups such as the National States' Rights Party and the National Socialist White Power Movement.[14]

Ever an extremist and the enemy of compromise, Savitri Devi supported the open Hitler cult of Jordan and Rockwell. She greatly regretted that Jordan and Tyndall had fallen out. By 1965, Françoise Dior had become the official WUNS representative in France, which in view of their close friendship, further cemented Savitri Devi's links with Lincoln Rockwell, his deputy Matt Koehl, and the American Nazi Party. Over and above the cause of its sectional European nationalisms, the WUNS was determined to present the racial idealism of National Socialism as a program of global Aryan power to a younger generation of new supporters. When, in the spring of 1966 Rockwell commenced publishing a new WUNS periodical entitled *National Socialist World* from his headquarters in Arlington, a new forum for her own international brand of Nazi ideology had at long last been created. This magazine was to play a crucial role in promoting Savitri Devi to the worldwide readership of the WUNS.

Rockwell had appointed as the periodical's editor Dr. William L. Pierce, a newcomer to the neo-Nazi movement. Pierce was a physicist by profession who had studied at Rice University and the California Institute of Technology, completed his doctorate at the University of Colorado, and then spent three years teaching at Oregon State University. From the outset *National Socialist World* cultivated its image and status as the leading international Nazi periodical with long articles and book reviews written for an educated and literate readership, as well as high standards of production. The magazine was intended as a quarterly, with each issue having more than one hundred pages. The first issue comprised a philosophical appraisal of National Socialism by Colin Jordan and an article by Lincoln Rockwell on the value of vulgar Nazi propaganda; pride of place was given to a condensed edition of Savitri Devi's *The Lightning and the Sun*. Pierce not only had decided to publish her alongside Rockwell and Jordan, the leaders of the WUNS, but had devoted nearly eighty pages of the inaugural issue to her.[15]

For Savitri Devi, this publication represented her literary debut in international neo-Nazi circles. Hitherto, her books extolling National Socialism had been published privately in Calcutta and in limited editions. These had then been given or distributed by means of personal contacts in England, France, and Germany, especially through her ODESSA contacts like Hans-Ulrich Rudel and Otto Skorzeny, as well as the numerous sympathizers and Nazi widows she regularly visited in the 1950s. But through Rockwell and Pierce, her ideas about National Socialism as a religion of nature, the Hindu cycle of the ages, and Hitler's world significance as an avatar were brought before a much wider readership in Western Europe, the United States, South America, and Australia. In the third issue, Pierce announced that the magazine had received such an enthusiastic response to its condensed version of *The Lightning and the Sun* that he had decided to offer its readers more of her writings; there followed excerpts from two chapters of *Gold in the Furnace* in 1967 and from *Defiance* in 1968.[16] This new prestige and notoriety can be traced back to her attendance at Colin Jordan's NSM summer camp and her founding membership of the WUNS in August 1962.

It was also during this period that Savitri Devi began to influence Ernst Zündel in the direction of Holocaust denial, for which he has now achieved worldwide notoriety. Born in Germany in 1939, Zündel had emigrated to Canada in 1958 and settled in Toronto. After meeting Adrien Arcand, the elderly prewar French Canadian fascist leader, Zündel became an ardent German nationalist and apologist for Nazism. Savitri Devi first wrote to Zündel, possibly at Arcand's suggestion, in 1961. Her letters and books made a deep and lasting impression on the budding neo-Nazi. Here, at last, he found that eloquent, high-flown praise of Adolf Hitler and the German people that he so earnestly sought. Savitri Devi's extravagant eulogies of National Socialist doctrine, the Nazi Party, and the SS as the vanguard and bastion of a regenerate Aryan race confirmed his sense of national identity and the German world mission. So impressed was Zündel by Savitri Devi's Aryan idealism that he visited her several times at Montbrison in the 1960s and remained in close touch with her until her final years.

At the time of their first meeting Savitri Devi was interested in Holocaust denial, namely, the attempt to whitewash Nazism by questioning the genocide of the Jews. The French fascist Maurice Bardèche (b. 1907) had been the first to take this view in his trenchant critique of the Allied war crimes trials *Nuremberg ou la terre promise* (1948), which claimed that the genocide of the Jews was mere propaganda. Bardèche's ideas were then taken up by Paul Rassinier (1906–1967), a French socialist who had actually been interned by the Nazis during the occupation in the Buchenwald and Dora camps. Given his left-wing credentials and the fact that he had been a Nazi victim, Rassinier's denial of the genocide was even more attractive to neo-Nazis. The titles of his early books refer to Ulysses's tall stories on his return from legendary lands. That Rassinier was also a vehement anti-Semite was also evident from his writings. He published his denials in *Le mensonge d'Ulysse* (1950), *Ulysse trahi par les siens* (1962), *La véritable procès Eichmann* (1962), and *Le drame des juifs européens* (1964).[17] The controversy over Rassiner's books in France was at its height during the early 1960s; his views would have instantly appealed to Savitri Devi as a neo-Nazi alibi.

Savitri Devi was the first to suggest to Zündel that the Nazi genocide of the Jews was untrue. Zündel went on to make a career out of Holocaust denial, publishing Thies Christophersen's notorious *Auschwitz: Truth or Lie?* (1974) and Richard Harwood's *Did Six Million Really Die?* (1974) in several languages in editions running into many hundreds of thousands. After his initial arraignment in 1983 under an old Canadian statute for publishing falsehoods, Zündel convened the leading theorists of Holocaust denial from across the world as expert witnesses for his appeal trial in 1988. This major revisionist lineup in court consisted of Ditlieb Felderer, Thies Christophersen, Bradley Smith, Mark Weber, Joseph G. Burg, Udo Walendy, Robert Faurisson, and the well-known British historian David Irving. Fred A. Leuchter, an American execution technology specialist, carried out a forensic investigation during the Polish winter on-site at Auschwitz.[18] Thanks to the glare of world media, the existence of these hitherto sectarian neo-Nazi ideas became almost common knowledge. When she relayed this myth of French origin to the young Zündel in the 1960s, Savitri Devi could scarcely have imagined the world audience that he would gain for Holocaust denial through his court cases and appeals by the end of the 1980s.

Throughout the 1960s Savitri Devi continued to reside in France. Between January 1961 and November 1963 she taught in Montbrison and at the same time worked on a new book with the title *Hart wie Kruppstahl* (Hard as Krupp steel). This phrase recalled Hitler's eulogy of National Socialist youth, and her book was intended as a paean to German militarism. She nearly lost her next post in a school at St. Etienne because of opposition from a local league against anti-Semitism as a result of her pro-Nazi statements in class, which included denying the Holocaust. Between 1965 and 1967 she taught in Firminy, just outside St. Etienne, but continued to live in Montbrison. She usually spent her summer holidays visiting old Nazi comrades in Germany and regularly stayed in Bavaria, often at Berchtesgaden in spiritual proximity to her idol Hitler. In September 1968 she was the focus of another friendly gathering of Nazi sympathizers, this time at Munich. Hans-Ulrich Rudel and his wife, Uschi; John Tyndall, now prominent in the National Front, a new far right party in Britain; and Beryl Cheetham, a former Mosleyite and veteran of the Narford and Cotswold camps, spent a happy reunion dinner with Savitri Devi. She later traveled with John Tyndall and Miss Cheetham to the Austrian border for a rendezvous with Fred Borth. Since 1963 he had become involved with pro-German terrorists fighting in South Tyrol (an Austrian province with a German-speaking majority ceded to Italy in 1919) and was now wanted by the German police.

In 1969 a job in Ireland beckoned, but again she was frustrated by the British ban on her entry, and she traveled on to Greece, where she took a small job and gave some private lessons. Since 1968 she had been working on a book of her reflections and memoirs in the French language, and in October 1970 she accepted an invitation from her old friend Françoise Dior to stay and write at her home in Ducey in Normandy. Dior had divorced Colin Jordan in October 1967. Her stormy career in the 1960s included a number of anti-Semitic incidents in London, culminating in her being sentenced in January 1968 at the Old Bailey to eighteen months in Holloway prison for conspiring to commit arson on synagogues. While "inside" she enjoyed the nickname of "Nazi Nell" among fellow inmates.

Savitri Devi had now passed her sixty-fifth birthday and had no further prospect of earning her living in French state schools. However, she had built up a small pension entitlement from the past nine years' service, and the question arose as to where she should now spend her retirement and continue writing on such slender means. The cost of living was very high in France, Britain was closed to her, and despite her well-wishers in America, she had no prospects of an U.S. residence permit. A return to India had much to commend it. She had spent many years in the country and enjoyed its ambience. She still had the friendship of her husband, who now lived in Delhi, even if they had long lived separate lives. A number of supporters provided her airfare, and on 23 June 1971 Savitri Devi flew from Paris to Bombay. She arrived in Delhi in August and stayed for a while in the guest rooms of the Hindu Mahasabha office, completing the manuscript of *Souvenirs et réflexions d'une aryenne*, an intellectual autobiography combined with her final statement of Aryan racist religion.

Once she and her husband had found a new home in Delhi, she resumed writing, returning as ever to the racial basis of history and her abiding obsession with the Jews. A new book in French, entitled *Ironies et paradoxes dans l'histoire et la légende*, was begun. This was an anthology of historical curiosities, including the strongly Christian upbringing of Josef Goebbels, against which he had rebelled. But the book was chiefly concerned with the apparent paradoxes of Jewish history. These included the Jews' acquisition of banking skills from the Aryan Kassite dynasty during the period of their Babylonian exile under Nebuchadnezzar. But for the destruction of the second Temple by Titus (A.D. 70) and the dispersal of the Jews by Hadrian (A.D. 135), she was certain that the Jews would have been overwhelmed by Islam in the seventh century. By this time, however, they had been dispersed in comparative safety around the Mediterranean and in the Germanic world, and so Europe inherited the "Jewish Question." Although physically remote, she still busily corresponded with Colin Jordan, Matt Koehl, Ernst Zündel, and others around the world. It was in this fashion that her ideas were passed on to a new generation of mystical neo-Nazis from the late 1970s into the 1990s.

12

LAST YEARS AND LEGACY
Nazis, Greens, and the New Age

Once again Savitri Devi lived in the tropical world of faraway India. This was the country to which she had first traveled in search of the Aryan race in 1932 and where she had remained, throughout all her hopes of the Third Reich, until 1945. Now she had returned as a sixty-six-year-old pensioner. New Delhi was planned by Sir Edwin Lutyens when the British moved their imperial capital from Calcutta to the northern plain in 1911. This spacious and gracious city of modern palaces, extensive parks, and broad avenues still bristled with old forts, towers, mosques, and temples recalling India's legends, gods, and dynasties. She and her husband first lived in New Delhi in a small apartment on South Extension Park One until 1973, when they moved to similar accommodation at C-23 on South Extension Park Two. This crowded suburb lay five miles south of the old walled city but within walking distance of the diplomatic enclave. Such meager income as they enjoyed was derived from her French pension and earnings as a teacher at a French school until the summer of 1977. After a period of illness, her husband died on 21 March 1977. From Delhi, Savitri Devi continued to follow the fortunes of neo-Nazi groups and parties in Europe and America and conducted a busy correspondence with her die hard comrades scattered around the world. Through these links she maintained her continuing influence and reputation in the international Nazi movement. But there is more. Her association with Hinduism and oriental religions, her biocentric view of nature and fanatical concern with animal welfare have offered present-day Nazis the opportunity to disguise their entry into the occult, Green, and New Age movements.

From Toronto Ernst Zündel wrote to her proposing a new edition of her books and outlining his plans to record an extensive interview with her. Since the early 1970s his neo-Nazi publishing house Samisdat had been issuing tracts on Holocaust denial, including Thies Christophersen's *Auschwitz: Truth or Lie?* (1974), which was a runaway success among anti-Zionists, the far right, and German patriots in the United States. It also had made money for Zündel and established Samisdat as a flourishing underground Nazi publishing concern. By the summer of 1979, more than 100,000 copies of the book in five languages had been sold. At this time Zündel was also pandering to the market for mysteries and occultism with books on Nazi UFOs that were based at secret German postwar bases in Antarctica. Willibald Mattern, a German émigré in Santiago de Chile, had spun a powerful tale of Nazi resurgence. His book, *UFOs: Unbekanntes Flugobjekt? Letzte Geheimwaffe des Dritten Reiches* (UFOs: Unidentified flying object? Last secret weapon of the Third Reich) (1974), described how thousands of Nazi UFOs will one day fly forth from the South Pole to restore German world power against a scenario of increasing racial chaos and economic catastrophe in a final act of deliverance.[1]

Mattern's work was a resounding underground success in West Germany, linking the market for mysteries and extraterrestrial visitations with millenarian myths of German salvation. Zündel lost no time in publishing an abridged English-language version, which introduced yet more occult speculations. Did the Nazis in Antarctica gain access to the "Inner Earth," long ago described in Nordic legends and sagas and assiduously cultivated by the Thule Society? Had the Nazis discovered long-hidden secrets on their expeditions to the Himalayas and Tibet? Perhaps extraterrestrials from other galaxies had assisted the Germans with the saucer projects, having recognized their receptiveness to the new technology. Perhaps this collaboration was based on some shared ancestral kinship. Zündel recalled Reinhold Schmidt's account of a "Saturnian" spacecraft, whose crew spoke German and behaved like German soldiers, and speculated whether the German nation was indeed a colony of Saturn, long since settled on Earth. Why were the Germans so "different"? Could this explain why the Germans always excel as soldiers, engineers, and technologists? Was Hitler planted on this planet to pull back Western civilization from the brink of degenerate self-extinction?[2]

Besides the Mattern book, Samisdat also published Zündel's own books on the German Antarctic theme, *Secret Nazi Polar Expeditions*

(1978) and *Hitler am Südpol?* (1979). In the former, Zündel dilated on
the enigma of extensive German wartime activity involving bases,
mountain troops, and U-boat patrols within the Arctic Circle. He asked
whether there was a shortcut from the Arctic to Antarctica. Had the
Nazi expeditions discovered a more direct way to Antarctica via Green-
land, Spitzbergen, or the North Pole? "Only time will tell us what is
really up there or down there, or should we say, IN there?"[3] Further
titles in the planning stage on the secrets of the poles included *The
C.I.A.-U.F.O. Cover-Up*, *The Antarctica Theory*, and *The Last Battal-
ion*. In 1978 Zündel sent out a large mailing to readers in North
America and West Germany, advertising a proposed Samisdat Hollow
Earth Expedition to Antarctica on a specially chartered Boeing 747 to
search for Nazi UFO bases and the entrances to the Inner World. The
idea of Nazi UFOs caught on fast. The British author W. A. Harbinson
wrote a best-selling novel *Genesis* (1980) on the theme, which was
reprinted five times in three years. Harbinson has since expanded this
novel into a tetralogy, *Projekt Saucer* (1991–1995), and also published
a nonfiction study, *Projekt UFO: The Case for Man-Made Flying Sau-
cers* (1995). Several heavily documented studies about the Nazi UFOs
were published by Hugin, a neo-Nazi research group in the Ruhr.[4]

The mystical ideas of Savitri Devi, the aged Aryan Hindu prophetess,
now fitted well into Samisdat's publishing program. Her identification
of Hitler as an avatar, her celebration of ancient Vedic texts as Aryan-
Nazi scripture, the whole mythological and devotional cast of her
thought concerning her beloved Führer and the Third Reich were a
perfect complement to Mattern's Hitler-survival myths and Nazi UFO
apocalyptic. Ernst Zündel decided to relaunch Savitri Devi with a new
illustrated Samisdat edition of *The Lightning and the Sun* (1979), the
result of her lifelong meditations on history and religion. In a short
preface, he remembered the privilege and pleasure of meeting the pro-
phetic and talented Aryan writer years before in southern France. She
was, he recalled, a true revelation and a source of many mysteries to
him, the embodiment of ancient Aryan India, the repository of the
Aryan racial memory. Her gifts of psychic vision and insight had enabled her to express better than anyone else the meaning of Adolf
Hitler and National Socialism, not only for Germany, or even for the
white race, but for all mankind. "The name, Savitri Devi, will be remembered in White History as one of the truly great names of Our
Race, when our history is once again written by White historians."[5]

Besides giving details of a further six Savitri Devi titles, an appendix announced an appeal to raise funds to republish *Pilgrimage*.

Zündel also produced a set of five two-hour audiocassettes recording extended interviews with Savitri Devi to coincide with the publication of the book. Already in November 1978 he had arranged for a German agent to fly from Frankfurt am Main to Delhi to conduct taped interviews with his old mentor from the 1960s. "Discovered alive in India: Hitler's guru!" read one of his sales flyers, and it was indeed a strange experience to hear the harsh, self-confident voice of Savitri Devi speaking clearly amid the raucous, bustling squalor and street sounds of distant India. For ten hours she related the story of her youth in France and her mission to India in the 1930s. The excitement of her propaganda tours in occupied Germany, arrest and imprisonment, and contacts with the neo-Nazis in the 1960s completed the chronicle of her Aryan pagan mission across the decades. It was another Samisdat masterstroke of surprise and publicity, precisely because Savitri Devi was such a strange and exotic veteran of the Nazi movement. Just how many neo-Nazi sympathizers knew what had become of her since her WUNS days in the mid-1960s? Even if Zündel could not find Hitler in Antarctica, he had produced his forgotten priestess in a fabulous and faraway country.

But Savitri Devi had remained in regular contact with the Anglo-American leaders of the neo-Nazi movement. Matt Koehl, who had become leader of the National Socialist White People's Party (NSWPP) and the WUNS in 1967 after Rockwell's assassination, was making his movement into a full-blown Hitler cult and had a particular affinity for Savitri Devi. For him, Nazi ideology was a creed and a new faith that would lead to an upheaval of unprecedented magnitude.[6] Besides his periodicals *White Power*, *The National Socialist*, and *NS Bulletin*, Koehl promoted a variety of books by Hitler, Alfred Rosenberg, Rudolf Hess, and Colin Jordan, and Savitri Devi's *Souvenirs et réflexions d'une aryenne* to his international WUNS mailing list. His books, *The Future Calls* (1972) and *Faith of the Future* (1995), set forth the "racial idealism" of modern Hitlerism, regularly invoking religious mythology and symbolism. On the occasion of Hitler's birthday in April 1987, he recalled the words of the *Bhagavad Gita*, that "ancient book of Aryan wisdom and insight" according to Savitri Devi: "Age after age, when justice is crushed, when evil reigns supreme, I come; again am I born on Earth to save the world." Mingling Hindu, pagan, and Christian motifs, Koehl ruminated on nature's eternal message of renewal and resurrection.[7]

William Pierce's publication of her writings in *Nationalist Socialist World* (1966–1968) had brought her new admirers in the United States like the violent Nazi fanatic James N. Mason. Born in 1952, Mason spent an alienated youth in Ohio before joining Rockwell's Nazis in 1966. By 1968 he had a full-time job in the Arlington headquarters. When the party split into various factions in 1970, Mason initially remained loyal to Koehl's NSWPP but later rejected the mass strategy of electioneering in favor of subversive terrorism. His inspiration was Joseph Tommasi (b. 1951), a young leader of the NSWPP in southern California who had founded the National Socialist Liberation Front (NSLF) in 1974. Aping the militant left, Tommasi called for a guerrilla war with racial killings and direct attacks on "the Jewish power structure" of the United States. The NSLF maintained overseas links with the extremist British Movement in England. The NSLF's advocacy of armed struggle would not be matched for a decade in the United States until the terrorist outrages of The Order in the mid-1980s, based on William Pierce's novel about a global white revolution, *The Turner Diaries* (1978). In 1980, Mason revived the NSLF (lapsed after Tommasi's assassination in 1975) as a forerunner of new militant American white-supremacist movements committed to armed struggle against the so-called Zionist Occupation Government.[8]

Mason now relaunched the NSLF journal *Siege*, in which he preached violence, racial strife, and an all-out war against the hated "system." In his quest for extremist mentors, Mason next became obsessed with Charles Manson (b. 1934), the notorious psychopathic killer serving life imprisonment for conspiracy in the murders of the actress Sharon Tate and others in 1969. By the late 1970s Manson had begun to assume an underground cult status as the supreme outlaw who had taken direct action against a corrupt society. He claimed the "system" was killing the world: human survival depended on a simple ecological philosophy based on air, trees, water, and animals. Meanwhile he had carved a swastika on his forehead as a badge of his renegade spirit. By 1982 James Mason had adopted Manson as the spiritual leader of his new Nazi group, the Universal Order (the name came from Manson), and its campaign of destruction against the alleged insanity of liberal American society. The Universal Order's insistence on the balance of nature coupled with a call for apocalyptic violence against a rotten mankind bears an uncanny resemblance to the sentiments of Savitri Devi. In the pages of *Siege* Mason paid extravagant tribute to Hitler, Tommasi, Manson, and Savitri Devi.[9]

But Savitri Devi also had her admirers in Britain. Her old friend John Tyndall was meanwhile a prominent leader of the National Front (NF) in England. Founded in 1967 as an alliance of racial populist parties, the new party experienced electoral surges as a result of immigration scares involving the Ugandan Asians (1972) and Malawi Asians (1976). Until its decline after the 1979 general election, the NF threatened to become the third party in British politics.[10] Savitri Devi was excited by this prospect, but her favorite contact in England remained the hard-core Nazi Colin Jordan.

In 1968 Jordan had reorganized the National Socialist Movement as the British Movement (BM) and recruited street toughs, skinheads, and soccer hooligans from the ranks of alienated white urban youth as shock troops for racial attacks on immigrants. During the 1970s the BM was at the forefront of terrorist efforts to provoke a color war in Britain, destabilize the state, and prepare the way for a neo-Nazi coup. Scorning the NF's parliamentary ambition, the BM reflected Jordan's long-standing obsession with Hitler and National Socialism, backed by a violent private militia. Through all the splits on the British Nazi scene, Savitri Devi had always followed Jordan's extreme lead. Jordan still recalled her memory years after her death. On the hundredth anniversary of Hitler's birth, Jordan used her terminology and wrote "The Man against Time" in a commemorative article for Matt Koehl's *NS Bulletin*.[11]

Jordan retained his admiration for Savitri Devi and often recommended her writings to his more literate BM members. One of his young bodyguards, David Myatt (b. 1952), was so enthused by the eulogy of Nazi values in *The Lightning and the Sun* that he recalled its impact in an interview more than twenty years later.[12] A violent neo-Nazi activist, Myatt started his own National Democratic Freedom Movement in 1974 and was twice imprisoned for public order offenses in the 1970s. He meanwhile embraced satanism as an extreme expression of Nazi paganism and was involved in Jordan's "Vanguard Project" to create Nazi rural communes in the mid-1980s. Since the early 1990s Myatt has reemerged as the publicist of an "Aryan religion" that owes much to the idealized Hitlerism of Savitri Devi. His Nazi sect Reichsfolk acts as a cadre of the current British neo-Nazi scene, which now imitates American terrorist models and calls for a white racial enclave in East Anglia. Myatt and his Nazi satanic group, the Order of Nine Angles, are close to a similar cult in New Zealand, the Ordo Sinistra Vivendi, whose leader Kerry Bolton has published a condensed edition of *The Lightning and the Sun* (1994), promoting it alongside an interview with James Mason.[13]

Following Zündel's new publicity, Savitri Devi even received visits in Delhi from young neo-Nazi pilgrims. One of these was Christian Bouchet from France. Born in 1955 into a radical-right family with strong Vichy and OAS links, Bouchet had been involved in monarchist, fascist, and nationalist groups since his early teenage years. During the 1970s he was a member of the Organization Lutte du Peuple and the Groupes Nationalistes Révolutionnaires. Through the mystical fascist writings of Julius Evola (1898–1974), he discovered tantricism and Shivaism and visited India three times, staying for a year. During this time he sought out Savitri Devi to learn more about the Kali Yuga and the Hitler avatar. In 1991, Bouchet founded Nouvelle Résistance, a new revolutionary nationalist movement, and the European Liberation Front, which revives the ideas of Francis Parker Yockey for a fascist continental bloc. He now busily liaises with Libyan nationalists and Mexican national revolutionaries, while his magazine *Lutte du Peuple* promotes the idea of an alliance between Third Way movements in Britain, Spain, Italy, Germany, and Russia. He has issued editions of Savitri Devi, Yockey, Gabriele D'Annunzio, Jean-François Thiriart, Louis Auguste Blanqui, José Antonio Primo de Rivera, Pierre Drieu La Rochelle, and Robert Brasillach. Bouchet is also involved in magic, fringe masonry, and gnosticism. He publishes an esoteric journal, *Thelema*, and his imprint carries titles by Aleister Crowley and his followers, Jack Parsons, Frater Achad, and Austin Osman Spare.[14]

A regular correspondent from Germany was Lotte Asmus of Sylt in Schleswig-Holstein. Her family had been dedicated Nazi supporters during the Third Reich, and she had been a keen member of the Bund Deutscher Mädel during the 1930s. At some stage in the late 1970s she had discovered the books of Savitri Devi and begun writing to her. Lotte Asmus was married to a retired Italian headmaster and had good links to neofascist circles in Italy because she and her husband spent part of the year at Terracina near Rome. She proposed to translate Savitri Devi into German and sought a publisher. Her first choice for translation, *Gold in the Furnace*, recalled her own postwar impressions of defeated Germany and its privations. In 1982, Edizioni di Ar published Asmus's German-language edition of Savitri Devi's *Gold in the Furnace* in its "Sturm" series. Its narrative is suffused by her glowing account of the unbroken Nazi spirit of the various individuals she befriended and their undimmed enthusiasm for Hitler and the Third Reich. The book was distributed in Germany by Thies Christophersen's Kritik-Verlag in Mohrkirch in Schleswig-Holstein. The text made a strong propaganda offering to a new generation of young German neo-Nazis looking for new ideological tools to glorify the Nazi past.

Savitri Devi's publication by Edizioni di Ar marked her arrival as a author in the Italian neofascist scene, renowned for both its terrorism and intellectual following. Franco Freda, the notorious Italian neofascist finally tried in 1978 for his part in the bombings of 1969, originally founded Edizioni di Ar in Padua in 1964. Its list includes memoirs by Léon Degrelle, Goebbels, and the French fascist Drieu La Rochelle; a three-volume work by Hitler entitled *Idee sul destino del mondo*; and new critical editions of works by such conservative revolutionaries as Julius Evola, Oswald Spengler, Werner Sombart, and Othmar Spann. The imprint consciously cultivates the idea of a pagan Aryan heritage through the Romans and the European peoples with artwork showing prehistoric artifacts of Indo-European origin. Edizioni di Ar also publishes an annual review, *Risguardo* (1980–), which contains articles on the ancient Aryans, the New Europe, and Third Position. Its fourth volume carried an article by Lotte Asmus and Vittorio De Cecco devoted to Savitri Devi as the "missionary of Aryan paganism," with a review of her life, works, and influence.[15]

Savitri Devi's work had already appeared in Italian translation with the publication of *L'India e il Nazismo* by Edizioni all'insegna del Veltro of Parma in 1979. The publisher, Claudio Mutti, is a prominent member of the Italian far right. Formerly a lecturer in East European languages at Padua University, he had edited an edition of Julius Evola's *L'autenticité dei Protocolli provata della tradizione ebraica* (The authenticity of the Protocols as proven by the Hebrew tradition) for Edizioni di Ar in 1976. He also published a new edition of the *Protocols* with his own introductory essay entitled "Hebrews and Hebrewdom." An admirer of Islamic fundamentalism and Franco Freda's brand of armed right-wing terrorism to provoke revolution, Mutti styles himself a "Nazi Maoist." His own imprint, Veltro, offers a wide range of books on symbolism, tradition, golden-age myths, paganism, and Islam, together with works by Nazis and fascists, including Horia Sima, Corneliu Codreanu, and Robert Brasillach, and Holocaust denial texts. Steeped in the antimodernist sentiment of Julius Evola, Mutti is drawn to the works of the Traditionalists René Guénon and Frithof Schuon as a negation of the secular world.

As a Muslim convert and Third Positionist, Mutti combines anti-Semitism with virulent anti-Westernism, mirrored in his editions of Rûhollâh and Imâm Khomeyni, and the Iranian Mujâhidîn and its declaration of a holy war against the infidels. In his introduction to Savitri Devi's *L'India e il Nazismo*, a translation of the tenth chapter of her *Souvenirs et réflexions d'une aryenne* (1976), Mutti claims that while "the spiritual dimension of Nazism has been ignored in the West, it is intuitively understood by those traditional peoples of India, North Africa, Japan, and Afghanistan who have a concept of holy war." He suggests that Savitri Devi's "Hitlerian esotericism" throws new light on the Hindu regard for Hitler as an avatar of Vishnu, and sees a similar motive in his honorific title *hâjj* (pilgrim) among Muslims. Mutti mentions Hitler's own recognition of his providential status among non-European peoples ("Already Arabs and Moroccans are mingling my name with their prayers," *Hitler's Table Talk*, 12/13 January 1942). Mutti wholeheartedly agrees with Savitri Devi's conception of Hitler as a "Universal Restorer" of a pristine order akin to the Kalki avatar or the Mâhdi.[16] By this means Claudio Mutti assimilates Savitri Devi into his own neofascist war against the profane West. It is perhaps noteworthy that Mutti first encountered Savitri Devi through reading the fervent prose of *Pilgrimage* as an idealistic teenager.

Further Italian translations of her work have been published in *Arya*, an émigré neofascist journal published by Vittorio De Cecco in Montreal.[17] De Cecco was a former member of Unità Italica, a Canadian section of the far-right Italian terrorist group Ordine Nuovo (New Order). This organization was founded in the early 1960s by Pino Rauti, formerly of the fascist MSI party, and led by Stefano delle Chiaie, who was responsible for many ultraright bombings intended to create a state of tension propitious for a military coup in the early 1970s. The Canadian section was active as an émigré support group from 1964 to 1971. Graduating to the philosophical sources of Italian terrorism, De Cecco founded a Canadian affiliate of the Centro Studi Evoliani (Genoa) in 1976 to promote Evola studies in Montreal. But De Cecco soon broadened his brief to embrace an outspoken neo-Nazism and began publishing *Arya* to reflect this political line. The articles on Savitri Devi were duly characteristic of his attempts to popularize a pan-Aryan universal Nazism among Italian émigrés (and terrorist fugitives) in North America.

Savitri Devi has also become known in the Spanish-speaking world. Through the WUNS she came into contact with Franz Pfeiffer, a German Nazi who had fled to Chile after the war. In 1963 he had founded the Partido Nacional Socialista Obrero Chileno (National Socialist Chilean Workers' Party), which joined the WUNS. During the Allende era, Pfeiffer edited a clandestine fascist newsletter, and after the 1973 coup he published a monthly journal. He too corresponded with Savitri Devi and received copies of her books for publicity in his journal. It is most probable that Miguel Serrano, the retired Chilean diplomat and author of several devotional books on Hitler, first encountered her work through his fellow fascist and countryman Franz Pfeiffer. Serrano's own occult brand of neo-Nazism presents a heady brew of ancient Teutonic mysteries, Hinduism and yoga, Jungianism, Gnosticism, and the Western esoteric tradition. He also adopts Savitri Devi's idea of Hitler as the divine avatar of the Aryan race. This unique constellation has led to the introduction of Nazi mysticism among occult and New Age groups.

Born in 1917, Serrano had already joined the Chilean Nazi Party in 1939 and edited a pro-Axis periodical *La Nueva Edad* (The new age) in Santiago during the early war years. He subsequently entered the diplomatic service as Chilean ambassador in India (1953–1962), Yugoslavia (1962–1964), and Austria (1964–1970). During this time he acquired an international reputation as a poet and mystical writer and formed friendships with Hermann Hesse and Carl Gustav Jung. Following his summary dismissal in 1971 by the new Marxist government in Chile, Serrano reverted to his fascist past and articulated a new cult of "Esoteric Hitlerism." While living as an exile in Switzerland, he wrote *El Cordón Dorado: Hitlerismo Esotérico* (The golden band: Esoteric Hitlerism) (1978), which presented a convoluted Nazi mythology involving the Knights Templar, the Cathars, the Holy Grail, and the Rosicrucians. The trilogy was completed by *Adolf Hitler, el Último Avatāra* (Adolf Hitler, the last avatar) (1984) and *Manú: "Por el hombre que vendra"* (Manu: "For the man who will come") (1991). During the 1970s Serrano befriended many old Nazis in Europe, including Léon Degrelle, Otto Skorzeny, Hans-Ulrich Rudel, and Hanna Reitsch, the famous aviatrix. He visited Julius Evola in Rome and Herman Wirth, the aged former director of Himmler's Ahnenerbe, in West Germany. He also knew the former French Waffen-SS man and author, Saint Loup, whose novels about the "Nazi mysteries" had given him much inspiration.

Serrano's neo-Nazi mythology may be traced to his wartime enthusiasm for Hitler, anti-Semitism, and initiation into a Chilean esoteric order practicing yoga, tantricism, and a Nietzschean will to power. He elaborates a Gnostic doctrine describing the celestial origin of the Aryans, the bearers of divine light, and a global conspiracy against them by the evil demiurge, the regent of our planet and all base matter, personified by the Jews. Serrano claims that Hitler was an avatar, an archetypal eruption of the Aryan racial unconscious against the reign of the demiurge and his minions. He took this idea from Carl Gustav Jung's notion of the collective unconscious as a store of ancestral racial memory. Serrano well understood how Jung's ideas owed much to his interest in Mithraism and other supposed Aryan cults, gleaned from Theosophy and the occult-*völkisch* milieu of the early 1900s.[18] Serrano's Aryo-Nordicist inspiration is plainly evident in his assimilation of the Aryans' polar home, Sanskrit terminology, and yoga. Meditation, mudras, and mantras are supposed to repurify the blood to its former quality of divine light, transforming the Aryan into a god-man. For instance, Serrano interprets the Hitler salute as a mudra for drawing cosmic energy into the *chakras*, the subtle energy centers of kundalini yoga.[19]

Although he gave the Hitler avatar a Gnostic-Jungian slant, Serrano had evidently immersed himself in Hindu mythology and Savitri Devi's *The Lightning and the Sun*. Like her, Serrano also identified Hitler as an avatar of the gods Vishnu, Shiva, or Wotan, come to lead the heroic Aryans back to their long-lost divinity.[20] Serrano paid frequent tribute to Savitri Devi and has twice published an account of her own visit to the Externsteine and ritual death and reawakening in the Tomb Rock. He described her "as the greatest fighter after Adolf Hitler, Rudolf Hess, and Josef Goebbels . . . the first to discover the secret and spiritual power behind Hitlerism." He noted her belief in the incompatibility of Nazism and Christianity, predicting that posterity would revere her as a pioneer of "Esoteric Hitlerism" and "the priestess of Odin."[21] Serrano combined his thoughts on the Hitler avatar with Nazi UFO myths. He claimed that Hitler had escaped from the Berlin bunker and remained some years at a secret base in Antarctica before his translation to Venus and thence to the Black Sun, the original home of the extraterrestrial Aryans before their Gnostic descent into time, space, and matter.[22]

By early 1980, Savitri Devi was regularly corresponding with Miguel Serrano, who had returned from Switzerland to Chile after Allende's fall. She expressed great interest in his "Esoteric Hitlerism" but worried about Serrano's disagreement with Manfred Roeder, with whom she also corresponded, about the Russian potential for neofascism and made a plea for good relations within the embattled neo-Nazi camp. Most of her long letters revolved around the themes of her books, such as the coming of the last avatar (Hitler now being accounted the last but one) and England's betrayal of Hitler's peace plan. As retribution, she prophesied that England would disappear within three hundred years in a chaos of racial confusion and vice. She also sent Serrano her martial poem "And Time Rolls on," a bitter postwar memoir of her grief at the defeat of the Third Reich, which ends with the refrain "Faithful when all become unfaithful—while we never forget, never forgive." Serrano praised her extravagantly as a warrior and thanked the gods that he knew about her. It was, he considered, a privilege to have lived at the same time as her and their Führer.[23]

Serrano's Esoteric Hitlerism trilogy was originally published in Chile, Colombia, and Spain, but there is evidence that his ideas have now begun to percolate through the rest of world. A German translation of *El Cordón Dorado; Hitlerismo Esotérico* was published in 1987 by Richard Schepmann's Teut-Verlag in Wetter, West Germany, which specializes in reprints from the SS Ahnenerbe's Nordland press and dossiers on Nazi UFOs. Serrano was the subject of long in-depth illustrated interviews in the Spanish neofascist journal *Cedade* and the Greek far-right magazine *TO ANTIΔOTO*.[24] More recently, he has been featured in the underground literature of the Black Order, a small international neo-Nazi organization with lodges in Britain, the United States, Italy, Sweden, Australia, and New Zealand. The Black Order combines Hitlerite mythology with Nazi satanism in a Nordic pagan denial of the Christian roots of Western civilization.[25]

Serrano's mystical neo-Nazism and references to Savitri Devi have a distinct appeal to the younger generation. Here Nazism becomes a pop mythology, severed from the historic context of the Third Reich. The Gnostic Cathars, Rosicrucian mysteries, Hindu avatars, and extraterrestrial gods add a sensational and occult appeal to powerful myths of elitism, planetary destiny, and the cosmic conspiracy of the Jews that culminate in a global, racist ideology of white supremacism. In interviews Serrano seeks to engage a younger audience by juxtaposing his magical vision of National Socialism with a corrupt, saturated image of modern liberalism, a contrasting that appeals to Green and New Age audiences. Using heroic and epic metaphors, Serrano opposes the mystique of archetypes, ancient Aryan gods, and lost continents to the Jewish "black magic" of money, computerization, nuclear power, and ecological degradation.[26] His numerous references to Savitri Devi have fostered interest in her work as a precursor of his, and a new edition of *The Lightning and the Sun* was published by Renaissance Press for the Black Order in 1994. Books by Serrano and Savitri Devi are now circulating among neopagans, satanists, skinheads, and Nazi metal music fans in the United States, Scandinavia, and Western Europe.[27]

By the time of her taped interviews for Zündel's Samisdat in November 1978, Savitri Devi was already suffering from one cataract and her eyesight deteriorated further over the following year. Myriam Hirn, a middle-aged clerk from the French embassy, befriended her and looked after her with regular house visits. By early 1981 Savitri Devi had cataracts in both eyes and underwent an operation that left her nearly blind. Following a stroke, she suffered partial paralysis of her right leg and hand. Myriam Hirn now read her mail aloud to her and also wrote on her behalf to Serrano and other correspondents. However, her powers of recovery were not to be underestimated and she rallied. In the meantime, Zündel's publicity and appeals for charity had led to several offers of financial help and health care. Encouraged by this response, Savitri Devi decided to leave India and travel once again to Germany, her land of hope for an Aryan revival.

With the aid of friends, Savitri Devi was able to return to Germany in October 1981 and first stayed at a Bavarian home for the elderly. She moved on to stay with Frau Elisabeth Ettmayr, an old friend who lived in Traunstein near the Chiemsee in Upper Bavaria. It was at this time that she first met Lotte Asmus, who traveled to Prien on the Chiemsee to visit her. There were also other contacts in Munich. Later, in the spring of 1982, Savitri Devi lived at an old people's home in Alix near Lozanne (Rhône) in France but she soon wanted to be on the move again. In late June she returned to Germany, staying for more than a month with Georg Schrader and his wife in Steinen near Lörrach. In August she returned with the Schraders to Frau Ettmayr, and together they visited Hans-Ulrich Rudel in Kufstein just over the Austrian border. She had not seen her hero Rudel since the late 1960s when visiting Bavaria during school holidays; it was to see such old Nazi comrades that she had wished to return to Germany.

It was however evident to all concerned that Savitri Devi was stranded in Europe with scant means of support. Rudel generously offered to pay for Savitri Devi's return flight to India but she seemed in no hurry to leave. Frau Schrader's impression is that she intended to return to India in due course but was excited at the prospect of revisiting more old contacts. After another short stay in Traunstein, she visited friends in Munich, and then traveled on to France. While staying with friends in Nantes, word came from Matt Koehl in Arlington, Virginia, that a visa and funds were available for her to travel and stay in the United States. He had arranged for her to address American racist and Nazi groups in seven or eight cities. Savitri Devi was immensely proud of this invitation and quickly accepted Koehl's offer. Although half blind and lame, unable to read and write, she took the view that she could still lecture. Despite her acute infirmity, Savitri Devi saw this trip as a fitting finale of her lifelong Nazi witness and secretly indulged thoughts of martyrdom at the hands of a Jewish or Negro assassin. In the meantime, she made a stopover in England, to visit her oldest friend, Muriel Gantry.

On Sunday, 17 October 1982, Savitri Devi arrived by taxi from London's Victoria station at Moira Cottage, Muriel Gantry's cozy small home in the sleepy Essex village of Sible Hedingham. It was an expensive fare, but Miss Gantry had already been alerted to her impending arrival by the police, who still kept a watchful eye on Savitri Devi's entries to Britain. Although the two elderly women had not met since the 1960s, they had regularly kept in touch by letter. Their friendship extended back to London in 1946 when a common enthusiasm for Akhnaton and ancient Egypt had brought them together. It was perhaps one of Savitri Devi's few nonpolitical friendships, for Miss Gantry had no time for Hitler or National Socialism. Muriel Gantry had visited Savitri Devi and her mother at Lyons in autumn 1950 and twice traveled to stay with her in Athens, in February 1953 and again in the summer of 1961. The two women spent the next couple of days happily sharing reminiscences before an roaring coal fire. Savitri Devi was eagerly anticipating her visit to the United States and even hoped to see Japan on the return leg of her journey to India.

But Savitri was unwell. Wearing only a thin white sari, she looked fragile in the English autumn weather. At noon on Thursday she was complaining of fever. Miss Gantry called a doctor, who thought the problem was mainly due to recent changes in diet and water supply. Later that night, just after midnight, Muriel Gantry heard Savitri Devi breathing heavily and shortly afterward found her dead in her bed in the front room of the cottage. It was 12:25 A.M. on Friday, 22 October. The doctor recorded the causes of death as myocardial infarction and coronary thrombosis. After a long delay, occasioned by fruitless police inquiries after next of kin, official permission was granted for her cremation. As Muriel Gantry began to make the arrangements, she received a visit from Tony Williams, a wealthy young supporter of Nazi causes, who was acting on Colin Jordan's behalf. He provided money and later attended the simple funeral ceremony with two fellow Nazis, all three dramatically dressed in black. On 7 December 1982 at Colchester crematorium, Miss Gantry read her own tribute to her friend while the press cameras popped and flashed. Savitri Devi's simple floral wreath was decorated with a Man-rune, the sign of life; the inverse Yr-rune (death) commonly marked SS graves in the war.[28]

By an odd irony of fate, Savitri Devi's mortal remains continued their journey around the world. The great finale took place in the United States. By a prior arrangement, Muriel Gantry sent an inscribed urn containing Savitri Devi's ashes to Matt Koehl, who placed them in his Nazi hall of honor at Arlington, purportedly next to those of Lincoln Rockwell. To mark this occasion Koehl held a formal New Order memorial service replete with memorabilia and Nazi bathos. Pious tributes by leading American comrades were interspersed with rousing music from the Third Reich. Behind the funerary urn hung the black, white, and red colors of a gigantic swastika banner, while a picture of Savitri Devi was draped with a funeral sash said to have belonged to Adolf Hitler. A report of the proceedings in Koehl's *NS Bulletin* stated that "[her] extraordinary loyalty and devotion to our cause has earned her a place for all time in the pantheon of National Socialist heroes and heroines."[29] Thus did Savitri Devi, the nomadic

Nazi and Hitler worshiper, enter the Valhalla of the former American Nazi Party.

Savitri Devi's influence on international neo-Nazism and other hybrid strains of mystical fascism has been continuous since the mid-1960s and beyond her death into the 1990s. But the very eccentricity of her thought, combining as it does Aryan supremacism and anti-Semitism with Hinduism, animal rights, and a fundamentally biocentric view of life, has led to strange alliances in radical ideology. Indications of her potential appeal to occult, neopagan, ecological, and New Age groups are apparent in the interest shown by Myatt, Bouchet, Serrano, and Mason in her ideas. In their writings paganism, magic, and the natural order act as a foil for a cleansing wave of fascist violence that will sweep away a corrupt humanity, leaving only Aryans in possession of a pristine world. Their thought is undeniably fascist in inspiration, but her ideas also hold an appeal for "alternative" movements whose inspiration is far removed from such sources.

In 1954 the Ancient and Mystical Order of the Rosae Crucis (AMORC), America's leading Rosicrucian occult order, published a second edition of A Son of God. Founded in 1915 by H. Spencer Lewis (1883–1939), AMORC offers a nondenominational approach to ancient wisdom teachings. In his early years the American founder had been involved in Theosophy and several occult lodges in Britain as well with Aleister Crowley and his magical Ordo Templi Orientis (OTO). Lewis received a formal Rosicrucian initiation at Toulouse in 1909, but he also laid emphasis on the arrival of traditional Rosicrucians in North America in the 1690s.[30] He was versed in Theosophical lore concerning rounds, root races, and Aryans, and also held the ancient Egyptians in great esteem, especially Akhnaton.[31] From its Californian headquarters comprising an entire city block built with sphinxes, domes, and porticoes in San Jose, AMORC now runs a very successful nonprofit educational foundation with tens of thousands of members worldwide, seeking health, happiness, and human progress. Its influence in the New Age movement has been enormous.[32] As a key volume in the AMORC Rosicrucian Library, Savitri Devi's book is always available, last reprinting in 1992.

From the late 1960s onward growing numbers of individuals began to dissent from the values and institutions of modern Western society. The hippie movement of 1965–1973 celebrated drugs, Eastern religions, and other forms of exotic enlightenment against the "false civilization" of denominational religion, reason, and industrial modernity. By the 1970s, there was more widespread concern about the unchecked exploitation of the earth's limited resources, urbanization, and the destruction of the environment. The Marxist critique traced these ills to the power of the bourgeoisie and international capital, but these scapegoats were giving way to a broader condemnation of urban-industrial culture by the 1980s. With the advent of the New Age movement, man was felt to have lost his roots in nature, leading an artificial life among machines and automated processes that robbed him of his humanity and a meaningful life. Rudolf Bahro, a leading left-wing Green and an important New Age figure, identifies patriarchy, the Judaeo-Christian religious tradition, and the entire rationalist and scientific praxis of the West as the root causes of man's alienation.[33]

Green thinkers are especially pessimistic about the effects of human population on nature. New advocates of Malthusianism—the doctrine that species proliferate until they exhaust their food resources—oppose liberal and Christian notions of aid to the needy. In the 1970s there were widespread appeals for zero population growth or decline, if necessary backed by repressive measures, especially in Third World countries. The Environmental Fund, a prestigious international grouping, took the view that sending food aid to the hungry only encouraged their population growth. Other organizations like Zero Population Growth, the Campaign to Check the Population Explosion, and Planned Parenthood/World Population also focused attention on the overbreeding in poor nations. Paul Ehrlich's bestseller, *The Population Bomb* (1970), suggested tax penalties for childbearing and breaking off relations with a Vatican opposed to birth control. A rhetoric using inflammatory terms of violence ("bomb," "explosion") was matched by a contempt for humans ("plague," "people pollute"). Many ecologists identified the teeming colored races of Africa, Asia, and South America as the root cause of the world population problem.

An extreme school of ecological catastrophism regards all human civilization as deleterious and evil. Such antihumanist sentiment, coupled with an idealization of animals and nature, represents a break with liberal thought. Many radical ecologists believe that human population must be drastically reduced because humans have simply become too numerous, placing an intolerable burden upon their natural environment. Edward Callenbach's novel *Ecotopia* (1978) described a revolutionary ecological regime in the Pacific Northwest that secedes from the United States. Its ecocentric policy is enforced through a variety of repressive, violent, and exclusionary measures against any opposition. Once human beings are stigmatized as a threat to Mother Nature, Christian and Enlightenment notions of human equality and the sanctity of human life start to retreat. Nazi modes of thought concerning "unfit life" (the old, sick, and indigent), hierarchies of human value, and eugenic programs find ready acceptance among those who despair of mankind.[34]

The American movement of Deep Ecology betrays an uneasy resemblance to Savitri Devi's biocentric vision. Its precepts of community and cooperation are belied by romantic irrationalism and the assertion that all nature is equal. In his pioneering work *The Arrogance of Humanism* (1978), the leading U.S. biocentrist David Ehrenfeld rejects the humanist foundation of modern life, denying that any part of nature has more value than another. Due to man's global health schemes, the pox virus is now an endangered species.[35] Inspired by the Norwegian philosopher Arne Naess (b. 1912), Bill Devall and George Sessions, both American professors, have publicized Deep Ecology and biocentrism as a fundamentalist movement opposed to the pragmatic approach of reform ecology. In their influential book *Deep Ecology* (1985), man is regarded as a degenerate and artificial creature in painful opposition to wild, untamed nature. Only a radical revaluation of human importance can avert the grim future of a teeming, polluted planet. Man must give up his privileged position as the lord of the earth and seek a new accommodation with nature, at once harmonious, modest, and subordinate.

The hero of Deep Ecology is Thomas Malthus (1766–1854), while the philosophies of humanism, rationalism, and Enlightenment are blamed for man's vanity and ecological destruction. Devall and Sessions approvingly quote Theodore Roszak, the doyen of the American counterculture: "Humanism is the finest flower of urban-industrial society; but the odor of alienation yet clings to it and to all culture and public policy that springs from it." And again, with the philosopher Pete Gunter: "Pragmatism, Marxism, scientific humanism . . . the whole swarm of smug antireligious dogmas emerging in the late eighteenth and nineteenth centuries and by now deeply entrenched in scientific, political, economic, and educational institutions . . . make nature an extension of and mere raw material for man."[36] The sources of Deep Ecology are variously sought in mysticism, Christianity (especially St. Francis of Assisi), the Eastern religions of Hinduism, Taoism, and Zen Buddhism, and Native American spirituality. Devall and Sessions also trace their ideas in the literary tradition of naturalism and pastoralism in America (Walt Whitman, Henry Thoreau, Robinson Jeffers, and John Muir).[37]

All nature has intrinsic worth and equality, and whatever science that remains should be nondominating. But if Devall and Sessions couch Deep Ecology in gentle words, their biocentrist epigones use a sterner language. Dave Foreman, the founder of the radical movement "Earth First!" conflates romanticism and brutality in a manner reminiscent of Savitri Devi. Primitivist sentiments such as "dream the bison back, sing the swan hither" and "back to the Pleistocene" punctuate Foreman's views that starving Ethiopians should be left to die and Malthus was right: "There are too many people on the earth."[38] He agrees with Arne Naess that the earth's human population should be reduced to about 100 million. Another contributor to his magazine has recommended a drastic 80 percent reduction in the global human population, while praising AIDS as a valuable ecological weapon.[39] The German Green leader, Herbert Gruhl, has even echoed Savitri Devi's passion for nuclear destruction: because only Westerners are amenable to birth control programs, the overcrowded peoples of the Third World will one day regard "the atom bomb no longer as a threat but as a liberation."[40]

Left-wing writers have been the fiercest critics of Deep Ecology, which they accuse of smuggling "fascist" discourse into liberal society. "People are shit," a recent quote from the German ecomagazine *Instinkte*, illustrates the left-wing claim that biocentrism denies the moral basis of any human rights to equality and support. By rejecting man's claim to distinctiveness from animals and plants, either through spiritual transcendence or social consciousness, biocentrism reduces mankind to mere biomass, a burden on nature. And by blaming humanity collectively for ecological disaster, Deep Ecology deflects any critique of capitalism and authority, thereby frustrating genuine social emancipation.[41] Marxist ecologists regard such doctrine as the ideological ally of monopoly capitalism. Only by denying the special status of man and his anthropocentric traditions of Judaism, Christianity, humanism, and socialism can capitalism soften up democracy to accept the mass dying of Third World populations, as well as the euthanasia of the elderly, ill, poor, and redundant in the rich North. Such a countertranscendent strategy will facilitate the exploitation of human beings as raw material in twenty-first-century industries based on genetic engineering, embryo farming, and cloning.

Ideological parallels between Deep Ecology and the prefascist currents of Social Darwinism and mystical *Lebensreform* (the natural-living movement in pre-1914 Germany) are also highlighted by Marxist critics. At the end of the nineteenth century the ugly, unhealthy, and harmful effects of industrialization—destruction of nature, slums, disease—were attributed by its romantic bourgeois critics not to capitalism but to decadent civilization in general. Rather than demanding the emancipation of the working class, German *Lebensreformer* embraced health diets, natural remedies, nudism, and vegetarianism, and founded alternative colonies on the land and in the cities. Ideas of civilizational decadence found a ready ally in Darwinist ideas of degeneration, which could be countered only by healthy rural living, Aryan racism, and eugenics, as advocated by the Social Darwinist Wilhelm Schallmayer (1857–1919) and the *völkisch* biologist Willibald Hentschel (1858–1947). Marxist and anarchist ecologists detect the same romantic reactionary thought in Deep Ecology today. However, whereas German *Lebensreform* is burdened by its links to Nazism, Deep Ecology can supply a similar prefascist discourse from an blameless Anglo-American source.[42]

Nature is divinized, man is relegated. The ultraright-wing Noontide Press in California has recognized this receptivity to the Nazi religion of nature by bringing out a new edition of Savitri Devi's *Impeachment of Man* (1991). Presented by the publisher as an indictment of the values and mores of our modern human-centered "produce and consume" society, the book attempts to popularize Savitri Devi's conviction that divinity manifests itself in all of nature, that man is nothing special, and that his recent ideas of universal equality and entitlement to prosperity at the expense of the rest of nature are fundamentally wrong. The beautiful tiger, the great banyan tree, the lithe felines, according to Savitri Devi, these are noble creatures, but not all "two-legged mammals" qualify. Only the strong, intelligent Aryan is fit to survive in a redeemed biocentric order. The publisher's foreword gives a brief account of her life, mentioning her lifelong devotion to Nazism and her books in which "she portrayed Hitler and National Socialism as expressions of transcendent spiritual truth." Such an edition is a telling example of the new entryism the far right is currently pursuing in its appeal to Green and New Age audiences.

But Savitri Devi's emphasis on nature and animal rights against the claims of mankind could evoke a wider response in mass urban society. Ecological sentiment often owes more to an urbanized lifestyle than any authentic awareness of nature. Here one might note that anti-hunting and animal rights activists have their bases of support in large towns and cities. Their sentimental image of animals and nature is informed by modern media and synthetic enclaves like "wild life parks" but hardly ever anchored in the genuine countryside, where farming, animal husbandry, hunting, and practical conservation schemes are pursued as a way of life. The shrill and often violent demands for the protection of animals from human exploitation typically come from social groups with no living connection to the land. Given the over-whelming preponderance of urban over rural populations in modern Western society, these attitudes are set to become ever more prevalent.

The growing practice of vegetarianism and its active proselytism amongst the young often derive from the sentimental and squeamish sensibilities of urban populations. Advanced technological societies no longer regard food as rural produce: the sanitized image of hygienic food packaging in the suburban supermarket replaces livestock, slaugh-terhouses, and butchers' shops in the modern imagination. Once city dwellers are reminded of the bloodstained background to meat produc-tion, the horrified flight into vegetarianism only reinforces the contin-uing retreat from nature. Constantly serviced by television and computers, modern man inhabits an electronic "virtual" reality drained of organic natural content. The sensory poverty of a synthetic order devoid of life could well lead to contempt for mankind and a compen-sating idealization of animals. Here again, one may detect the reviving appeal of Savitri Devi's vehement misanthropy. A computerized and superurbanized humanity might long for contact with nature while entertaining violent visions of hatred and destruction for its own spe-cies.

Nor is Savitri Devi's vision of the noble Aryan far removed from primitivist currents of New Age thought. The German *völkisch* and youth movements in the period 1890–1930 mixed paganism and nature worship with reverence for barbarian virtue. Ancient Germans, racial

purity, and national revival were all bound up with the merits of nature.[43] Many New Age groups rehearse the nativist aspects of these
Nazi precursors in a eulogy of the primitive. The movement began in
the 1970s with European support for the cultural struggle of the North
American Indians, but politics soon gave way to mythology. Navajo,
Hopi, and Sioux Indians were credited with a natural wisdom long lost
among the rational, technologically advanced peoples of the West. In
the 1980s Indian deputations and medicine men plied their trade of
esoteric workshops and conferences across Germany and Switzerland.
So long as the idealized groups were marginal, alien, or oppressed, such
New Age sentiment was generally left-wing or anarchist. However
once the models were sought closer to home in the prerational, mythical past of Western culture, *völkisch* ideas could make a fashionable
return.

By the early 1980s the enthusiasm for North American Indians and
their ecological-esoteric wisdom had spread to the ancient European
tribes—the "Indians of the West." In the New Age movement there
are now numerous groups devoted to reviving the wisdom of the ancient Celts and Teutons. Druids and old Germanic priest-kings, witches,
and priestesses now provide New Age precursors closer to home and
Western identity. Books, workshops, and conferences on paganism,
shamanism, runes, and magic proliferate. The Anglo-American Ásatrú
Free Assembly and Odinists revived neo-Germanic paganism, while in
Germany neo-*völkisch* groups such as the Goden (est. 1957) and Ar-
manenschaft (est. 1969), a revival of the Guido von List Society, swiftly
reoriented themselves toward the New Age concern with feminism,
ecology, and esoteric lore. The Aryan mysticism of Julius Evola was
rediscovered by New Age publications. Nostalgia for a lost golden age
and apocalyptic hopes of its revival recall the ideological foreground of
earlier demands for fascist renewal.[44]

Deep Ecology, biocentrism, nature worship, and New Age paganism
reflect a hostility toward Christianity, rationalism, and liberalism in
modern society. Although these radical movements often have their
roots in left-wing dissent, their increasing tendency toward myth and
despair indicate their susceptibility to millenarian and mystical ideas
on the far right. Neo-Nazi and fascist activists now actively seek to
infiltrate the ecological and esoteric scene. The cybernetic encirclement
of man and his complete divorce from nature could well foster a more

fundamental alienation. In a congested and automated world, Savitri Devi's sentimental love of animals and hatred of the masses may find new followers. The pessimism of the Kali Yuga and her vision of a pristine new Aryan order possess a perennial appeal in times of uncertainty and change.

NOTES AND REFERENCES

NOTES TO THE INTRODUCTION

1. Illustrated advertisement for books (Buffalo, N.Y.: Samisdat Publishers, circa 1982), card flyer.

2. Matt Koehl, "Adolf Hitler: German Nationalist or Aryan Racist?" *National Socialist World*, no. 4 (summer 1967), pp. 13–22.

NOTES TO CHAPTER 1

1. Savitri Devi, *Defiance* (Calcutta: A. K. Mukerji, [1950]), pp. 12, 58.

2. Savitri Devi, *Pilgrimage* (Calcutta: Savitri Devi Mukherji, 1958), pp. 12, 142f.

3. Savitri Devi, interview, New Delhi, November 1978, Cassette 1A.

4. Irving Putter, *The Pessimism of Leconte de Lisle: The Work and the Time* (Berkeley and Los Angeles: University of California Press, 1961), pp. 277–287; Alison Fairlie, *Leconte de Lisle's Poems on the Barbarian Races* (Cambridge: Cambridge University Press, 1947), passim.

5. Richard Clogg, *A Short History of Greece*, 2d ed. (Cambridge: Cambridge University Press, 1986), pp. 105–110; Edward S. Forster, *A Short History of Modern Greece, 1821–1945*, 2d ed. (London: Methuen, 1946), pt. 2.

6. Savitri Devi, *Defiance*, p. 59; Savitri Devi, interview, New Delhi, November 1978, Cassette 1A.

7. Quoted in Clogg, *Short History of Greece*, p. 76.

8. The following account of the Anatolian campaign is drawn from Clogg, *Short History of Greece*, pp. 112–121, and Forster, *Short History of Modern Greece*, pp. 135–147.

9. Savitri Devi, *Pilgrimage*, p. 105.

10. Savitri Devi, *Defiance*, p. 60.

11. *Athen-München*, ed. George Himmelheber (Munich: Bayerisches Nationalmuseum, 1980).

12. E. M. Butler, *The Tyranny of Greece over Germany: A Study of the Influence Exercised by Greek Art and Poetry over the Great German Writers of the Eighteenth, Nineteenth and Twentieth Centuries* (Cambridge: Cambridge University Press, 1935).

13. Savitri Devi, *Pilgrimage*, pp. 105f.

14. Savitri Devi, *Defiance*, p. 58.

15. Biographical material for the following account of Kaïres's life is drawn from *Philosophics of Theophilos Kaires (Greece's new Socrates)*, ed. and trans. Peter Thetis (New York: Pageant Press, 1960), pp. 9–33. An earlier biography written by Demetrios P. Paschales, *Θεόφιλος Καΐρης* (Athens, 1928) was acknowledged by Maximiani Portas in her thesis.

16. Maximiani Portas, *Essai critique sur Théophile Kaïris* (D. Litt. thesis, University of Lyons, [1935]). The thesis was revised in the summer of 1931. Maximiani dated her introduction at Athens in October 1931 with an acknowledgment to her friend Kyria Marika Kaloyerikou for hospitality, affection, and kindness during the previous years in the capital.

17. Heinrich Schliemann, *Troy and Its Remains* (London: John Murray, 1875), pp. 102, 119–120.

18. Malcolm Quinn, *The Swastika: Constructing the Symbol* (London and New York: Routledge, 1994), pp. 22–26.

19. Sir Charles Eliot, *Hinduism and Buddhism*, 3 vols. (London: Edward Arnold, 1926), 1:41.

20. Savitri Devi, *Defiance*, pp. 69–70.

NOTES TO CHAPTER 2

1. Leconte de Lisle, "L'Arc de Civa," in *Poèmes Antiques* (1852), quoted in Savitri Devi, *Defiance* (Calcutta: A. K. Mukerji, [1950]), p. 431.

2. Savitri Devi, *Defiance*, p. 379.

3. Ibid., p. 69.

4. Léon Poliakov, *The Aryan Myth* (London: Sussex University Press and Heinemann, 1974), pp. 183–188. A. Leslie Willson, *A Mythical Image: The Ideal of India in German Romanticism* (Durham, N.C.: Duke University Press, 1964) traces the growth of interest in India among the German Romantics.

5. J. P. Mallory, *In Search of the Indo-Europeans* (London: Thames and Hudson, 1989), pp. 9–11.

6. Poliakov, *Aryan Myth*, pp. 188–190.

7. Ibid., pp. 190–192.

8. Ibid., pp. 192–199.

9. Malcolm Quinn, *The Swastika: Constructing the Symbol* (London and New York: Routledge, 1994), pp. 22–38, 45. All the swastika symbols collected for the

Paris Exposition display were illustrated in the journal article by Michael von Zmigrodzki, "Zur Geschichte der Suastika," *Archiv für Anthropologie* 19 (1890): 173–181, tables 4–7. Thomas Wilson, a delegate at one of the conferences, was the curator of the Department of Prehistoric Anthropology at the Smithsonian Institution in Washington, D.C. His comprehensive study *The Swastika: The Earliest Known Symbol, and Its Migrations* was published in the *Annual Report of the Board of Regents of the Smithsonian Institution, 1894* (Washington, D.C. 1896), pp. 757–1011.

10. Helena Petrovna Blavatsky, *The Secret Doctrine*, 2 vols. (London: Theosophical Publishing Company, 1888), 2:6–12, 300f., 433–436; 98–101, 585f.

11. The contribution of Theosophy to the German *völkisch* movement is fully documented in Nicholas Goodrick-Clarke, *The Occult Roots of Nazism: Secret Aryan Cults and Their Influence on Nazi Ideology*, 2d ed. (New York: New York University Press; London: I. B. Tauris, 1992).

12. Erich Biehahn, "Blondheit und Blondheitskult in der deutschen Literatur," *Archiv für Kulturgeschichte* 46 (1964): 309–333.

13. Savitri Devi, *Gold im Schmelztiegel*, trans. Lotte Asmus (Padua: Edizioni di Ar, 1982), p. 21.

14. Details of B. G. Tilak's career may be found in *Dictionary of National Biography*, ed. S. P. Sen, 4 vols. (Calcutta: Institute of Historical Studies, 1972–1974), 4:352–356.

15. Bâl Gangadhar Tilak, *The Arctic Home in the Vedas* (Poona: Kesari, 1903), pp. 453–455, 464.

16. A concise account of the Aryan settlement of India appears in Romila Thapar, *A History of India*, vol. 1 (Harmondsworth: Penguin, 1966), chap. 2, "The Impact of Aryan Culture," pp. 28–49.

17. Savitri Devi, *L'Etang aux lotus* (Calcutta: author, 1940), pp. 62–68.

18. Ibid., pp. 74–86.

19. Ibid., pp. 167–171.

20. Ibid., pp. 19–25, at p. 25.

21. Savitri Devi, *Defiance*, pp. 100–102.

22. Savitri Devi, *Souvenirs et réflexions d'une aryenne* (New Delhi: Savitri Dêvi Mukherji, 1976), pp. 282f.

23. Lotte Asmus and Vittorio De Cecco, "La 'missionaria' del paganesimo ariano," *Risguardo* 4 (1984): 64–70, at p. 65.

NOTES TO CHAPTER 3

1. The origin and development of these movements are discussed in the masterly study by Christophe Jaffrelot, *The Hindu Nationalist Movement and Indian Politics: 1925 to the 1990s* (London: Hurst, 1996), pp. 11–35.

2. Savitri Devi, *Souvenirs et réflexions d'une aryenne* (New Delhi: Savitri Dêvi Mukherji, 1976), pp. 35–40.

3. Details of V. D. Savarkar's career may be found in *Dictionary of National Biography*, ed. by S. P. Sen, 4 vols. (Calcutta: Institute of Historical Studies, 1972–1974), 4:92–95.

4. V. D. Savarkar, *Hindutva*, 2d ed. (New Delhi: Central Hindu Yuvak Sabha, 1938), pp. 7f.

5. Vincent A. Smith, *The Oxford History of India*, 4th ed., ed. Percival Spear (Delhi: Oxford University Press, 1981), pp. 405–407.

6. Savarkar, *Hindutva*, pp. 69f.

7. Smith, *Oxford History of India*, pp. 407–415.

8. Savarkar, *Hindutva*, pp. 71, 72f.

9. This act symbolized the victory of Maratha nationalism and Hinduism over the old Muslim order in India. A plate of the event provided the frontispiece for Savarkar's longer history of the Marathas. V. D. Savarkar, *Hindu-Pad-Padashahi or a Review of the Hindu Empire of Maharashtra* (Poona: Manohar Granth-Mala, 1942).

10. Smith, *Oxford History of India*, pp. 439–442.

11. Savarkar, *Hindutva*, pp. 56f.

12. Ibid., pp. 102, 103, 105ff., 111ff.

13. Ibid., pp. 126, 144.

14. Jaffrelot, *Hindu Nationalist Movement and Indian Politics*, pp. 32, 53f.

15. V. D. Savarkar, *Hindu Sanghatan: Its Ideology and Immediate Program* (Bombay: Hindu Mahasabha, 1940), pp. 11, 13f., 23–30.

16. Ibid., pp. 43–47, 60–67.

17. Ibid., p. 83.

18. G. D. Savarkar, Foreword to *A Warning to the Hindus* by Savitri Devi (Calcutta: Hindu Mission, 1939), p. ix.

19. Savitri Devi, *Warning to the Hindus*, pp. 7, 17.

20. Ibid., pp. 46–48.

21. Ibid., p. 50.

22. Ibid., p. 51.

23. Ibid., p. 54.

24. Ibid., pp. 34, 35.

25. Ibid., pp. 41f.

26. Ibid., pp. 43f.

27. Ibid., p. 55.

28. Ibid., pp. 57f.

29. Ibid., p. 61.

30. Ibid., pp. 68–73; cf. Savarkar, *Hindu Sanghatan*, p. 80.

31. Savitri Devi, *Warning to the Hindus*, pp. 73–75.

32. Biographical details of K. B. Hedgewar may be found in *Dictionary of National Biography*, ed. S. P. Sen, 4 vols. (Calcutta: Institute of Historical Studies, 1972–1974), 2:161–162; Jaffrelot, *Hindu Nationalist Movement and Indian Politics*, pp. 33f.

33. The RSS is fully documented in Walter K. Andersen and Shridhar D. Damle, *The Brotherhood in Saffron: The Rashtriya Swayamsevak Sangh and Hindu Revivalism* (Boulder, Colo.: Westview Press, 1987), and Tapan Basu et al., *Khaki Shorts and Saffron Flags: A Critique of the Hindu Right* (New Delhi: Orient Longman, 1993). See also Jaffrelot, *Hindu Nationalist Movement and Indian Politics*, pp. 35–79.

34. Andersen and Damle, *The Brotherhood in Saffron*, p. 38.

35. Jaffrelot, *Hindu Nationalist Movement and Indian Politics*, pp. 65–68.

36. Ibid., pp. 51f.

37. M. S. Golwalkar, *We, or Our Nationhood Defined* (Nagpur: Bharat Prakashan, 1939), pp. 19, 35, 59, quoted in Jaffrelot, *Hindu Nationalist Movement and Indian Politics*, pp. 52–53.

38. Golwalkar, *We, or Our Nation Defined*, p. 37.

39. Jaffrelot, *Hindu Nationalist Movement and Indian Politics*, pp. 72–74.

40. Savitri Devi, *Warning to the Hindus*, p. 142.

41. Ibid., p. 146.

42. Ibid., p. 63.

43. Savitri Devi, *Defiance* (Calcutta: A. K. Mukerji, [1950]), p. 60.

44. Savitri Devi, *Warning to the Hindus*, title page; cf. *Defiance*, pp. 379–380.

45. Savarkar, *Hindu Sanghatan*, pp. 114–126. Savarkar discussed the pan-Hindu flag, ibid., pp. 140–42, and also wrote the tract "The Pan-Hindu Dhwaj" about its design and symbolism.

46. Jaffrelot, *Hindu Nationalist Movement and Indian Politics* is the definitive study of the later history of the RSS and the Hindu national parties. The Babri Masjid incident is described in detail, pp. 453–458.

NOTES TO CHAPTER 4

1. Adolf Hitler, *Mein Kampf*, intro. D. C. Watt, trans. Ralph Manheim (London: Hutchinson, 1969), p. 602.

2. *Hitler's Table Talk, 1941–44* [the so-called Heim-Bormann notes], ed. H. R. Trevor-Roper, 2d ed. (London: Weidenfeld and Nicolson, 1973), 8–10.8.1941, 17–18.9.1941, 10.1.1942, 12–13.1.1942, 3.3.1942, 27.6.1942, 22.8.1942. For a full review of Hitler's thinking on India, see Milan Hauner, *India in Axis Strategy: Germany, Japan, and Indian Nationalists in the Second World War* (Stuttgart: Klett-Cotta, 1981) (Publications of the German Historical Institute London, vol. 7), pp. 26–34.

3. Alfred Rosenberg, *Der Mythus des 20. Jahrhunderts* (Munich: Hoheneichen-Verlag [Franz Eher Verlag], 1934), pp. 660–664.

4. Hauner, *India in Axis Strategy*, pp. 56–70.

5. Quoted, ibid., p. 66.

6. Jean Parvulesco, *La spirale prophétique* (Paris: Guy Trédaniel, 1986), p. 99; Savitri Devi, *Souvenirs et réflexions d'une aryenne* (New Delhi: Savitri Dêvi Mukherji, 1976), pp. 41, 274f.

7. Biographical details of Asit Krishna Mukherji are drawn from Savitri Devi, interview, New Delhi, November 1978, Cassettes 1A, 1B.

8. The ideology, membership, and political influence of the Thule Society are fully discussed in Nicholas Goodrick-Clarke, *The Occult Roots of Nazism: Secret Aryan Cults and Their Influence on Nazi Ideology*, 2d ed. (New York: New York University Press; London: I. B. Tauris, 1992), pp. 135–152.

9. Savitri Devi, *Defiance* (Calcutta: A. K. Mukerji, [1950]), pp. 39f.

10. Ibid., p. 148.

11. Ibid., pp. 39f., 434f.

12. Ibid., p. 161.

13. Ibid., p. 453.

14. Ibid., p. 342.

15. Ibid., pp. 126, 149–151, 226.

16. The ensuing account of Savitri Devi's life in wartime India is based on Savitri Devi, interview, New Delhi, November 1978, Cassette 2B.

Notes to Chapter 5

1. The following account of Subhas Chandra Bose's life and political career is drawn mainly from Leonard A. Gordon, *Brothers against the Raj: A biography of Indian Nationalists Sarat and Subhas Chandra Bose* (New York: Columbia University Press, 1990). Further material has been gleaned from Milan Hauner, *India in Axis Strategy: Germany, Japan, and Indian Nationalists in the Second World War* (Stuttgart: Klett-Cotta, 1981) (Publications of the German Historical Institute London, vol. 7).

2. Gordon, *Brothers against the Raj*, pp. 32–35.

3. Ibid., pp. 37–41.

4. Ibid., pp. 40, 42–49, 52–54.

5. Ibid., pp. 55–63.

6. Ibid., chaps. 3, 4, and 5, passim, pp. 234–235.

7. Ibid., pp. 269–285; Hauner, *India in Axis Strategy*, p. 61.

8. Gordon, *Brothers against the Raj*, pp. 286–288.

9. Ibid., pp. 293–309; Hauner, *India in Axis Strategy*, p. 62.

10. Gordon, *Brothers against the Raj*, pp. 316f., 325–331, 338–349.

11. Ibid., pp. 349–353.

12. Ibid., pp. 370f., 372–392, 399–402, 416f.; Hauner, *India in Axis Strategy*, p. 64.

13. Hauner, *India in Axis Strategy*, p. 239; Gordon, *Brothers against the Raj*, pp. 410, 420.

14. Hauner, *India in Axis Strategy*, pp. 240–249; Gordon, *Brothers against the Raj*, pp. 421–428, 441–445.

15. Hauner, *India in Axis Strategy*, pp. 246f.

16. Ibid., pp. 187–189, 193–213.

17. Ibid., pp. 249, 255–258.

18. Ibid., pp. 259–274, 357–361.

19. Gordon, *Brothers against the Raj*, pp. 450–452.

20. Hauner, *India in Axis Strategy*, p. 251.

21. Ibid., pp. 250–253, 363f., 368–371; Gordon, *Brothers against the Raj*, pp. 447f., 453–455.

22. Hauner, *India in Axis Strategy*, pp. 366–368, 371f., 576–592; Gordon, *Brothers against the Raj*, pp. 456–460, 486.

23. Hauner, *India in Axis Strategy*, pp. 409–413, 433f., 437–439, 489–493; Gordon, *Brothers against the Raj*, pp. 462–472.

24. Hauner, *India in Axis Strategy*, p. 415.

25. Ibid., pp. 417f. The invitation to Bose to come to Asia was repeated in March and again at the Bangkok conference of Indian nationalists in June, pp. 434, 489–493; Gordon, *Brothers against the Raj*, pp. 468–470.

26. Hauner, *India in Axis Strategy*, pp. 423–436, cf. above, chap. 4, n. 2; Gordon, *Brothers against the Raj*, pp. 461f.

27. Hauner, *India in Axis Strategy*, pp. 382–390, 391–406.

28. Ibid., pp. 484–487; Gordon, *Brothers against the Raj*, pp. 484f.

29. Hauner, *India in Axis Strategy*, pp. 487–489, 558–562; Gordon, *Brothers against the Raj*, pp. 486–490.

30. Gordon, *Brothers against the Raj*, pp. 491–504.

31. Ibid., pp. 507–23, 534–43.

32. Ibid., pp. 604–610.

NOTES TO CHAPTER 6

1. Savitri Devi, *Defiance* (Calcutta: A. K. Mukerji, [1950]), p. 451.

2. Ibid., pp. 345f.

3. Cyril Aldred, *Akhenaten: King of Egypt* (London: Thames and Hudson, 1988), provides a comprehensive account of the rediscovery of Akhnaton and his new capital.

4. Arthur Weigall, *The Life and Times of Akhnaton, Pharaoh of Egypt* (Edinburgh and London: William Blackwood and Sons, 1910).

5. In her taped interview of 1978 (Cassette 5B), Savitri Devi recalled a trip to Syria and Iraq by ship and train in 1937. This journey probably included a stop-over in Egypt, for there are some passing references to ancient and modern Egypt in *A Warning to the Hindus* (Calcutta: Hindu Mission, 1939), pp. 58–61. She also mentions rail travel in Egypt in *L'Etang aux lotus* (Calcutta: author, 1940), p. 46.

6. Savitri Devi, *A Son of God* (London: Philosophical Publishing House, 1946), p. 16.

7. Ibid., pp. 19–25.

8. Ibid., pp. 25–27.

9. Ibid., p. 35.

10. Ibid., pp. 35, 40–42.

11. Ibid., pp. 126–128.

12. Ibid., pp. 129–130.

13. Ibid., p. 243.

14. Ibid., pp. 245f.

15. Ibid., p. 247.

16. Ibid., p. 248.

17. Ibid., p. 253.

18. Ibid., p. 254.

19. Ibid., pp. 255f.

20. Ibid., p. 253.

21. Ibid., pp. ix-xiii.

22. Savitri Devi, *Defiance*, p. 347.

23. Savitri Devi, *Impeachment of Man* (Calcutta: Savitri Devi Mukherji, 1959), chaps. 1, 2.

24. Ibid., pp. 16, 52.

25. Ibid., p. 59.

26. Ibid., pp. x-xi, 13–14.

27. Ibid., p. 59.

28. Ibid., pp. 148f.

29. Savitri Devi, *Impeachment of Man*, p. 141.

30. Savitri Devi, *Impeachment of Man*, pp. xi, 189–193.

31. Savitri Devi, *Defiance*, pp. 184–186, 203–204, 456–457.

32. Savitri Devi, *Impeachment of Man*, p. [iv].

NOTES TO CHAPTER 7

1. Savitri Devi, *Souvenirs et réflexions d'une aryenne* (New Delhi: Savitri Dêvi Mukherji, 1976), pp. 33–35, 39, 285–287. Srimat Swami Satyananda also quoted in Savitri Devi, *Defiance* (Calcutta: A. K. Mukerji, [1950]), pp. 375–377, and in-terview, New Delhi, November 1978, Cassettes 4B, 5B.

2. Agehananda Bharati, *The Ochre Robe* (London: George Allen & Unwin, 1961), p. 214.

3. Agehananda Bharati, "Hindu-Faschismus," *FORVM* 33, Heft 387/394 (30 September 1986): 29–35.

4. Horace Hayman Wilson, *The Vishńu Puráńa, a System of Hindu Mythology and Tradition* (London: John Murray, 1840), pp. 21–26 (bk. 1, chap. 3). The text is also discussed in John Muir, *Original Sanskrit Texts on the Origin and History of the People of India*, 2d ed., 5 vols. (London: Trübner, 1868), 1:43–49.

5. Quoted in Muir, *Original Sanskrit Texts*, 1:142–146.

6. Wilson, *Vishńu Puráńa*, pp. 621–626 (bk. 6, chap. 1).

7. Savitri Devi, *The Lightning and the Sun* (Calcutta: Savitri Devi Mukherjee, 1958), pp. 21, 20.

8. Ibid., pp. 4–15.

9. Ibid., pp. 17f.

10. Ibid., p. 18.

11. Ibid., pp. 36f.

12. Ibid., pp. 37–41. The first part of this book presents the story of Genghis Khan, pp. 57–126.

13. Ibid., p. 126.

14. Ibid., pp. 41–47.

15. Savitri Devi, *A Son of God* (London: Philosophical Publishing House, 1946), p. 215.

16. The complex mythology and theology of the avatar receives its definitive study in Geoffrey Parrinder, *Avatar and Incarnation*, 2d ed. (New York: Oxford University Press, 1982).

17. *Bhagavad Gita*, 4, verses 7–8. This couplet is quoted by Savitri Devi repeatedly in *Pilgrimage* (Calcutta: Savitri Devi Mukherji, 1958), pp. [v], 7, 28, 31, 52, 173, 188–189, 261, and in *Lightning and the Sun*, passim and p. 416.

18. Savitri Devi, *Lightning and the Sun*, pp. 215–216, 222–224.

19. Ibid., pp. 349–351. August Kubizek, *Young Hitler: The Story of Our Friendship*, trans. E. V. Anderson, 2d ed. (Maidstone: George Mann, 1973), pp. 64–66.

20. Savitri Devi, *Pilgrimage*, pp. 10f.

21. Ibid., pp. 28, 31.

22. Savitri Devi, *Lightning and the Sun*, pp. 220f.

23. Ibid., p. 235.

24. Ibid., p. 403.

25. *Bhagavad Gita*, 3, verses 19, 25, quoted in Savitri Devi, *Pilgrimage*, p. 199.

26. *Bhagavad Gita*, 2, verse 38, quoted in Savitri Devi, *Lightning and the Sun*, pp. 405f. Otto Ohlendorf's example in Savitri Devi, *Pilgrimage*, pp. 252f. Interestingly enough, Ohlendorf was also a Theosophist and may well have studied the *Bhagavad Gita*.

27. Savitri Devi, *Lightning and the Sun*, pp. 204f., 246–249.

28. Ibid., pp. 251, 265, 362f.

29. This cosmic vocabulary owes something to Hitler's fascination with prehistory, diluvial myths, and cosmology. He enthused over Edgar Dacqué, *Urwelt, Sage und Menschheit* (Munich: R. Oldenbourg, 1924), which related diluvial myths to prehistoric cataclysms and Hanns Hörbiger's glacial cosmogony. Hitler also supported Hörbiger's theories. James Webb, *The Occult Establishment* (La Salle, Ill.: Open Court, 1976), pp. 326–333.

30. Adolf Hitler, *Mein Kampf*, trans. James Murphy (London: Hurst and Blackett, 1939), pp. 76, 316.

31. Savitri Devi, *Lightning and the Sun*, pp. 230f., 236.

32. Ibid., p. 256.

33. Ibid., p. 244.

34. Ibid., p. 258.

35. Wilson, *Vishńu Puráńa*, pp. 483f. (bk. 4, chap. 24).

36. Savitri Devi, *Lightning and the Sun*, pp. 431f.

Notes to Chapter 8

1. Savitri Devi, *Pilgrimage* (Calcutta: Savitri Devi Mukherji, 1958), pp. 193–195.

2. This story is narrated in Savitri Devi, interview, New Delhi, November 1978, Cassette 4B.

3. Leconte de Lisle, "Le Runoïa," in *Poèmes Barbares* (1862), quoted in Savitri Devi, *Defiance* (Calcutta: A. K. Mukerji [1950]), pp. 495–497.

4. Detlef Brennecke, *Sven Hedin: Mit Selbstzeugnissen und Bilddokumenten* (Hamburg: Rowohlt, 1986).

5. Ibid., pp. 116–123.

6. Savitri Devi, *Gold im Schmelztiegel*, trans. Lotte Asmus (Padua: Edizioni di Ar, 1982), pp. 65ff.

7. Ibid., p. 67.

8. Ibid., pp. 195–204, 233–246, 248–263.

9. Savitri Devi, *Defiance*, p. 50.

10. Savitri Devi, *Gold im Schmelztiegel*, pp. 233–239.

11. Ibid., pp. 131–137.

12. The full story of conditions in Allied POW camps in postwar Germany was not published until the late 1980s. James Bacque, *Other Losses: An Investigation into the Mass Deaths of German Prisoners at the Hands of the French and Americans after World War II* (London: Macdonald, 1990).

13. Savitri Devi, *Gold im Schmelztiegel*, pp. 239–246, *Defiance*, pp. 574f., and *Pilgrimage*, pp. 244f.

14. Savitri Devi, *Gold im Schmelztiegel*, pp. 315–340.

15. Ibid., pp. 248–263.

16. Text of handbill quoted in English in Savitri Devi, *Defiance*, pp. 1ff. The German original appears in Savitri Devi, *Gold im Schmelztiegel*, p. 261.

17. Savitri Devi, *Defiance*, pp. 158–161. At this hearing Wassmer was sentenced to six months' imprisonment. The incident and a description of Savitri Devi's leaflets were reported in the British press, "Nazi Leaflets in Cologne," *The Times*, 15 March 1949, p. 3.

18. Savitri Devi, *Defiance*, pp. 69–71.

19. Ibid., pp. 188f.

20. Ibid., pp. 169, 104, 190.

21. Ibid., pp. 211–212.

22. Details of Belsen and its liberation are recounted in Douglas Botting, *In the Ruins of the Reich* (London: George Allen & Unwin, 1985), pp. 28–36. Robert H. Abzug, *Inside the Vicious Heart: Americans and the Liberation of Nazi Concentration Camps* (New York: Oxford University Press, 1985), describes the universal shock at the discovery of the concentration camps and their publicization.

23. Savitri Devi, *Gold im Schmelztiegel*, p. 121.

24. Details of the female wardresses appear ibid., pp. 128–130. Ehlert's Auschwitz service is mentioned in *Defiance*, p. 273.

25. Savitri Devi, *Defiance*, pp. 117–118.

26. *Trial of Josef Kramer and Forty-Four Others (The Belsen Trial)*, ed. Raymond Philips (London: William Hodge, 1949), pp. 227–241, 709–711. Trial picture of Hertha Ehlert, No. 8, facing p. 352.

27. Savitri Devi, *Gold im Schmelztiegel*, pp. 122–125.

28. Ibid., p. 126.

29. Savitri Devi, *Defiance*, pp. 463f.

30. Ibid., pp. 562–575.

NOTES TO CHAPTER 9

1. Savitri Devi, *Pilgrimage* (Calcutta: Savitri Devi Mukherji, 1958), p. 13.

2. Extensive details of Adolf Hitler's life at Linz may be gleaned from August Kubizek, *Young Hitler: The Story of Our Friendship*, trans. E. V. Anderson, 2d ed. (Maidstone: George Mann, 1973); Franz Jetzinger, *Hitler's Youth*, trans. Lawrence Wilson, 2d ed. (Westport, Conn.: Greenwood Press, 1976); John Toland, *Adolf Hitler* (New York: Doubleday, 1976).

3. Savitri Devi, *Pilgrimage*, p. 16.

4. Ibid., p. 17.

5. Ibid., pp. 23–27. Other witnesses of the young Adolf Hitler's behavior in Leonding are quoted in Jetzinger, *Hitler's Youth*, pp. 59–60, 74–76. One of Hitler's teachers at the Realschule in Linz, which he attended between 1900 and 1904, recalls him as having talent but also as willful, arrogant, and irascible. Another

remembers his open expression, bright eyes, and, perhaps evidence of his love of nature, how he would converse with trees. Ibid., pp. 68–70.

6. Savitri Devi, *Pilgrimage*, p. 32.

7. Ibid., p. 34.

8. Ibid., p. 42.

9. Ibid., pp. 43–48.

10. Ibid., pp. 48–54.

11. Toland, *Adolf Hitler*, pp. 142f., 211f., 219, 229.

12. The history and development of the Obersalzberg is documented in Josef Geiß, *Obersalzberg*, 17th ed. (Berchtesgaden: Anton Plenk, 1985). Copious pictures, aerial photographs, and maps appear in *Der Obersalzberg im 3. Reich* (Berchtesgaden: Anton Plenk, 1982), *Das Kehlsteinhaus* (Berchtesgaden: Anton Plenk, 1986), and *Obersalzberg: Bilddokumentation* (Berchtesgaden: Anton Plenk, 1983).

13. Savitri Devi, *Pilgrimage*, pp. 64–66.

14. Ibid., p. 67.

15. Ibid., pp. 71–80.

16. Ibid., pp. 101–111.

17. Ibid., pp. 112f.

18. Ibid., pp. 114–121, 126–129, 131–133.

19. The political circumstances of this softening line on Nazi war criminals and an account of the paroles at Landsberg are described fully in Tom Bower, *The Pledge Betrayed* (New York: Doubleday, 1982), pp. 343–354, and T. H. Tetens, *The New Germany and the Old Nazis* (New York: Random House, 1961), pp. 197–209. Mention of Savitri Devi's contribution to the appeal is made in *Pilgrimage*, pp. 161, 256.

20. Savitri Devi, *Pilgrimage*, pp. 152–162.

21. Ibid., pp. 203–214.

22. Ibid., p. 217.

23. Ibid., pp. 223–230, 239–247, 251–258.

24. Ibid., pp. 270–294.

25. Ibid., p. 302. For the historical background to Ernst von Bandel and the Hermannsdenkmal, see George L. Mosse, *The Nationalization of the Masses: Political Symbolism and Mass Movements in Germany from the Napoleonic Wars through the Third Reich* (New York: Howard Fertig, 1975), pp 58–61.

26. The Irminsul and rock-hewn grave are attributed by modern scholars to a Christian hermitage established at the Externsteine, possibly by the bishop of Paderborn, Henry II, around 1115. Wilhelm Teudt identified the Tomb Rock as an ancient Germanic structure in his book *Germanische Heiligtümer* (Jena: Eugen Diederichs, 1929).

27. Savitri Devi, *Pilgrimage*, pp. 320–323.

28. Ibid., pp. 341–345, 348–352.

NOTES TO CHAPTER 10

1. Quoted in Ib Melchior and Frank Brandenburg, *Quest: Searching for Germany's Nazi Past: A Young Man's Story* (Novato, Calif.: Presidio Press, 1990), pp. 219–222.

2. Hans-Ulrich Rudel describes his experiences in the postwar period 1945 to 1951 in *Trotzdem: Kriegs- und Nachkriegszeit* (Preußisch Oldendorf: Karl Schütz Verlag, 1987) and *Mein Leben im Krieg und Frieden* (Rosenheim: Deutsche Verlagsgesellschaft, 1994).

3. Jörg Friedrich, *Die kalte Amnestie: NS-Täter in der Bundesrepublik* (Frankfurt am Main: Fischer, 1984), pp. 216f.

4. Kurt P. Tauber, *Beyond Eagle and Swastika: German Nationalism since 1945*, 2 vols. (Middleton, Conn.: Wesleyan University Press, 1967), 2:1114–1115 (chap. 7, n. 179).

5. Ibid., 1115; T. H. Tetens, *The New Germany and the Old Nazis* (New York: Random House, 1961), pp. 73–75; Friedrich, *Die kalte Amnestie*, p. 217; William Stevenson, *The Bormann Brotherhood* (New York: Harcourt Brace Jovanovich, 1973), pp. 123–128.

6. Tauber, *Beyond Eagle and Swastika*, 2:1113 (chap. 7, n. 178).

7. For Johannes von Leers's contacts in Munich, see Anna Bramwell, *Blood and Soil: Walther Darré and Hitler's "Green Party"* (Bourne End: Kensal Press, 1985), pp. 49–50. Von Leers's introduction of Herman Wirth to Heinrich Himmler is documented in the standard history of the Ahnenerbe: Michael H. Kater, *Das "Ahnenerbe" der SS 1935–1945* (Stuttgart: Deutsche Verlags-Anstalt, 1974), pp. 16, 26, 363, 366, 387. On Karl Weisthor, see Nicholas Goodrick-Clarke, *The Occult Roots of Nazism: Secret Aryan Cults and Their Influence on Nazi Ideology*, 2d ed. (New York: New York University Press; London: I. B. Tauris, 1992), pp. 177–191.

8. Otto Skorzeny's wartime career is described in Otto Skorzeny, *Skorzeny's Special Missions* (London: Robert Hale, 1957), and Charles Foley, *Commando Extraordinary* (London: Longmans, Green, 1954). Details of his shadowy postwar activities are reported in Stuart Christie, *Stefano delle Chiaie: Portrait of a Black Terrorist* (London: Anarchy Magazine/Refract Publications, 1984) (Black Papers No. 1), pp. 156–161. See also Angelo del Boca and Mario Giovana, *Fascism Today: A World Survey* (London: Heinemann, 1970), pp. 79–82.

9. Savitri Devi, *Souvenirs et réflexions d'une aryenne* (New Delhi: Savitri Dêvi Mukherji, 1976), pp. 219–221.

10. For biographical details and wartime career, see Léon Degrelle, *Denn der Hass stirbt . . . Erinnerungen eines Europäers* (Munich: Universitas, 1992).

NOTES TO CHAPTER 11

1. Angelo del Boca and Mario Giovana, *Fascism Today: A World Survey* (London: Heinemann, 1970), pp. 89–90.

2. The ensuing account of far-right political groups associated with Colin Jordan in the period 1958–1962 is based on Martin Walker, *The National Front* (London: Fontana, 1977), chap. 2, pp. 25–50.

3. Friedrich Borth's career is described in del Boca and Giovana, *Fascism Today,* pp. 87–89, 208–209.

4. Colin Jordan, *Britain Reborn: The Policy of the National Socialist Movement* (London: National Socialist Movement, [1962]).

5. The following biographical details are drawn from William L. Pierce, "George Lincoln Rockwell: A National Socialist Life," *National Socialist World,* no. 5 (winter 1967), pp. 13–36, and his own autobiography *This Time the World* (Arlington, Va.: author, 1962).

6. Rockwell, *This Time the World,* pp. 154–155.

7. Ibid., pp. 296–302. Rockwell's communications with the Atlanta suspects are discussed in Melissa Fay Greene, *The Temple Bombing* (London, Jonathan Cape, 1996), pp. 219–223.

8. Rockwell, *This Time the World,* pp. 309–310.

9. Newspaper coverage of the camp included "Home Office Ban Entry of Nazi Delegates," *The Times,* 2 August 1962, p. 10; "Foreign Nazis Banned," *The Daily Telegraph,* 2 August 1962, p. 1; "Secret 'Nazi' Camp," *The Daily Telegraph,* 6 August 1962, p. 9; "Inquiry on Visit by U.S. Nazi," *The Times,* 7 August 1962, p. 8; "Yard Search for U.S. Nazi Leader," *The Daily Telegraph,* 7 August 1962, p. 1; "Jackboots in an English Glade," *The Daily Telegraph,* 7 August 1962, pp. 1, 16.

10. "Camp Abandoned by British Nazis," *The Daily Telegraph,* 8 August 1962, p. 1; "Deportation Order on U.S. Nazi," *The Times,* 8 August 1962, p. 8.

11. "U.S. Nazi Caught in London," *The Daily Telegraph,* 9 August 1962, p. 1; "American Nazi Detained in London," *The Times,* 9 August 1962, p. 8.

12. "2-hour Yard Raid on Nazi HQ," *The Daily Telegraph,* 11 August 1962, p. 1.

13. George P. Thayer, *The British Political Fringe* (London: Anthony Blond, 1968), pp. 13–14.

14. Richard C. Thurlow, *Fascism in Britain: A History, 1918–1985* (Oxford: Basil Blackwell, 1987), pp. 268–269.

15. Savitri Devi, "The Lightning and the Sun" (condensed ed.), *National Socialist World,* no. 1 (spring 1966), pp. 13–90.

16. Savitri Devi, "Gold in the Furnace," *National Socialist World,* no. 3 (spring 1967), pp. 59–71; Savitri Devi, "Defiance" (excerpts), *National Socialist World,* no. 6 (winter 1968), pp. 64–87.

17. The early French history of Holocaust denial is recounted in Deborah E. Lipstadt, *Denying the Holocaust: The Growing Assault on Truth and Memory* (London: Penguin, 1994), pp. 50–64.

18. Robert Lenski, *The Holocaust on Trial: The Case of Ernst Zundel* (Decatur, Ala.: Reporter Press, 1989). The story of Ernst Zündel's first trial is told in Michael A. Hoffman II, *The Great Holocaust Trial* (Torrance, Calif.: Institute for Historical Review, 1985).

NOTES TO CHAPTER 12

1. Willibald Mattern, *UFOs: Unbekanntes Flugobjekt? Letzte Geheimwaffe des Dritten Reiches?* (Toronto: Samisdat Publishers, [1974]), pp. 142–149. An English-language edition was published in 1975.

2. Willibald Mattern and Christof Friedrich [i.e., Ernst Zündel], *UFOs: Nazi Secret Weapon?* (Toronto: Samisdat Publishers, [1975]), pp. 143–146. Schmidt's otherwise typical alien abduction experience took place at Kearney, Nebraska, in November 1957. Reinhold O. Schmidt, *The Kearney Incident and to the Arctic Circle in a Spacecraft* (Kearney, Nebr.: author, 1959).

3. Christof Friedrich [i.e., Ernst Zündel], *Secret Nazi Polar Expeditions* (Toronto: Samisdat Publishers, [1978]), p. 97.

4. Walter Kafton-Minkel relates the extensive background of Nazi polar mythology in the chapter "The Nazis and the Hollow Earth," in his *Subterranean Worlds: 100,000 Years of Dragons, Dwarfs, the Dead, Lost Races and UFOs from inside the Earth* (Port Townsend, Wash.: Loompanics Unlimited, 1989), pp. 217–242, and Joscelyn Godwin, *Arktos: The Polar Myth in Science, Symbolism and Nazi Survival* (Grand Rapids, Mich.: Phanes Press; London: Thames and Hudson, 1993), offers the definitive and most comprehensive account of the traditions about the poles and the postwar Nazi myths surrounding them. The Hugin Nazi UFO publications comprise D. H. Haarmann, *Geheime Wunderwaffen*, 3 vols. (Wetter: Hugin, 1983–1985); O. Bergmann, *Deutsche Flugscheiben und U-Boote überwachen die Weltmeere*, 2 vols. (Wetter: Hugin, 1988–1989); and a dossier of two hundred press reports over four decades, *UFO Dokumenten-Sammlung* (Wetter: Hugin, 1986).

5. "A commentary by Christof Friedrich," in Savitri Devi, *The Lightning and the Sun* (Buffalo, N.Y.: Samisdat Publishers, [1979]), [pp. iii-iv].

6. Matt Koehl, "Some Guidelines for the Development of the National Socialist Movement," *National Socialist World*, no. 6 (winter 1968), pp. 8–17, at pp. 12, 14f.

7. Matt Koehl, "Resurrection," New Order brochure, reprint of an editorial in *NS Bulletin* (April 1987).

8. James N. Mason, *Siege: The Collected Writings of James Mason* (Denver: Storm Books, 1992), pp. xi-xxvii.

9. Ibid., pp. 281–322. For Savitri Devi, see *Siege* 11, no. 10 (October 1982), reprinted ibid., pp. 304ff.

10. For the electoral rise and fall of the National Front in the 1970s, see Stan Taylor, *The National Front in English Politics* (London: Macmillan, 1982).

11. Colin Jordan, "Adolf Hitler: The Man against Time," *NS Bulletin* Special Centennial Issue (1989), reprinted in Colin Jordan, *National Socialism: Vanguard of the Future* (Aalborg: Nordland Forlag, 1993), pp. 25–29.

12. David Myatt, *Cosmic Reich: The Life and Thoughts of David Myatt* (Wellington: Renaissance Press, 1995), p. 1.

13. "An Interview with James Mason," *The Flaming Sword* (Wellington), no. 2 (April 1994), pp. 2–4.

14. "An Interview with Christian Bouchet," *The Nexus* (Wellington), no. 6 (November 1996), pp. 1–6.

15. Lotte Asmus and Vittorio De Cecco, "La 'missionaria' del paganesimo ariano," *Risguardo* 4 (1984): 64–70.

16. Savitri Devi, *L'India e il Nazismo* (Parma: Edizioni all'insegna del Veltro, 1979) (Quaderni del Veltro 11), pp. 5–7.

17. De Cecco has published *Omaggio a Savitri Devi* as *Arya* 2 (1978). Her article "Shinto (La via degli dei)" appeared in *Arya* 4 (July 1980) (written in 1979 and based on an article of Asit Krishna Mukherji in *New Mercury* [circa 1936]). An Italian translation of her book on Paul of Tarsus, introduced by "Wittekind," was published under the title *Cristianesimo e Giudaismo (Paolo di Tarso)* in *Arya* 5 (January 1981).

18. Miguel Serrano, *Adolf Hitler, el Último Avatāra* (Santiago: Ediciones La Nueva Edad, 1984), pp. 33f., 94–97, 119–124, 129–132. Jung's own occult sources are discussed in Richard Noll, *The Jung Cult: Origins of a Charismatic Movement* (Princeton: Princeton University Press, 1994), pp. 64–69, 109–137.

19. Serrano, *Adolf Hitler*, pp. 210, 243, 254, 281.

20. Ibid., pp. 95, 124, 131, 139, 232.

21. Ibid., pp. 481, 497f., 620. Savitri Devi's visit to the Externsteine is described ibid., p. 497, and illustrated in Miguel Serrano, *La Resurrección del Heroe* (Santiago: author, 1986), p. 79. The latter book is also dedicated to Savitri Devi with a portrait and verse. For these quotes, see "Miguel Serrano στο ΑΝΤΙΔΟΤΟ," *TO ANTIΔΟΤΟ* no. 29 (n.d.), pp. 23–31, at p. 27.

22. Serrano, *Adolf Hitler*, pp. 145f., 149, 487.

23. Personal correspondence between Savitri Devi and Miguel Serrano.

24. Javier Nicolás, "Miguel Serrano: Una visión mágica del NS," *Cedade* (Barcelona), July-August 1985, pp. 28–33, and "Miguel Serrano στο ΑΝΤΙΔΟΤΟ," *TO ANTIΔΟΤΟ* no. 29 (n.d.), pp. 23–31.

25. The *TO ANTIΔΟΤΟ* interview was reprinted in *The Flaming Sword*, no. 3 (August 1994), pp. 5–9. A further interview has been published as "Miguel Serrano: 'Esoteric Hitlerist,'" *The Flaming Sword*, no. 4 (November 1994), pp. 4–8,

and no. 5 (February 1995), pp. 4–10. The latter interview was reprinted as a booklet in 1995.

26. Miguel Serrano, *Imitación de la Verdad: La ciberpolítica, Internet, realidad virtual, telepresencia* (Santiago: author, 1995).

27. A eulogy of Savitri Devi has appeared in one of Britain's leading Nazi "skinzines." "Heart of Gold, Spirit of Light, Will of Steel," *The Order*, [no. 14, early 1996?], cover headline: "No Surrender to ZOG!" [pp. 5–7]. Cover title and article "Priestess of Hitlerism: Savitri Devi," *The Nexus*, no. 9 (August 1997), pp. 1–4.

28. *Searchlight*, no. 91 (January 1983), p. 3.

29. *Searchlight*, no. 97 (July 1983), p. 10.

30. Christopher A. McIntosh, *The Rosicrucians: The History and Mythology of an Occult Order*, 2d ed. (Wellingborough: Thorsons, 1987), pp. 129–141.

31. Harvey Spencer Lewis, *Rosicrucian Questions and Answers with Complete History of the Rosicrucian Order*, 15th ed. (San Jose, Calif.: AMORC, 1981; 1st ed., 1929), pp. 52–60, 292–294.

32. J. Gordon Melton, Jerome Clark, and Aidan A. Kelly, *New Age Encyclopaedia* (Detroit: Gale, 1990), pp. 16–17.

33. Rudolf Bahro, *Avoiding Social and Ecological Disaster: The Politics of World Transformation*, trans. David Clarke (Bath: Gateway Books, 1994). The first German edition was published as *Die Logik der Rettung: Wer kann die Apokalypse aufhalten?* (Stuttgart: Weitbrecht, 1987).

34. The ideologies of "ecofascism" are discussed in David Pepper, *The Roots of Modern Environmentalism* (London: Croom Helm, 1984), pp. 204–213.

35. David Ehrenfeld, *The Arrogance of Humanism* (New York: Oxford University Press, 1978), pp. 207–211.

36. Theodore Roszak, *Where the Wasteland Ends: Politics and Transcendence in Postindustrial Society* (London: Faber and Faber, 1973), p. xxx, and Pete Gunter, "Man-Infinite and Nature-Infinite: A Mirror-Image Dialectic" (MS, North Texas State University, 1980), quoted in Bill Devall and George Sessions, *Deep Ecology* (Salt Lake City: Gibbs Smith, 1985), pp. 53–54.

37. Devall and Sessions, *Deep Ecology*, pp. 79–108.

38. Dave Foreman, "Around the Campfire," *Earth First!*, 21 June 1987, p. 2; "Whither Earth First!?" *Earth First!*, 1 November 1987, p. 20.

39. Miss Ann Thropy, "Population and AIDS," *Earth First!*, 1 May 1987, p. 32.

40. Herbert Gruhl, *Himmelfahrt ins Nichts: Der geplünderte Planet vor dem Ende* (Munich: Langen Müller, 1992), p. 244. Gruhl is citing René Jules Dubos, *Die entfesselte Fortschritt: Programm für eine menschliche Welt* (Bergisch Gladbach: Lübbe, 1970), p. 166. This title was originally published in English as *So Human an Animal* (New York: Scribner's, 1968).

41. Jutta Ditfurth, *Entspannt in die Barbarei: Esoterik, (Öko-)Faschismus und Biozentrismus* (Hamburg: Konkret Literatur, 1996), pp. 124–134.

42. Dieter Asselhoven and Andrea Capitain, "Wenn Gedanken wie Wildgänse

rauschen: Die Reinkarnation der präfaschistischen Lebensreform," *ÖkoLinX*, no. 25 (spring 1997), pp. 11–15.

43. George L. Mosse, *The Crisis of German Ideology: Intellectual Origins of the Third Reich* (New York: Grosset and Dunlap, 1964; London: Weidenfeld and Nicolson, 1966), provides a concise survey of the *völkisch* movement.

44. The correspondences between *völkisch*, fascist, and New Age thinking have been chiefly noted by German writers to date. See, for example, Eduard Gugenberger and Roman Schweidlenka, *Mutter Erde, Magie und Politik: Zwischen Faschismus und neuer Gesellschaft* (Vienna: Verlag für Gesellschaftskritik, 1987), and Karlheinz Weißmann, *Druiden, Goden, Weise Frauen: Zurück zu Europas alten Göttern* (Freiburg: Herder, 1991). A Marxist critique is offered by Ditfurth, *Entspannt in die Barbarei.*

BIBLIOGRAPHICAL NOTE

The primary sources for this study of Savitri Devi and the new Hitler cults have been identified in the notes. This list of Savitri Devi's works is intended to serve as a chronology of her works.

Maximiani PORTAS, afterward SAVITRI DEVI MUKHERJI

Savitri Devi's first published works were her two doctoral theses presented at the University of Lyons, which appeared under her maiden name Maximiani Portas.
Essai critique sur Théophile Kaïris (Lyons, [1935])
La simplicité mathématique (Lyons, [1935])

All her subsequent publications appeared under her new Hindu name Savitri Devi. The books relating to Hinduism and India were written in the 1930s after her arrival there.
L'Etang aux lotus (Calcutta: author, 1940) [written in 1935–1936]
A Warning to the Hindus (Calcutta: Hindu Mission, 1939) [written in 1937–1939].
    Translations into Bengali, Hindi, Marathi, and other Indian languages.
The Non-Hindu Indians and Indian Unity (Calcutta: Hindu Mission, 1940)
During the war years she wrote at length on Akhnaton and his solar cult; the earlier books were published in Calcutta; the others were published in London after her return to Europe in 1945.
Akhnaton's Eternal Message: A Scientific Religion 3300 Years Old (Calcutta: A. K. Mukherji, [1940])
Joy of the Sun: The Beautiful Life of Akhnaton, King of Egypt. Told to Young People (Calcutta: Thacker, Spink and Co. [1933] Ltd., 1942)
A Son of God: The Life and Philosophy of Akhnaton, King of Egypt (London:

Philosophical Publishing House, 1946); subsequent editions were published under the title *Son of the Sun: The Life and Philosophy of Akhnaton, King of Egypt*, 2d ed. (San Jose, Calif.: Supreme Grand Lodge of AMORC, 1956); 3d ed. (London: Hazell Watson and Viney Ltd., 1957); 4th ed. (San Jose, Calif.: Supreme Grand Lodge of AMORC, 1981); 2d printing, 1992.

Akhnaton: A Play (London: Philosophical Publishing House, 1948)

Her books on Hitler and National Socialism were first written after the war. The first editions were typically published in India to avoid censorship and other restrictions.

Defiance (Calcutta: A. K. Mukerji, [1950]). Excerpts from the work were published in *National Socialist World*, no. 6 (winter 1968), pp. 64–87.

Gold in the Furnace (Calcutta: A. K. Mukherji, 1953) (written in 1948–1949). Excerpts, comprising chapters 3 and 13, were published in *National Socialist World*, no. 3 (spring 1967), pp. 59–71. A German translation was published under the title *Gold im Schmelztiegel: Erlebnisse im Nachkriegsdeutschland*, trans. Lotte Asmus (Padua: Edizioni di Ar, 1982). The same edition was simultaneously published by Nordwind Verlag at Mohrkirch under the auspices of Thies Christophersen.

Paul de Tarse, ou Christianisme et juiverie (Calcutta: Savitri Devi Mukherji, 1958) (written in 1957). An Italian translation, introduced by "Wittekind," was published under the title *Cristianesimo e Giudaismo (Paolo di Tarso), Arya* 5 (January 1981) (Montreal: Arya, 1981)

Pilgrimage (Calcutta: Savitri Devi Mukherji, 1958) (written in 1953–1954)

The Lightning and the Sun (Calcutta: Savitri Devi Mukherjee, 1958) (written in 1948–1956). A condensed edition was published in *National Socialist World*, no. 1 (spring 1966), pp. 13–90. Second edition (Buffalo, N.Y.: Samisdat Publishers, Ltd. [1979]). Third edition (Paraparaumu Beach, Wellington, New Zealand: Renaissance Press, circa 1994).

Impeachment of Man (Calcutta: Savitri Devi Mukherji, 1959) (written in 1945). Second edition (Costa Mesa, Calif.: Noontide Press, 1991)

Hart wie Kruppstahl (not known) (written in 1961–1963)

Long Whiskers and the Two-Legged Goddess, or The True Story of a Most "Objectionable Nazi" and . . . half-a-dozen Cats (Calcutta: Savitri Devi Mukherji [n.d.]) (written in 1957–1961)

Souvenirs et réflexions d'une aryenne (Calcutta: Savitri Dêvi Mukherji, 1976) (written in 1968–1971). The tenth chapter of this book was translated into Italian and published as *L'India e il nazismo* (Parma: Edizioni all'insegna del Veltro, 1979) (Quaderni del Veltro 11).

Shinto (La via degli dei), Arya 4 (July 1980), (Montreal: Arya, 1980) (written in 1979 and based on an article of Asit Krishna Mukherji in *New Mercury* [circa 1936]).

Further biographical material is contained in the five audiocassettes of an interview with Savitri Devi in November 1978, in New Delhi, published by Samisdat Publications of Toronto in 1979. Arya of Montreal has published *Omaggio a Savitri Devi* as *Arya* 2, and the article by Lotte Asmus and Vittorio De Cecco, "La 'missionaria' del paganesimo ariano," *Risguardo* 4 (1984): 64–70 (published by Edizioni di Ar, Padua) contains interesting details.

INDEX

ABOUT THE AUTHOR

Nicholas Goodrick-Clarke was educated at Lancing College, Berlin, and Bristol University, gaining a starred first class honors degree in German, Politics, and Economics. His doctoral research at Oxford in German intellectual history resulted in the definitive study, *The Occult Roots of Nazism: Secret Aryan Cults and Their Influence on Nazi Ideology* (also published by NYU Press and translated into many languages). He has held a number of teaching and senior administrative posts at colleges in Scotland, Germany, and Oxford University and also worked in real estate finance with the Chase Manhattan Bank.

Dr. Goodrick-Clarke has traveled widely in Central Europe and the Near East since the 1970s. He is a consultant for TV films on the Third Reich and World War II and a full time author and historian. He also lectures internationally on Renaissance neo-Platonism and has a particular interest in the Western esoteric tradition. He is Series Editor of the HarperCollins "Essential Readings" series including volumes on John Dee, Jacob Boehme, Robert Fludd, Emanuel Swedenborg, and the author of *Paracelsus,* a study of the life and thought of the sixteenth-century magus. He is a regular contributor to the London *Times* and other European journals.

Nicholas Goodrick-Clarke lives on the Berkshire Downs in Wessex, England.